U-BOATS
ATTACK!

U-BOATS ATTACK!

THE BATTLE OF THE ATLANTIC WITNESSED BY THE WOLF PACKS

JAK P. MALLMANN SHOWELL

SPELLMOUNT

This book is based on original logbooks, written at the time as the action unfolded and the additional annotations come from the numerous files from the German U-boat Museum.

First published in 2011

The History Press
The Mill, Brimscombe Port
Stroud, Gloucestershire, GL5 2QG
www.thehistorypress.co.uk

British Library Cataloguing in Publication Data.
A catalogue record for this book is available from the British Library.

ISBN 978 0 7524 6188 5

Typesetting and origination by The History Press
Printed in the EU for The History Press.

CONTENTS

INTRODUCTION

U-BOAT LOGBOOKS

Anyone studying the Second World War will quickly discover that many facts seem to get lost in a deliberate perpetuation of myths; in fact it is easy to find that a high proportion of well-established stories are totally without foundation. Many historians, even those who publish their results on stone epitaphs, seem to be happy to repeat figments of the imagination and, to make matters worse, even embroider these with their own fantasies. Those who do check original records discover very quickly that a number of well-established facts seem to be based on material first presented by the Allied propaganda systems, rather than on events of the war. Eyewitness reports, so favoured by the media, are even worse. Many come entirely from the deepest imagination rather than fact. The stories in this book are different. They are based on original logbooks, written at the time when the action unfolded.

War logs (*Kriegstagebücher* or KTB) differ from ordinary naval diaries in that they were regarded in Germany as legal documents and had to be signed personally by commanders every four hours. In addition to the main log, officers also carried small observation books for recording personal information.

As far as is known, there were only two cases where logbooks were deliberately falsified. The most famous is the first ship (the *Athenia*) sunk by a U-boat during the Second World War. Hitler ordered this incident to be eradicated from the records and the crew sworn to secrecy. The other incident took place during the Spanish Civil War, when some U-boats operated off Spain as part of an international peacekeeping force. It would appear that there are logs indicating that boats were in the Arctic seas, while in reality they were off Spain. Changing the logs in this case was thought necessary because the information in them had to be handed over to foreign governments participating in the international peacekeeping activities.

At times it is exceedingly difficult to interpret the words written in logs and there have been a number of cases where, long after the war, senior officers could no longer understand what they themselves had written in the heat of conflict. Naval terminology and code words are not easy to follow.

Recent high-level public inquiries have made people aware that some important leaders are allowed to be 'economical' with the truth. This means they are allowed to deliberately withhold information in order to mislead the general public. This must have happened during the war as well and one wonders how many things were spotted but not recorded. However, for most of the time one can take U-boat logs as an accurate account of what happened and it is very interesting to compare them with logs kept by the opposition. Often the Allied reports and the U-boat logs fit snugly together, like a perfect jigsaw puzzle. Of course all these logs fell into Allied hands after the war and there is evidence that some pages, possibly containing critical information, were then removed.

The accounts in this book are based on original U-boat logs. The additional annotations come from the large number of files in the International U-boat Museum (Formerly U-boat Archive) in Cuxhaven-Altenbruch (www.dubm.de). Allied information comes mainly from the secret Anti-Submarine Reports released by the British Anti-Submarine Warfare Division of the Naval War Staff. These were issued each month only to officers involved with hunting U-boats.

Once a U-boat returned to port, staff from the U-boat Command would have interviewed the commander and added comments to the log. Following this, six or seven copies were made and generally distributed as follows:

1.	Operational Flotilla,
2.	U-boat Command,
3. & 4.	Supreme Naval Command,
5.	Second Admiral for U-boats (Training and Administration),
6.	AGRU-Front (Units responsible for final training of U-boat crews),
7.	27th U-boat Flotilla, responsible for training.

The Supreme Naval Command not only employed a large staff to file the logs, but also sent terse letters to flotilla chiefs when they found any unaccounted periods in the logs. Even when the boats were being repaired in ports, the skeleton crew was expected to record what was happening.

Although Hitler ordered all logs to be destroyed shortly before the end of the war, Naval Command took the view that it had nothing to hide and therefore did not pass on these instructions. As a result American forces captured a vast stock of German naval records towards the end of the war. Many of these logs were later microfilmed (on 35mm film) and made available through the American National Archives. There is a complete set in the Deutsches U-Boot-Museum. I am most grateful to Horst Bredow for allowing me to dig through his archive and for helping in interpreting the complicated language of the logbooks. Much of what is in them has been discussed with ex-U-boat men and I am also most grateful to everyone who has helped with the interpretation of the logs. Photographs have come from the author's collection and from Deutsches U-Boot-Museum in Cuxhaven-Altenbruch (www.dubm.de).

1

COMMENCE HOSTILITIES AGAINST ENGLAND

Readers might cringe at the use of the word 'England' in the title, but this old generic name for the United Kingdom has been used here to keep the atmosphere of the period. Even long after the war, Germans were happy to use terms such as 'English soldiers from Scotland', when describing the first British troops in the shipyards of Hamburg.

During the middle of August 1939, U-boat flotilla commanders were ordered to implement the Three Front War Programme for a possible conflict in the Baltic, North Sea and Atlantic. This involved moving as many units as possible out of ports to prevent them from being locked in by superior blockading forces. Kptlt. Alexander Gelhaar recorded the exact details of how U45 perceived the start of the war. Like many other boats, U45 left the Elbe estuary on 19 August 1939, two weeks before the beginning of the war, in order to take up a waiting position in the North Atlantic among the column furthest west from Ireland. Of course, in addition to these official orders, crews were also well within range to receive normal radio broadcasts.

25 August 1939: 1714 hrs
Notification was sent to all units at sea that special announcements were due to follow. The reason for such a warning signal was that many merchant ships did not man their radio room all the time.

27 August: 1830 hrs
Received via the German Ocean Weather Forecast:

> To all German ships.
> Make use of all advantages to reach a German port during the next four days. If this is not possible then go to a Spanish, Italian, Russian, Japanese, Dutch or other neutral port. In no circumstances make for the USA. From Naval Command.

31 August: 2100 hrs
The following decoded signal was handed to the commander:

1. Start hostilities against Poland in home waters on 1 September at 0445 hrs.
2. Not certain how the western powers will react.
3. Should the western powers declare war then our own forces are to react only in self-defence or on receipt of special orders.
4. Pocket battleships are to remain in their waiting positions; no attacks, not even against Polish ships.

The pocket battleships at sea were: *Admiral Graf Spee* with a supply ship in the South Atlantic and *Deutschland* with a supply ship in the North Atlantic. They were not given permission to commence hostilities until the end of the month.

3 September: 1226 hrs
The following decoded signal was handed to the commander:

> To all Atlantic units.
> Commence hostilities against England immediately.

Same day: 1743 hrs

> To all Units from the Naval War Staff.
> Since 1700 hours France has considered itself to be at war with Germany. For the time being our own units may engage only in self-defence.

5 September: 0042 hrs

A general radio broadcast reported the sinking of the passenger liner *Athenia* and shortly after that came:

> To all Units from the Naval War Staff.
> On orders from the Führer, passenger ships are not to be attacked, even if they are sailing in convoy.

7 September: 2054 hrs

The following decoded message was handed to the commander.

> To all units from the Naval War Staff.
> All boats from 6th and 7th U-boat Flotillas, except U53, are to make their way back home at the fastest possible speed allowed by their fuel reserves via the north of England without regard of other boats' operations areas. Take advantage of any attack opportunities as long as these comply with operation orders. New operation orders make this return necessary.

Thus a few simple radio messages plunged the world into war for the second time within about thirty years.

Alexander Gelhaar and his entire crew returned home only once. U45 was the 6th U-boat to be sunk during the Second World War. It went down on 14 October 1939 with all hands during its second war voyage as a result of having been depth charged by the destroyers HMS *Inglefield*, HMS *Intrepid* and HMS *Icarus*.

2

MINING THE LION'S DEN

U26 set out before the beginning of the war with a sealed envelope containing orders from the Supreme Naval Command to lay mines in the approaches of Weymouth Harbour on England's south coast.

The small staff controlling the U-boat war in the west arrived unexpectedly in Wilhelmshaven at around the same time as Britain and France declared war on Germany. There the only available space was in rather depressing wooden huts by a road leading to a military cemetery called Toten Weg. These may have been close to a substantial communications bunker, but this isolated conglomeration of naval offices still felt like a definite comedown. It was on the landward side of the town, a long way from the dockyard and even further from Germany's only purpose-built U-boat base. The squalid huts were nowhere near as prestigious as the highly mobile depot ship *Erwin Wassner*, which the staff had just vacated in the Baltic Sea. But then, the last weeks had been exceptionally hectic and the confusion created by the unexpected war preparations made the unavailability of more suitable accommodation understandable. The U-boat Command's new control headquarters in Sengwarden were still under construction and would not be ready for some time, so the men had no alternative other than shrugging off the inconvenience and hoping their stay would not be for long.

The location didn't even have the feel of the seaside. Only the persistent squawking of gulls gave any indication there might be salt water nearby. The men had not yet settled in when they realised that the huts had one great advantage: they looked too unimportant to make them a bombing target. The war had hardly been a day old when the pocket battleship *Admiral Scheer* shot down a Vickers Wellington, clearly demonstrating that the old imperial naval base was no longer out of reach of the enemy. *Admiral Scheer* hadn't gone to war with the rest of the fleet because much of the internal machinery was being dismantled for a major refit.

The light cruiser *Emden* also brought down a plane, but this one crashed onto the forecastle, making a hell of a mess and causing some loss of life. An irate officer threatened the unfortunate gunner with court martial, saying he should have waited for orders before opening fire. Kpt.z.S. und Kommodore Karl Dönitz, (Führer der Unterseeboote – Flag Officer for U-boats), took more than a casual interest in the controversial gossip. After all, four years earlier he had commanded the *Emden*, and had been looking forward to a promotion which might offer him the opportunity of leading a whole cruiser squadron. Instead of such a highly-regarded step up, he was shunted into these squalid huts, commanding a tiny band of stinking submarines. Dönitz was pleased that the arrogance of the irate officer was not his concern. His U-boat men didn't cultivate that sort of short-sightedness. During the four years since leaving *Emden*, he had been able to create an enthusiastic elite where common sense, self-discipline and perfect teamwork displaced the majority of bombastic naval regulations.

Dönitz knew that many people would be forced into adjusting their thinking. Things were definitely going to change and a good number of officers were in for a big shock. The arrogance of some juniors and the loftiness of many seniors had been making him uneasy for some time. How could anyone think that an aircraft with British markings dropping bombs on the town was not an acceptable reason for a rating to open fire? The peacetime routine, which demanded unquestioning automatons, was no longer appropriate. Dönitz had often told his superiors that the navy needed more quick-thinking men. He had survived the First World War and knew this one wouldn't go away again in a hurry. He was also certain that they were going to be exceptionally lucky if they were still alive when it ended. He had seen it all before. He knew it was going to be a long slog and that Britain was an unforgiving opponent. A military cemetery, with graves from the First World War, was just a few minutes' walk from the new headquarters and anyone doubting Britain's determination needed only to take a few steps to see the memorials to the masses that had died twenty-five years earlier, when the pathetic European leaders were so stupid that they ordered their best men to kill each other.

The war plans, which the Supreme Naval Command had ordered two weeks earlier, were not to Dönitz's liking. He wanted to make drastic changes. His argument was that if Britain had started evacuating children and valuable racehorses from London, then vulnerable targets would also have been withdrawn from the sea lanes before declaring war. Therefore the U-boats might as well be brought home to refuel and be ready for when British ships reappeared. There was no point having submarines at sea doing nothing. However, Dönitz's visions for a U-boat war couldn't be fully realised either. An embarrassing shortage of torpedoes meant that the U-boat Command would also need to fall back on the navy's generous stock of torpedo mines. The difficulty was that the majority of commanders who had been trained in laying these mines were now driving boats without the necessary mine laying modification to the torpedo tubes.

One of the boats already at sea with a load of torpedo mines was U26. Both Dönitz and Eberhard Godt (his chief of operations) considered the proposition in detail, wondering whether it might not be better to bring this boat home with the rest. Finally Dönitz decided against the move, although he still hated the idea of approaching so close to harbours. He had succeeded in cancelling another mining operation and diverting the boat (U53 under Kptlt. Ernst-Günter Heinicke) into the Atlantic. But despite this, U26 sailed with orders from the Supreme Naval Command to mine the approaches of Weymouth harbour on England's south coast. Intelligence suggested the port was likely to be earmarked as a wartime emergency disembarkation point for transports, but the high-ranking officials in Berlin seemed to have forgotten that this was also the home of the British anti-submarine school and it was therefore likely to have the best defences against U-boats. Dönitz didn't like sending his men so close to the lion's den, but he wasn't in full control and also had to obey orders.

U26 was one of only two boats belonging to the infamous Type IA, a class that had been replaced by the more stable Type VII. Both U26 and U25 had the disgusting habit of collecting air bubbles in their diving tanks and in bad weather they rolled about, adding to instability problems. In addition to this, when diving quickly, the centre of gravity seemed to creep forward, encouraging the boats to continue turning in a massive loop. This might be an impressive air-craft manoeuvre for amusing crowds at displays, but it was somewhat nerve wracking when 1,000 tons of submerged steel tried the same performance on its own. It proved especially irritating during chaotic alarm dives when the engineering officer could momentarily lose sight of exactly where the centre of the earth actually was. To make matters worse, this was Kptlt. Klaus Ewerth's first cruise with U26 and there hadn't been time to get him acquainted with the machin-ery or the men.

This last point didn't particularly worry Dönitz. The 32-year-old Ewerth had been in the navy since 1925 and had been with subma-rines since before the Diktat of Versailles allowed Germany to own them. Then, when U-boats first reappeared, he became commander of U1. He was one of the old guard; precise, confident and capa-ble of tackling anything. Ewerth was a quiet type who was respected because people liked him, not because they were impressed by his gimmicks or by the piston rings on his sleeve.

The Second World War was one week old on 10 September when the news spoiled Dönitz's Sunday lunch; the fact that it took two days for Berlin to relay the information made him even more furious. After all, one of the main naval communications bunkers was just a few yards from his office. The shattering news arrived just before midday, when the Supreme Naval Command phoned to say that two days ago the BBC had reported a successful attack against a mine-lay-ing U-boat in the English Channel and French radio had confirmed the news a few hours later. Two days! Two whole days later the Supreme Naval Command casually told the Flag Officer for U-boats. Dönitz wasn't the type to explode, but he had adequate vocabulary to ensure that the admirals were aware of his views on the system. This snail-like communication wasn't good enough. Godt wasn't so sure about his boss's brash approach and wished he would choose more diplomatic language when expressing his feelings. He could see the admirals clipping Dönitz's wings by shoving him sideways into a post where he would be less of an embarrassment.

The boat in question had to be U26. There were no other boats in the English Channel. Dönitz usually did not take his fury out on the men around him, but on this occasion he cursed Godt as well. Yet before slamming the phone down, it had already occurred to his quick-thinking mind that this couldn't be the straightforward sinking that Berlin was making it out to be. How could the British know that the submarine was laying mines? TMB mines (Torpedo Mine, type B), with time-delay fuses of several days, were ejected through torpedo tubes, making it impossible for anyone to work out what the boat was doing. Those tubes were submerged, even when the boat was on the surface – no one could see what was popping out of the ends. In any case, mines would have been ejected from a submerged position or from the surface during the darkest of nights when observers would have had problems spotting the low silhouette of a conning tower. So how could anyone know what the U-boat was doing? Had the crew been captured? No, he couldn't accept it. The intelligence people were having him on. The news had to be worse than Berlin made out. It couldn't have been a case of someone just sinking a U-boat. The Royal Navy could well have been on board! Otherwise how would they know about the mines? Did the crew talk to British interrogators? The potential consequences were spine chilling. Every boat carried a full library and if the opposition got into U26, then U-boat Command could write off every other U-boat operation there and then. For a start, it would give the Royal Navy the positions of all other boats and the radio code settings for the coming month. This problem could be overcome in future by sending mine-laying boats out with just enough documentation for one objective, but U26 was also carrying six torpedoes for the Western Approaches, which was considerable hitting power to sacrifice. U26 had enough supplies and fuel for a whole month, meaning that she could remain at sea until mid-October; therefore it might be a while before the

U-boat Command could discover what was really going on in the English Channel. Ewerth was the sort of bloke who had often disappeared during manoeuvres and then popped up, unexpectedly, just at the last moment; making Dönitz think he was probably still alive. He would have phoned home the moment he started running into trouble and his whereabouts became known to the enemy.

A couple of weeks earlier, on 29 August 1939, U26 passed through the smallest locks in Wilhelmshaven on a bright, hot summer's day. It was midday and the beach was already full of people taking advantage of the brilliant blue sky. The thought that some of them could well be on the payroll of the British navy had crossed the minds of more than one person. Ewerth was determined to give such characters a good run for their money. It was fairly obvious that someone would be keeping tabs on the traffic in and out of the naval base. Everything had to go through the locks and then along the narrow channel leading out into the North Sea, so it wasn't difficult. After making the usual trimming dive, U26 quickly resurfaced. Ewerth was determined to maintain the standard procedures, but he wanted to make sure watching eyes didn't lose track of the U-boat. Following the deepwater channel, U26 made for the distinctive red and white rocket-like lighthouse at Roter Sand (Red Sand), but Ewerth didn't go that far. Remaining within sight of the island of Wangerooge, he turned left towards the west, heading straight towards Dover.

Keeping the low outlines of the German Friesian Islands in sight, the boat continued its leisurely pace, but six hours later, when passing the Norderney lightship, the entire crew had been placed on a war footing. Ewerth closed in on Borkum, the last of the German islands. He wanted to get as close to Holland as the 3-mile limit allowed. Anyone with an interest in the boat leaving Wilhelmshaven might also have a set of eyes among the low sand dunes there and it would be helpful if observers thought the boat was heading west. Ewerth had planned drastic action. Shortly after dark, U26 made a sharp right turn and headed north. Fishing boats, the occasional destroyer, aircraft and an assortment of merchant ships were avoided by diving or by changing course. The North Sea seemed busier than usual. But it didn't matter. U26 remained unseen as it nosed into the colder, rougher waters of the Norsemen.

Ewerth was the perfect naval officer, a good weapons delivery man, outwardly calm, doing his duty and not allowing his innermost thoughts to interfere with his objective. A few days ahead of him was Kptlt. Herbert Schultze in U48. Although two years his junior, Schultze carried a totally different attitude. For a start, he had been with his men for longer and therefore was able to trust them better, and he had no qualms about committing his thoughts to paper. His dislike for the German radio propaganda was plain for all to see. What's more, even after the beginning of the war, U48 openly tuned in to the BBC and Schultze recorded his praise for the high standard of the British news service.

'Our own news is too simplistic and too transparent,' he wrote, 'and virtually unbelievable.' Neither Dönitz, nor anyone else in the high command was left in any doubt about Schultze's contempt for the poor quality of broadcasts coming from Berlin. Ewerth however allowed himself to make only one open criticism (which was more for his own good than for telling his superiors what he thought of them). In his log he pointed out that messages to U-boats were being transmitted with accuracy and precision, but the meaningless fill messages to confuse outside listeners came over in such a slovenly manner that any radio operator could easily tell the difference.

The monotonous routine in U26 continued until the boat was drawing close to the Shetland Islands. Shortly after midday on 3 September the engineering officer appeared on the bridge, dodged a bit of spray and cursed. Then he told Ewerth that the British declaration of war, announced only minutes earlier by the radio, would need to be postponed. The oil pump lubricating the port diesel engine was giving trouble, which meant that it should be shut down for a while. Ewerth was prepared for even worse. He had noticed the nauseating clanking, but wasn't going to let such setbacks get him down. Instead he used the opportunity to practice an emergency dive and then gave his men the security of the depths for a peaceful lunch, after which engineers wrestled with the machinery.

The pump was quickly repaired, but the next problem was far more serious and had the potential for much more dangerous consequences. Responding to the call 'Commander to the bridge', Ewerth noticed the duty officer and lookouts were scrutinising a trail of oil in their wake. 'Stop, engines' ordered Ewerth.

As the froth behind them subsided and the surface of the water settled to the mirror-smooth surface of a duck pond, the men found a slight but noticeable trail shimmering in their wake. Ewerth's command, 'Engineer Officer to the bridge' was followed by the words, 'At once!' indicating that he was far from delighted by the colourful gloss on the water. The cause had to be a fracture between an oil tank and diving cell. Ewerth realised that the repairs would require a dry dock and that he, and he alone, had to make the decision whether to go on or turn back.

Seeing that the boat was surrounded by fairly thick fog, he decided to go on. They had been churning through the grey curtain for two full days and Ewerth knew that they were getting uncomfortably close to land. He also knew the south-west coast of England was no paradise for fools in ships. The cliffs were rugged, rocks sharp and currents treacherous. These hazards were well illustrated by an abundance of old wrecks. Bumping into something uncomfortable was far too easy. The radio navigation system had been working overtime, with men taking bearings on a variety of British transmitters, but this wasn't accurate enough for negotiating the dangers ahead. Ewerth needed an exact fix on some landmark or on stars or the sun. The sea had become noticeably calmer since coming around the southern tip of Ireland, but two days of mirror-smooth sea and constant fog had made it impossible to get a sighting on anything. It wasn't until the early evening of 9 September that a flash of light on their port flank caught the lookouts' attention.

So far U26 had avoided everything. The men knew they were on a special mission and Ewerth's order to turn the boat sharply towards the light was disturbing. The men confined to the inside of the stinking hull didn't like it. Why should the old man be making for a light? Lights are bad omens: in times of war everything should be blacked out. Ewerth didn't like it either. Spotting a light directly west suggested they had overshot their destination, and finding guiding lights shining so brightly was even more unnerving. The British government had declared war a week ago, meaning there had been ample time to switch them off. So why were the peacetime aids still on? Was it a trap? The timing of the flashes told the men the beam was not their destination off Portland Bill. Then illuminations spotted further along the coast indicated there was also a prominent town close by, tucked in behind a headland. The men had hardly taken bearings and come to the conclusion they were facing Berry Head by Brixham, when the darkened silhouette of a ship, showing only a few dull lights, brought the discussion to an abrupt halt. The U26 crashed below the waves. Realising they had been looking at the holiday resort of Torquay, the men were surprised that the peacetime illuminations had been left on.

Half an hour later, just after midnight, when the boat surfaced again, Ewerth headed in exactly the opposite direction, due east. The high cliffs of Portland Bill, with a lighthouse on top, were almost covering the flashes from the Shambles lightship while the Obersteuermann (Third Watch Officer and Navigator) took bearings on all positively identified landmarks. The men in the bow torpedo room were standing by to lay mines when words often found scribbled on public lavatory walls made them realise that not everything was as it should be. First the Obersteuermann bellowed down the voice pipe to ask for their course. Then he inquired who was at the helm. After that, he jumped down into the control room to check both magnetic and giro compasses for himself. Reappearing on the bridge, he confirmed Ewerth's suspicion: they were heading north-east instead of east. The currents were far stronger than they had imagined and the faint slither of black between Portland Bill and the mainland was now growing alarmingly larger, to stand out as an easily recognisable barrier.

Constant course corrections indicated that the old man was having problems. The men knew he could steer a submarine through a maze, but his skills were somewhat neutralised by the currents. This potent outside influence was made worse by the task in hand. Mines could only be laid at a slow, almost snail-like pace and maintaining such a crawl in these turbulent coastal currents was difficult at the best of times. Ewerth had no choice but to abandon his first objective and to creep around Portland Bill, hoping for more favourable conditions in the large bay to the east. Being the perfect naval officer, he didn't share his anxieties with his men. Instead, he remained calm, giving the impression everything was just as it should be.

U26 was still less than half a kilometre from the Shambles lightship when Ewerth looked at the illuminated dial of his watch before asking for confirmation of the time. U26 had been slowed down by the need to get an accurate fix on the lighthouse and by the current, and now he was wondering whether he was exposing his men to an unacceptable risk. It was getting late. It would soon be light. Yet Ewerth also had the special quality needed by a naval commander: that of not being put off his objective. He didn't fancy doing this twice and there was no way that he was returning during the following night for another go. So, with hardly a second thought, he allowed U26 to glide on into the lair of Britain's highly successful anti-submarine school.

To Ewerth's surprise, the opposition seemed to be asleep and nothing hindered the mission. There were no guard ships. No watchdogs. Nothing. Just a calm sea and a few illuminations on land. The first mine scraped out at 0523 hours and there were four course changes in 26 metres of water before the eighteenth and last mine was deposited just a little more than half an hour later. This meant they were spaced at about 120–150 metres. The astonishing point about this accomplishment is that not all of them fitted into the torpedo tubes at the same time; therefore the boat must have paused for reloading. What is more, during the course of the night, the men identified three different significant currents heading 108°, 120° and 49°, all moving at about 2 knots (nautical miles per hour). Bearing in mind the speed of the boat should have been not more than an outside maximum of 3 knots; one can see this mine laying was no mean effort. Navigation had to be perfect to drop the mines into the correct shipping channel otherwise they needn't have bothered. The water had remained calm with its mirror-smooth surface and the visibility gradually improved allowing ample compass bearings from fixed landmarks. Both Ewerth and the Obersteuermann were confident that their navigation was perfect. The mines were exactly where they should be.

The last mine had hardly been deposited when everybody on the bridge held their breath and a whispered order demanded more than total silence. Five hundred metres ahead, a darkened hulk appeared out of nowhere, blocking the escape. Strangely, it vanished as fast as it had emerged, leaving Ewerth to make full use of those powerful currents to his best advantage. Bringing U26 back into that strong surge which had troubled him earlier, he now gained extra speed to escape the mousetrap.

While heading out to sea U26 was running out of time and darkness. Soon it would be light, but now every minute was vital to get closer to deeper and safer water for diving. And yet, Ewerth could not run the risk of driving the boat too fast: he had to avoid displaying the giveaway white bow wave and wash at all costs. Remaining on the surface for as long as he dared, Ewerth eventually settled for a safer depth, clear of both the surface and the bottom, hoping that the current and electric motors would take them further out to sea. The calmness of the night didn't last long and soon an abundance of propeller noises started irritating the men inside U26. Thinking sound detectors had detected them while laying mines, they assumed half of the Royal Navy was now chasing them. The noises came closer. Too close for comfort. All machinery, including the gyrocompass and ventilator fans, was shut down. Men who had to walk around the interior wrapped their feet in rags, the cook was told they would give up eating for the day in preference to him clanking utensils and everybody was ordered to breathe through personal ventilators. These cumbersome contraptions were worn on the chest with a tube covering mouth and nose. A valve allowed air to be breathed directly from the surroundings but exhaled air passed through a tin containing potash for absorbing carbon dioxide.

Many men dropped off to sleep, exhausted after a long night's work. Those on duty found the surface activity becoming more determined. What's more they knew the early morning starry sky had indicated a clear day was to follow. The high-pitched whine of a destroyer stopped too frequently for comfort and shutting off its engine worried the men in U26. The water depth was only 60 metres. Aircraft flying overhead would probably see the submerged boat in the clearness of the Atlantic swell. Sunday, 10 September was neither a happy nor a comfortable day for the men in U26, yet it passed without serious incident. Of course, they didn't know it then, but the Supreme Naval Command had already written them off and Dönitz, their flag officer, was chewing over his lunch with similar ideas in his head. The high-pitched whining destroyer, which stopped to listen with its sound detectors, didn't hear the U-boat.

Less than twenty-four hours later the boot was on the other foot. With six torpedoes loaded in the tubes, U26 was ready, and, with deeper water under the keel, set course to pursue other targets. The first one was not as ill prepared as the peacetime illuminations on land had suggested. Running in zigzags, a steamer turned away at a distance of about 6 miles and then a small fishing boat with sails prevented U26 from giving chase on the surface. Several more of these obstacles were avoided before U26's honorary deputy commander, the port oil pump, dictated the course of action. Once again, the engine had to be stopped while the machinery was taken to pieces.

Although 13 September was a Wednesday, not a Friday, it still brought nothing but bad luck for the men in U26. A number of suitable targets appeared, but they either ran away at too great a distance or an abundance of small fishing boats with sails blocked the path. It was infuriating, but Ewerth and his men were pleased to be back in the Atlantic. There was something exceptionally unnerving about the drifting fog over those calm Channel waters.

Despite having accomplished their special mission and having successfully come back from the lion's den, the apprehension of war did not diminish. Having reloaded the six remaining torpedoes, they had to be withdrawn again because the radio ordered new settings to the heads. And then, those tiny nuisances continuously harassed U26; all of them small fishing boats with sails. There were too many of them and they could well be in direct communication with a big set of teeth in the form of destroyers or aircraft. The thought that they carried sound detection gear had occurred to the men in U26, but there was nothing they could do about it. Ewerth thought he might try creeping up on one, but that could bring more problems than it was worth and was not within his orders. The snag was that often there were more than one and knocking them off with torpedoes was hardly worth it. After all, one torpedo was almost bigger than the small pots and torpedoes were a good deal more expensive than these tiny fishing boats.

On one occasion, diving to avoid a trawler brought a positive advantage. U26's listening gear produced a faint far-off noise no one had heard before. A convoy. Ewerth immediately guessed it had to be the one reported earlier by U31 and, glancing around at the nervous fidgeting of his men, he jumped up and ordered 'battle stations'. From that moment on, seconds started dragging into an unbearable eternity. Everything appeared to be happening in slow motion, giving

Ewerth plenty of time to reflect on his decision. Might it not have been better to allow the target to slip away quietly? Approaching too close was not a good idea. Kptlt. Johannes Habekost in U31 had reported strong air cover and U26's sound detector heard the high-pitched whine of far-off destroyers. However, despite possible retribution, convoys made good targets. They could be attacked without warning and that was much safer than tackling lone ships. No matter what flag a lone ship might be flying, it had to be stopped and its papers inspected before any action could be taken. It could only be sunk if it was carrying war contraband, and even if it was, the crew still had to be given time to get off before launching an attack. On top of this, the submariners were supposed to assure the safety of the merchant sailors. So, convoys had some definite advantages.

Things were going to be tricky. What was more, U26's machinery was not being terribly cooperative and there was no point taking the usual precautionary look. Both periscopes were full of water and the raising mechanism of the attack periscope made enough noise to frighten the enemy. In addition to this, several threads of the steel cable for raising and lowering the periscope had snapped, suggesting the whole contraption might break altogether and leave an unwanted mast sticking up. Tension was high. Everybody knew what was at stake. U26 could surface uncomfortably close to something with a big bite. Ewerth jumped out onto the dripping conning tower, glanced over the protective wall to check that there was no one around and then gave the all clear for the lookouts to follow.

The convoy was some 4 or 5 kilometres on the horizon and Ewerth lost no time in aiming the boat at it. Then, quite suddenly, an unexpected opportunity presented itself. The men's stares were fixed on three overlapping freighters. They were a hell of a long way off, but looked like one large target. No one could miss it. Yet the IWO (First Watch Officer) was nervous. This was the first time he had done something like this for real. It took just over eight minutes for the sound of a detonation to reach their ears and then, almost immediately, the men tumbled back through the hatch while U26 dived to avoid an approaching fast warship. The term destroyer was rather alarming for men cooped up in the narrow confines of a submarine and the majority of commanders used less disturbing descriptions.

Four hours later, U26 was back on the surface, enjoying the fresh air over a hardly moving sea. The absence of a moon made everything seem blacker than normal, but not dark enough to miss a freighter on the horizon. Instantly the engines burst into life, pushing white surging foam away from the stern, but even with everything the boat had being thrust into driving the propellers, the freighter could not be caught and slowly vanished out of sight.

The great reward came at eight o'clock the following night when British radio announced the sinking of the 6,000-ton Belgian freighter *Alex van Opstal* in the English Channel. It had to be result of the mines laid near Weymouth. Then the radio also described the sinking of an 8,000-ton tanker in a convoy. For a time the men wondered whether this could have been their long-range attack against those three overlapping ships, but that has never been confirmed, suggesting that none of them went down.

There followed no shortage of ships, but the next one turned out to have been the United States freighter *Eglantine* on her way from Manchester to Houston (Texas). Germany wasn't at war with the United States, so she was allowed to proceed on her way. The next two ships sounded as if they were accompanied by the characteristic high-pitched whine of a fast warship's turbine and as it did not have a functioning periscope, it was better for U26 to remain submerged. The ship after that turned out to be another neutral, the Estonian *Otto Estri*, a small pot of less than 2,000 tons. Then U26 stopped the Swedish *Luzie Justero*. A bit bigger, but also not engaged in warring activities and she was allowed to continue her journey to pick up coal from Newcastle in England for the gas works in Stockholm. Finding out what the ship was doing and what cargo it was carrying was dangerous and time consuming. The submarine had to wait for the merchant seamen to lower a boat and row over with their ship's papers. At the best of times, the restless Atlantic was not an ideal place for this type of sailing. U-boat men didn't like it either; anyone could have attacked at the critical moments while they stood still. Some ships even retaliated by attempting to ram the submarine which was trying to stop them. However, the majority obeyed the grim international laws, known by the grand title of Prize Ordinance Regulations, which all German submarine commanders were ordered to follow to the letter.

Arriving back in the Jade Estuary made Ewerth curse again. The lightship didn't answer and it took a while before they dared approach the narrow channel leading to Wilhelmshaven. Those who felt like swearing did. The bright moon added a splendid silvery sheen to the water, making the low landline in the far distance stand out as a dominant streak, but Ewerth didn't dare approach any closer. He guessed the deep-water channel would now be well protected and he didn't wish to become a target for the Luftwaffe. So he waited patiently, bobbing around on moderate waves, until the authorities gave him permission to enter port. In any case, there was no point arriving in Wilhelmshaven unless the lock keepers were awake.

It wasn't until after he had made fast at 0300 hours on 26 September that he learned about the virtually non-existant coastal defences. Later he found out that his boss, Kapitän zur See und Kommodore Karl Dönitz had not been shunted sideways into a position where he had less cause to argue with his superiors in Berlin. Dönitz had in fact become a rear admiral and Ewerth had also been awarded another stripe, making him a Korvettenkapitän (Commander), but the promotion wasn't important at that moment. The best reward was being back home. Many historians have claimed that Dönitz's promotion came about as a result of U47's attack against the British battleship HMS *Royal Oak* in the Royal Navy's anchorage at Scapa Flow, but this is not correct as Dönitz had been wearing the rear admiral's stripe since 12 September 1939.

3

BATTLES AGAINST IMPOSSIBLE REGULATIONS

Kptlt. Wilhelm Rollmann joined the navy as an officer candidate in 1926 and took command of U34 almost one year before the beginning of the Second World War. U34 was one of the last seagoing Type VIIA boats to have been built at Germaniawerft in Kiel before production switched to the modified Type VIIB. It had a single hull instead of U26's double hull and was marginally smaller, but had been designed for roughly the same purpose.

In the middle of August 1939, the officer commanding the 2nd U-boat Flotilla (Flotilla Saltzwedel), ordered U34 to prepare quietly for war. U26 under Klaus Ewerth belonged to the same flotilla, based at Germany's only purpose-built U-boat station in Bant (Wilhelmshaven). These preparations were nothing new. Submarines had been put on war alert during previous political crises and this passed off as just another one of those irritating exercises. Outwardly everything looked calm, the same as it had always done, but this time U34 left with provisions for the considerably longer cruise of six weeks as well as six electric torpedoes of Type G7e and four faster varieties (G7a), driven by internal combustion engines. These had the advantage of requiring less maintenance but they left a noticeable trail of bubbles and oil as they sped through the water. Thus they could not be used during daylight, when the target could easily spot the eruption coming towards it.

At 0800 hours on 18 August, when U34 nosed out of the sea locks for trimming and diving trials, Rollmann still didn't know what all the fuss was about and it is highly likely that the flotilla commander wasn't any the wiser. They were obviously aware of problems flaring up with the Polish and British governments, but not many in Germany had any serious thoughts about war. Rollmann didn't even know where he was supposed to go or what he was supposed to do. The Supreme Naval Command in Berlin had drawn up the emergency Three Front War Programme, which the flotilla staff had been instructed to implement. The orders for this had been lying for some time in sealed envelopes, locked in safes. In order to preserve secrecy, very few knew the exact details. To make sure nothing leaked out, commanders were not allowed to open the envelopes until they were at sea and after they had received a special order to do so. This time, however, Rollmann didn't just take the envelopes to sea and bring them home again. He was also told to look inside. Things appeared serious, although the instructions were simple: put the boat onto a war footing and without being observed, take up a waiting position to the west of Ireland, roughly in line with Land's End in Cornwall (England).

The admirals of the German Navy left virtually nothing to the imagination and details of what was meant by 'war footing' was spelt out as well. It was a bit like putting up Christmas decorations in reverse; first everything detachable was removed from the outside. This included the huge bronze eagle on the conning tower, navigation lights and the identification plaques on the bows. Unscrewing these heavy bronze plates in their most inaccessible position was no easy matter and required someone with the agility of an acrobat. While that was going on, everything else, including the brightly-coloured life belts and the red and white rescue buoys, was painted dull grey. The huge white numbers on the side of the conning tower were also painted over to cover all identification marks. The rescue buoys had now become a dangerous liability because they had a telephone connection with a lamp on the top and a depth charge could blow them out of their fittings. If this happened they would automatically float to the surface and flash like a Belisha beacon. After all, they were designed to attract attention. So, many thought it would be better to remove the light bulb as well. As it happened, the sea was smooth and the wind added a light breeze to make this outside work almost enjoyable and certainly far better than sitting inside the tight confines of the pressure hull. Incidentally, the fitting-out instructions to the flotilla's quartermaster ensured that all necessary materials for this transformation were already on board.

Together with the navigation officer (the Obersteuermann), Rollmann calculated that the 1,700-sea mile (3,150-kilometre) journey to the waiting area at 9–11 knots would take at least nine days and use 20 tons of fuel, as long as there were not too many interruptions. The big problem was that U34 encountered such a large number of small fishing boats with sails that constant course changes were necessary. Once in position the men found a multitude of suitable targets to avoid, confirming that they were in just the right area if things came to a shootout. The signals to commence hostilities with England and France started arriving during the late morning of 3 September and made it necessary for Rollmann and his two watch officers to carefully read through the Prize Ordinance Regulations once more. Politicians conceived these unmanageable rules long before the war, but despite the impossibility of observing them, the German government signed the agreement and now a special order from the Supreme Naval Command reminded everybody that they were to be obeyed to the letter. The regulations ruled out any attacks against lone merchant ships. These could not be sunk without the attacker first seeing to the safety of the merchant crew and only if there was enough space in the submarine to take any additional men on board. So, Rollmann concluded that it would be best if they concentrated on troop transports, warships or merchant ships sailing with escort or in convoys. There were no clues however as to how one should distinguish a troop transport from a passenger ship carrying civilians. It was exactly this tricky problem that was the first one to land the U-boat arm in serious trouble. The first ship to be sunk by a U-boat turned out to be the passenger liner *Athenia*, which Kptlt. Fritz-Julius Lemp of U30 identified as a troop transport.

Luckily U34 managed to avoid such a confrontation. On the second day of the war, lookouts on U34 spotted a merchant ship without a flag and without any form of identification. Rollmann didn't attack it because of the Prize Ordinance Rules. The same thing happened a few hours later. This time the ship was identified as the SS *Browning*, sailing west from Britain. Rollmann remarked that if things continued like this, then he would use up all his fuel and provisions without ever having a chance of shooting any torpedoes. At around the same time, U34 received another warning signal from headquarters saying that passenger ships were not to be attacked under any circumstances, even if they were sailing in convoy.

The great bane of life on U34 remained those dreaded small fishing boats. Eight, and at times even more, were in sight at any one time, making the task of remaining unseen most difficult. It felt like being surrounded by a swarm of flies, where even swatting them wouldn't have made much difference other than revealing one's presence. The rules and regulations were infuriating and these were made worse by constant reminders and additions from Germany. The war was only two days old when the Supreme Naval Command prohibited attacks against French ships and, at about the same time, the radio operators discovered that the signals being transmitted on shortwave were different to what was being broadcast on longwave, although both should have been identical. As a result the radio room had to put on a double watch. Life certainly wasn't easy.

Things changed most dramatically on 7 September, when at 1120 hours the lookouts spotted smoke coming towards them. The weather was so brilliant that the beaches back home would have already started filling up with people eager to cool off in the sea. The zigzagging ship looked most suspicious. Its earlier peacetime colours had been covered hastily with black paint, but traces of the original underneath were still clearly visible. Later, having noticed the U-boat by its side, the crew prepared to lower lifeboats while the ship made a sharp turn towards U34 in what looked like a ramming attempt. Rollmann still wasn't sure how he should react and allowed to target to pass over the top of him. Then, resurfacing, he found the ship had stopped and the crew had taken to the lifeboats. Yet, he still obeyed his instructions and set a signal ordering the ship to stop and not use its radio. Just to make doubly sure that the merchantmen knew what was afoot, he also put a shot from the 88mm deck gun across the bows. Then he closed in on one of the lifeboats, only to discover that he was by the side of the 5,809 GRT freighter *Pukkastan* on her way from

Cape Town to Devonport with a load of mutton and maize. Despite the tension, there was nothing in the rules which allowed him to sink it. The rules stated quite clearly and definitely that he must first see to the safety of the crew. There was no way he could take so many men on board and Rollmann was on the verge of ordering the men back onto their ship, when another freighter, this time one flying a neutral flag, approached. That immediately sealed the fate of *Pukkastan* and a G7a torpedo was launched to hit it amidships. This made it the 6th target to be sunk by a U-boat during the Second World War and the newcomer was left to pick up the men in the lifeboats.

Fighting a war according to Prize Ordinance Regulations was no easy matter and many commanders found themselves in a quandary as to what to do with the merchant crews. The regulations stated that lifeboats were not regarded as a safe means of transport on the high seas, so it was a case of hopefully meeting neutral ships to help out with rescuing. If this was not possible then the ship had to be allowed to continue or U-boats had to operate close enough to land that lifeboats could safely reach it. U35, under Werner Lott, went even further to comply with these laws and, to many people's astonishment, landed a number of seamen in neutral Ireland.

This saga started on 9 September, when the war was less than one week old. U35, also a seagoing Type VIIA similar to Rollmann's U34, left Wilhelmshaven together with two small coastal boats, U23 (Otto Kretschmer) and U21 (Fritz Frauenheim), tagging on behind. They had just passed the Weser lightship when Lt.z.S. Roters ordered full speed ahead and a sharp turn to port. Lott scrambled up to the top of the conning tower to see a torpedo running a few metres ahead of the bows and, at the same time, another one sped past, only a short distance behind the stern. This proved that the lookouts were definitely fully awake and the Second Watch Officer reacted quickly, calmly and correctly to save the boat and everybody inside it. Lott wrote in the log that this was a 'waschechte Feuertaufe' – a term which can hardly be translated with the right sentiment, although it means 'genuine baptism of fire'. Other than sending an immediate warning signal to the other U-boats, there wasn't much that U35 could do; U-boats were not equipped with the necessary machinery for finding other submerged submarines. The only course of action was to get away as quickly as possible. The snag was that Lott was heading west for the Straits of Dover and now knew that everybody there would have been warned that three U-boats had just put to sea. Such an advertisement didn't feel good.

Werner Lott had commanded U21 for six months, and U32 for four months, before taking on U35. He may not have been to war before, but he was well experienced in handling submarines. Despite this, he found the next hours most unsettling because there were so many ships to avoid. Approaching Ostend in Belgium made matters even worse. He had expected the navigation aids there to be shining brightly, but straight ahead he noticed a number of lights appearing and disappearing in the murk, but was unable to make out what they were. Then, just before midnight at the end of 11 September, a mysterious shadow about as high as U35's conning tower came into sight. It appeared to be closing in and an emergency avoidance manoeuvre was ordered before the men realised they were sailing past what were either the bows or stern of a wreck sticking up into the sky. A strong tidal current created a wake around the wreck and the combination of U35's abnormally high speed of sailing and this swell gave the impression that the stationary object was coming towards them. This had only just been digested when a real irritation, a British destroyer, came into sight. The sea was rough enough to suggest that an attack might fail and Lott decided it would be better to dive and avoid confrontation. Yet, although the destroyer hadn't reacted to the U-boat on the surface and it seemed as if U35 had not been spotted, the threat wouldn't go away and its propeller noises accompanied the U-boat far too long for comfort.

A brisk force 7 north-north-westerly was still blowing heavy rain over a rough sea at midday on the 12th when the sound detector reported more propeller noises approaching. Had the destroyer heard the U-boat when it dived? Could it have called in reinforcements? The frightening situation of hearing sounds but not daring to surface for a closer look came as the last straw after a constant chain of lights and shadows had made Lott wary of going any further. Instead of proceeding to break through the narrow Straits of Dover, he ordered U35 to turn and sail to the southern Irish Sea via the north of Scotland. A long way round, but at that stage it felt like a considerably safer option. The reputation that this treacherous stretch of narrow water with its infamous Goodwin Sands had acquired during the First World War had been deeply ingrained in the minds of many U-boat men. Lott's crew also breathed a deep sigh of relief when they heard about the change of course. Almost exactly one month later, U16, under Horst Wellner, perished on those perilous Goodwin Sands, close to Dover. Lott probably made a wise decision.

Shortly after midday on 18 September U35 dived after lookouts sighted smoke on the horizon. It surfaced again later next to what turned out to be an armed trawler, the 271-ton *St Albis* from Hull, whose crew was so shocked that they immediately abandoned ship. The only lifeboat at their disposal may have been suitable for when the boat was fishing but it was much too small for the additional military specialists on board. It was lying so low in the water that it would not have got very far and would have foundered if towed. Lott sent a prize crew over with the order to throw all the trawler's equipment overboard and then, to comply with Prize Ordinance Regulations, he allowed the crew back on board. He would have been well within his rights to sink it. According to Prize Ordinance Regulations there was no need to assure the safety of crews from warships, troop transports or merchant ships sailing in convoys and an armed trawler could be classified as a warship. The Germans were rather surprised that this boat had obviously been rigged for combat and that two children as young as fifteen or sixteen were employed for such hazardous work. The skipper of the *St Albis* rewarded Lott for sparing the crew by telling him that the aircraft carrier *Ark Royal* was close by. Earlier in the day he had seen three of its planes pass overhead. A few minutes later U27 confirmed the statement, saying an aircraft carrier was lying about 100 nautical miles to the south.

About six hours later, at 1800 hours, this drama repeated itself. This time U35 surfaced next to the fishing boat *Arlita* from Fleetwood, whose crew was so keen on abandoning ship that the gear for lowering the lifeboat fell overboard as they tried to lower it. The crew were told to remain on board and to lower and discard their radio aerial. Then they were told to follow U35 to another cloud of smoke not too far away. Astonishingly enough, the small *Arlita* of 326 GRT easily kept pace with the considerably bigger submarine. The smoke came from another Fleetwood trawler, the 229 GRT *Nancy Hague*, which was ordered to join U35's throng to investigate a third cloud of smoke. This turned out to be *Lord Minto*, another Fleetwood trawler of 295 tons. The crew wasn't quite so obliging because they had seen the U-boat approaching and therefore tried running away at high speed. They capitulated when an 88-mm shell exploded in their path. The oldest and slowest of the trio was the *Nancy Hague*, so Lott put all the men aboard her and sunk the other two. Scenes like this were not the easiest to comprehend because no one present could really understand the grounds for the war and no one had yet come to terms with the harsh reality which it made necessary. For that reason many U-boat commanders would allow only the oldest and most mature men on deck during such heartbreaking situations.

Shortly after lunch on 21 September, U35 stumbled into a magnificent opportunity to disregard the Prize Ordinance Regulations. For only the second time in the Second World War, a U-boat found itself confronted with a convoy and this one (OB4) was in exactly the right position for a submerged attack. All that was necessary was a little juggling of the position from which to launch it. This is where Lott became unstuck. Although lookouts had seen the approaching smoke from a long way off, they were prevented from making for that perfect position by what Lott described as a huge lumbering whale of a flying boat. It seemed highly likely that the aircrew had also spotted the U-boat because shortly after the dive, the convoy made a drastic change of course. Lott had his eye on a destroyer on the starboard flank, moving at the same speed as the merchant ships. His argument was that this was partly shielding the ships and could present rather an aggressive problem once the first torpedo detonated. Strangely, the torpedo aimed at it just vanished, as if someone had picked it out of the water.

One big problem with shooting from a submerged position was that the balance of the submarine was so critical that the weight of one man walking from one end to the other could easily upset the trim. Shooting a single torpedo lightens a boat by 1½ tons and masses of water have to be pumped into the compensating tanks to prevent it from rising to the surface. On this occasion the men were a bit on the generous side and U35 dropped down too deep, meaning that it was no longer possible to look out of the extended periscope.

By the time they were back in the right place, the nearest column, that containing the destroyer, had moved on far enough to be out of reach. However, two ships from the far column were still within range and two torpedoes were fired. One of these was heard to hit and Lott saw enough through the periscope to notice that the other ship was making a sharp turn. The explosion must have warned the merchantmen and lookouts might even have seen the approaching torpedo in the clear Atlantic waters. Not sure exactly what had happened, the men in U35 heard another loud detonation, suggesting that both targets had been hit. Unfortunately Lott could not stay to observe the results. A destroyer was now coming much too close for comfort. Ordering U35 down to 70 metres worked well, but the men did not manage to hold it at that depth. Instead it dropped deeper and then a severe shuddering followed by a grinding noise told them they had hit the bottom. This provided the opportunity of shutting down all noise emitting devices so that the men could concentrate on the whirling from the destroyers above them. Pulling the boat free presented more problems than the opposition did. Luckily the expected depth charges didn't materialise, despite one of the destroyers sitting right on top of the submarine.

Pulling free from the firm hold proved difficult and all efforts of blowing the tanks failed until suddenly there was a jerk and U35 started accelerating upwards. This time all attempts at preventing it from dashing to the surface failed as well and the boat lurched out of the water like a half drunken whale. The collision with the bottom had caused some damage, which could now be clearly seen because the interior was filling up with unwanted water and pumps had to be brought into use to blow the surplus weight out again. The strange thing was that the convoy had vanished, leaving U35 free to nurse its wounds. British records confirm that the 6,014 GRT freighter *Teakwood* was damaged during this attack, but a second ship was not identified, suggesting that the torpedo fell foul of its own shortcomings and detonated without hitting anything.

The astonishing part of U35's voyage is that the boat ventured eastwards along the English side of the Channel to a little beyond Beachy Head by Eastbourne in Sussex and Lott was even contemplating exploring the traffic running around Dungeness. So he was within a few miles west of the spot from which he had abandoned the breakthrough through the Straits of Dover. However, prospects of launching successful attacks there within Prize Ordinance Regulations were too remote and the tension among the crew was so high that he decided it would be better if they were to head west into more open waters.

The rest of the journey was most eventful with plenty of action, but the real crunch with Prize Ordinance Regulations came shortly after lunch on 3 October when the 4,990 GRT Greek freighter *Diamantis* was spotted approaching. Lott dived and a short burst of speed eventually brought him close enough to surface by the ship's side. A Morse message 'STOP AT ONCE – DO NOT USE YOUR RADIO' was flashed over. The target came to a halt but there wasn't much more of a response other than the radio started sending a chain of distress calls. The sea was too rough for dispatching a prize crew or for the master to bring his papers to the U-boat, so Lott ordered him to follow U35 closer to the Irish coast, where he hoped to find calmer conditions. One of the large shades of grey within the Prize Ordinance Regulations was the use of radio for sending distress calls with position. Although this was theoretically prohibited, many U-boat commanders withheld further aggressive action, despite the radio putting them in real danger of retaliation from superior forces.

Lott started losing his rag with his opponent's slovenly behaviour when there was no reaction to his 'FOLLOW ME' signal. This had been flying from the extended periscope for more than ten minutes before he ordered the gun crew on deck for a shot across the bows. This worked exceedingly well. The empty deck of the freighter erupted into sheer pandemonium, with the crew scurrying to get into the lifeboats; despite the U-boat's searchlight flashing an order for them to remain on board. The lifeboats were being launched haphazardly into a rough north-easterly wind of force 7–8.

The British propaganda system with its tales of cruel German U-boat men must have made a significant impact on the Greeks for them to attempt to leave their ship under such stormy conditions. The large lifeboat on the windward side capsized the moment it touched the waves, but the one on the other side remained afloat and another, smaller boat seemed to have been launched on the leeward side as well. The Germans on top of the conning tower and gun crew watched the ridiculous spectacle in amazement and started helping those in the water as soon as Lott brought the submarine close enough. Waves were constantly washing over the upper deck, often throwing the gun crew off their feet. This left some painful bruises, but the safety harnesses ensured that no one could slip off the deck. The length of the cables holding them in place were not adjustable and Lott was horrified when he saw the artillery officer and a warrant officer, both of whom should have been more sensible than the men, join the crew in unclipping their safety lines in order to reach further over the side to help stricken men in the water. Despite wearing lifejackets, Lott could see the possibility of losing them overboard. Yet he didn't want to interrupt their heroic effort either. Shouting down to them would have been difficult; the gale would have stolen his commands. Having plucked the men from the capsized boat from the water, U34's crew set about picking up the rest who were still clinging desperately to the precarious situation in their small boat.

Once on deck, the Greeks were so exhausted that some of them cried and others didn't seem to do much more than say their prayers, despite waves constantly crashing over them and threatening to wash them back into the sea. This mayhem continued until all but three Greeks had been brought below. The only way into the submarine was to climb up the back onto the gun platform and from there through the hatch on the top of the conning tower and then down two vertical ladders on the inside. This was no easy effort, especially as the men were cold, wet and totally exhausted. Opening the hatches in the deck would have been suicidal with water quickly flooding the interior. This little climbing manoeuvre and then squeezing into the tight interior was far worse than any modern fairground ride and many men must have thought that their last minute of life had come. Even once inside, in relative safety, the merchant seamen found themselves with hardly enough space to move. It all felt and smelt hostile. Three Greeks were still on deck when matters were made worse by the harsh shrill of the alarm bells. An aircraft had been sighted, probably flying in as a result of the earlier distress call. Strangely, despite the chaos, the alarm procedure worked reasonably well and left the Germans counting twenty-eight wet and cold Greeks. The entire crew had been saved.

The engineer officer, Lt.z.S. Stamer, actually brought the boat down to periscope depth without any repercussions from the aircraft, leaving Lott free to tear a strip off the master for his unprofessional conduct and for neither obeying the U-boat's instructions nor acknowledging them. Lott was particularly annoyed that the ship continued giving away its position by sending SOS signals. It appeared that the sighting of the U-boat created a near mutiny with the master telling the men to remain on board but with one of the officers ordering them to abandon ship.

The *Diamantis* was carrying manganese ores from Freetown in Africa to Barrow-in-Furness, thus putting it into a class which could be sunk. So, since the crew confirmed that everybody had got off and there was no sensible chance of getting them back on board, Lott dispatched three torpedoes, one after the other to sink the freighter. The first two didn't work. Then came the next problem of finding another ship to take the Greek prisoners on board. The weather was slowly getting worse and the prospects of getting rid of the additional men didn't look good. Lott didn't like it and described the inside of his boat as smelling awful, something like the beast of prey house in the zoo.

It was shortly before four o'clock in the afternoon when *Diamantis* went down and it took until eight to sort out the inside of U35. Besides drying clothing, feeding the Greeks and dealing with a number of minor injuries, there were five serious cases of men with high temperatures, displaying symptoms of malaria and obviously needing to be seen by a doctor. Lott saw himself with no alternative other than to make towards Ireland. The capsized lifeboats had by this time been found as well and the merchant navy airwaves started buzzing with details. In view of this, Lott saw himself compelled to report the incident to base in order to prevent the generation of horror stories of German submariners killing men in lifeboats.

The fact that two torpedoes failed to sink the stationary ship was more worrying than dealing with the additional bodies and Lott made doubly sure that the correct firing procedures had been carried out. The waves were now hitting the U-boat almost sideways on, making it roll most dramatically, something even the seasoned Greek seamen couldn't cope with and a number of them were painfully seasick. This nauseating condition lasted until three o'clock the following afternoon, when U35 nosed slowly into the isolated harbour of Ventry in Dingle Bay. It took an hour and a half to get all the passengers on land, despite cooperation from the locals, who appeared to be making a considerable effort to help the stricken seamen. Forty or more came down to the harbour to help and to stare in amazement. Such help was not always forthcoming and there were several cases of shipwrecked sailors being locked in prisons by African governments because they did not have passports with the necessary entry visas.

The Greeks were lucky to have been put ashore at that critical moment as conditions got considerably worse when U35 continued with its homeward journey. The lookouts found themselves in the most dire situation of having to cope with breakers washing right over the top of the conning tower, making it difficult and at times even impossible to hold binoculars in front of their eyes. While these conditions lasted, things also started deteriorating considerably down in the engine room. So far it had hardly been necessary to cruise faster than 11 knots and for most of the time the men managed to keep to an economical 9 knots. Despite not driving up to their maximum of 17 knots, the engines were now showing extensive signs of wear, making a number of difficult running repairs more than essential. To make matters worse, U35 reached a point where both engines gave out at the same time, meaning that there was nothing for it other than to drift with the weather and wind while the engineers struggled to get the heap of scrap home again. The only consolation was that rocky coasts were a long way off and there was no danger of meeting any uncomfortably hard projections to bring the voyage to an abrupt end. Long after the war several more senior U-boat officers remarked casually that the contribution made by engineers to the U-boat war was enormous and has never been fully recognised or acknowledged. On this occasion Lott certainly appreciated the efforts made by his engineers and recorded his admiration in the U-boat's log.

In addition to the ships mentioned in this chapter, U35 tackled six other potential targets. The most disappointing incident for the men was when a massive passenger liner ran into the perfect shooting position all on its own, without knowing it was only 500 metres from the end of four fully loaded torpedo tubes. This was the 45,000-ton liner *Aquitania*, sailing without lights at 24 knots. A few days earlier the Supreme Naval Command had prohibited attacks against passenger liners, even if they were sailing in convoy and therefore Lott withheld the order to shoot his torpedoes, despite being in the perfect position for hitting a ship that was normally too fast for U-boats. Lott knew from his handbook that the *Aquitania* had been used as a troopship during the First World War, but on this occasion he had no way of knowing what she was carrying. The most disappointing part of this accidental meeting came two days later, when the radio gave him permission to attack passenger liners if they were sailing without lights at night, but by then it was too late.

At 0840 hours on 1 October 1939, U35 stopped the Greek freighter *George M. Embiricos*, sailing from Bahia Blanca in Argentina to Antwerp in Belgium, but allowed it to continue because it was sailing neither under a British nor French flag and an inspection of the ship's papers revealed that it was not carrying contraband. At 1120 hours the Portuguese *Alferrarde*, sailing from Lisbon in Portugal to Antwerp, was stopped and allowed to proceed because it too was neither carrying contraband nor aiding a warring nation. However, the Belgian *Suzon*, on its way from Bordeaux to Cardiff with a load of pit props was sunk with a torpedo shortly after 1845 hours due to its listed cargo. On 6 October the Norwegian *Hird* was also stopped and allowed to proceed because it too was sailing under a neutral flag and not carrying any war goods. The most astonishing inspection according to Prize Ordinance Regulations took place on 19 October when the 800-ton four-mast schooner *Yxphila*, sailing from Weymouth in England to Raumaa in Finland was stopped. It was also sailing under a neutral flag and wasn't making any contribution to Britain's war effort, so it too was allowed to continue.

In those cases where ships were behaving according to the regulations and displayed clear neutrality markings or where their neutral flag was clearly visible, U-boats usually asked for the ship's papers to be brought over by the merchant crew. Hardly any of these ships carried powered boats, so several seamen had to row an officer with a briefcase to the submarine. Very few lifeboats would have had any form of shelter or any mechanical means of pumping out seawater. So it was a case of getting cold, wet and out of breath. One or two of the crew often had to use buckets for bailing out as well. Suspicious ships were more difficult to deal with inasmuch that the U-boat had to dispatch a prize crew for an inspection. Although some U-boats carried wooden dinghies, these were usually too small for such a large group of men and large inflatables had to be used. These often had soft bottoms for folding into small storage containers and jumping into them could result in the floor being torn out. This type of transport was far from ideal. Even on the calmest of days the men arrived at their destination wet, often comparatively poorly armed and not knowing what type of hostile situation they were stepping into. If the target turned out to be a genuine neutral without contraband it was allowed to proceed.

On his way back from his first war voyage, Rollmann of U34 found himself in a somewhat strange situation regarding his prize crew. He was still a long way out in the North Sea when at first light on 29 September 1939 lookouts sighted a number of ships. Shortage of fuel, rough seas and the fact that the ships were heading towards Norway suggested there was not much point in pursuing any and the U-boat continued on its way southwards to Wilhelmshaven. At 1230 hours, with the smell of lunch drifting through the boat the duty officer called the commander to the bridge in order to exchange recognition signals with U29 (Otto Schuhart). This was just a few days after U29 had sunk the aircraft carrier HMS *Courageous*, but there is no record in the log as to whether Lott knew this when they met at sea.

These identification signals were changed daily and the majority of U-boats had a small slate in the conning tower with details of the current code. Usually there was a column for the colour of any lights shot from signal pistols, flags to be set or Morse messages to be flashed with the signal lamp. This portable lamp could be plugged into a socket on the top of the conning tower and it had a basket-like resting place on the main periscope support. U29 was also making for Wilhelmshaven and hadn't gone too far when a neutral Norwegian freighter sailing to Antwerp was inspected by U34 and allowed to proceed on its way. Almost exactly an hour later another, an Estonian ship, the 1,781 GRT *Hanonia* from Kuresseore with a load of pit props to the value of 30,000 British Pounds and destined for Grimsby in England, was spotted coming out of the Skagerrak on U34's port side.

This was obviously contraband and so close to home that Rollmann decided to dispatch a prize crew with instructions to take the ship into Kiel. This in itself was not an easy undertaking and even collecting together the necessary equipment took some time. Surface ships had rooms with everything lying ready and close at hand, but in a U-boat equipment had to be stowed wherever there was room, often a long way from the main hatch in the conning tower. The following items were collected together and issued to the prize crew: four scuttling charges, each one inside its own special storage box, which took up considerable space in the already crowded dinghy; six fuses with time delay mechanisms; charts for the area from Skagen to Kiel; a naval flag with swastika; a set of signal flags for sending semaphore messages; a Morse lamp with details of the necessary recognition signals; a radio capable of picking up longwave transmissions; one pair of binoculars and five rubber life jackets. The prize crew consisted of five men: Oblt.z.S. Wilfried Prellberg, Bootsmaat Welling, Matrosenobergefreiter Buckermann, Maschinenobergrefreiter Aufurth and Torpedomechanikergefreiter Meiburg.

They hoisted the Estonian flag before leaving the scene at 1633 hours to head east at 7.5 knots in their new charge. Once it started getting dark, the men ensured that the flag was well illuminated to prevent unnecessary interception from the surrounding neutral countries. The big problem was that the radio room was still capable of calling in uncomfortable opposition. To prevent this, the Morse keys were removed and the guards told to keep a special eye on the door to ensure that no one got inside. In view of the crew not showing any great signs of hostility, it was thought that these simple measures would be sufficient. Prellberg guessed that the ship would be allowed to return to Estonia. If the cargo had been paid for by Britain then it could be unloaded in Kiel, otherwise it would return home with the ship, so there was no point in any serious destruction.

Hanonia's crew was under the impression that U34 was following on alongside with a torpedo ready in case things didn't go according to plan. However, this was not the case and only Prellberg could have had any inclination that Rollmann received a radio message ordering him to investigate a couple of ships sailing almost side by side a few miles to his rear. A north-north-westerly force 5 had been blowing for some time, making it sheer hell for the stern lookouts, but the boat was riding the waves exceedingly well. The violent rolling and pitching was not too uncomfortable for the rest of the crew. Now, however, he had to turn and fight against the nauseating wind, which made the boat react most violently with chaotic and often unpredictable movements in addition to some frightful noisy shuddering. The lookouts found the two ships at 1830 hours, but the U-boat had exhausted its entire store of sidearms and there were no more spare bodies for forming another boarding party. In any case, Skagen, the northern tip of Denmark, was living up to its reputation of not always being the most hospitable place on earth. Like the Goodwin Sands near Dover, this area harboured a large collection of wrecks to prove that many people had come unstuck there. The weather was far too rough for another inspection. Yet, despite the horrendous conditions, Rollmann ordered the ships to bring their papers over, despite the fact that he had no alternative other than to allow them to proceed. He remarked that U34 had not been supplied with a copy of *Lloyd's Register*, so checking the names presented some problems and he could not be sure that they were carrying genuine papers. On the other hand he didn't find anything suspicious either and the merchantmen behaved correctly, in an obliging manner, as far as the foul weather allowed.

The lookouts were still watching the small whaler plough through the waves back to their ship, when two more newcomers were observed. Just to complicate matters, they were both on the horizon at opposite ends of the lookouts' field of vision. These two were quickly joined by a few more and Rollmann remarked that they had not seen so many ships for a long time. A good number of them were probably nothing more complicated than fishing boats and there was no way he could check all of them. What was still bothering him was that he had met the Estonian *Hanonia* while she was streaming out of the Baltic and he wondered why the ship had been allowed to proceed so far without having been checked by patrols nearer home.

U34 now headed south along the Danish west coast and later made some attempt at contacting the visual signal station on the Friesen Island of Wangerooge, but at first got no reply. There were no patrol boats either. Despite the calm, Rollmann waited until he received permission to proceed along the narrow deep-water channel towards the locks at Wilhelmshaven, arriving there at 0900 hours on 29 September.

Prellberg wasn't experiencing any great difficulties in the meantime. *Hanonia*'s crew thought the U-boat was close by, they didn't have any weapons for tackling armed Germans and knew their best chance of survival depended on them arriving safely in some port. Even if they hadn't been told, it wasn't difficult to guess that this would be Kiel. The only problem lay in negotiating some Danish barriers and there were several occasions where a Swedish aircraft circled the ship, but otherwise showed no interest in the neutral freighter from Estonia. The airmen must have wondered why this ship was carrying a load of wood in what could only have been concluded to be the wrong direction. The huge timber exporting forests were in the east and there was no need for anyone there to import it. Prellberg must have felt pleased at 0630 on 27 September when he passed the Kiel lightship. At 0810 he was on the landward side of the narrows between Friedrichsort and the U-boat Memorial at Möltenort. Ten minutes later the *Hanonia* dropped anchor in the bay there in order to hand the ship over to the coastguards. Prellberg remained IWO of U34 until January 1940 when he was sent to commanders' school. Later he commanded U19 and then U31, the U-boat that was sunk twice during the Second World War. Everybody on board was killed when it was bombed in the Jade Estuary during diving trials in March 1940. It was raised and made ready again and Prellberg and all but two of his crew were lucky to escape when the boat was depth charged by the British destroyer HMS *Antelope* in November 1940.

U35 under Werner Lott returned to Wilhelmshaven on 12 October. U35, still with Lott in command, was sunk in November 1939 by HM destroyers *Kashmir* and *Kingston* to the east of the Shetland Islands and Lott has the distinction of being one of only a few prisoners who were kept locked in the Tower of London for some time. Both Lott and Prellberg survived the war. Wilhelm Rollmann was killed in action as commander of U848 on 5 November 1943, when four Liberator aircraft bombed it.

4

THE START OF THE SUCCESSFUL TIME

Shortly after the beginning of the war, Werner Hartmann (Commander of the 6th U-boat Flotilla (Flotilla Hundius) also based at Bant in Wilhelmshaven) took command of U37, not through demotion, but as one of U-boat Command's early moves to set up a wolf pack on the high seas. U37 was the first ocean-going Type IXA, launched in May 1938 at Deschimag AG Weser in Bremen and differed from the majority of the later Type IXA boats by having special communications and navigation facilities to accommodate the leader of such a group. Yet, despite the additional facilities, the interior was too cramped to accommodate extra staff officers; therefore Hartmann had to command both the pack and the boat. During the pre-war years it was thought that an on-the-spot commander should lead wolf packs at sea, but radios had become so reliable and efficient that a seagoing commander proved to be unnecessary and virtually all group attacks were directed from a land-based Operations Room at U-boat Headquarters.

Shortly after lunch on 7 May 1940 Hartmann held his last crew inspection before handing command to Victor Oehrn, a remarkable officer about whom too little is known. Born in Caucuses near the Caspian Sea, meaning that his first name was spelt the Russian way with a 'c', rather than the German with a 'k', he joined the still fledgling Reichsmarine in 1927, six years before Hitler came to power and eight years before the U-boat Arm was re-founded. Oehrn quickly made himself indispensable with his clear thinking and highly methodical mind. He was the brain behind the famous raid on Scapa Flow, finding the way in and persuading the Flag Officer for U-boats (Kpt.z.S. und Kommodore Karl Dönitz) to launch the audacious attack where U47 under Kptlt. Günther Prien sank the battleship *Royal Oak* in October 1939. Later, while working as staff officer, he re-designed the U-boat Command's logbook to prevent officers randomly dictating or writing what they had done. Instead he provided a template where the daily occurrences had to be recorded in the same pattern each day. This has been a terrific boon for historians unravelling the history of the war at sea. His method was certainly far better than the mishmash recorded before he brought in this system.

Some book authors and Internet sites have stated that Oehrn was appointed as commander of U37 in order to restore the morale of the U-boat Arm, which is not true. It happened that his first voyage in U37 did just that and became a significant milestone in U-boat history. There certainly wasn't much of an indication at first that this was going to be a successful voyage and when he left no one was expecting him to come back with such huge successes. At first the boat sailed backwards and forwards between Wilhelmshaven and Heligoland several times and became a regular visitor at the naval ship yard, where the crew went as far as arranging several booze-ups for their faithful and patient repair workers. Although flotilla quartermasters appeared to count every calorie of food they issued, U37 had been around long enough to acquire whatever was needed and the men didn't find it too hard to accidentally withdraw just a little too much. In any case, wartime shortages had not yet started to bite in Wilhelmshaven, so it wasn't a case of helping destitute workers but having enough of the right drinks to make repairs progress smoothly.

U37 finally set out with Victor Oehrn in command during the late afternoon of 15 May 1940. By that time things had changed considerably with the war in general, but particularly with the Prize Ordinance Regulations. Both the east coast of the United Kingdom as well as the international waters of the Irish Sea and west of Cornwall had been declared a war zone by the German government. In May the area was enlarged to include the English Channel, waters to the west of Scotland and much of the Bay of Biscay. The final stage came in August of 1940 when the seas from Irish territorial waters to 20° west were included as well. This meant U37 was making for a clearly defined war area where merchant ships could be sunk without warning and without having to see to the safety of the crews.

The German invasion of France, Belgium and Holland started five days before U37 set out and the famous British evacuation of Dunkirk had come to an end by the time the boat came home again. So U37 was away during a momentous time in history. Today historians tend to emphasise the fact that Germany ignored Belgian neutrality and trampled over the small country in order to circumnavigate the French Maginot Line for their march into France. Oehrn and his contemporaries would have looked upon this in a slightly different light. They would have known that Belgian troops invaded Germany during the 1920s to ensure that both food, coal and other materials were exported as war reparations, despite many Germans being without heating, adequate food or proper clothing during cold winters. They would also have heard about several incidents where foreign troops, occupying parts of Germany, opened fire against unarmed civilians, turned them out of their homes and plundered personal possessions. So, 'neutrality' had a slightly different meaning in those days to what is understood by the term today.

Getting to that war zone, to the west of Britain, wasn't easy and Oehrn received his first baptism of fire on his first full day at sea. An aircraft attacked twice, dropping one bomb on each occasion. It didn't find the U-boat's exact position and the detonations were so far away that they didn't cause any noteworthy damage. Werner Hartmann, the boat's second commander, was awarded the Knight's Cross of the Iron Cross a few days after handing over command to Victor Oehrn, indicating that the men of U37 had seen plenty of action and been at the receiving end of far more shattering action than these half-hearted attempts, which they passed off without comment.

A more serious problem cropped up later, when U37 had resumed its voyage on the surface. The boat passed a drifting mine with so much seaweed attached that it looked like a remnant from the First World War. It was sunk by gunfire. A large number of such rusty mines appeared the following day, all in various stages of decay, some even with their lids missing. In addition to avoiding these, U37 spent an hour or so cruising through a mass of timber. This consisted of decent planks, about 10–20cm wide and in such good condition that they couldn't have been in the water long. Just the sort of thing the average handyman could have done with back home. This floating graveyard must have been some 6–9 sea miles (over 10km) long and come from a ship of some size. The deeply worrying point was not what was floating on the water, but the sky immediately above it. Towards the end of the afternoon this took on a thin layer of haze, making it impossible to see the horizon or any aircraft approaching from it. The surface of the sea remained clear, meaning it would be easy for aircraft to spot the U-boat. Oehrn did not take any chances and slowed down so as to make his wake as small as possible. Aircraft were more likely to spot the wake long before making out the ship creating it. The wake reduction worked well for a while, but during the following morning one of the lookouts failed to spot an approaching aircraft. This not only dropped three depth charges, but also advertised the presence of the U-boat. As a result the seas would be swept clear of shipping for the next few days. Oehrn was told about the discovery of his position by U-boat Command in Wilhelmshaven, which in turn received the news from the German Radio Monitoring Service. During those early days of the war the B-Dienst under Heinz Bonatz was most efficient at decoding Royal Navy messages.

Despite this prominent announcement, U37 discovered a target of about 5,000 tons shortly before first light the next day. It was too dark for a submerged attack, so Oehrn surfaced and ordered the IWO to shoot one G7a torpedo, the type with internal combustion engine, leaving a trail of bubbles. These hardly mattered on this occasion because the torpedo announced itself after a run of 75 seconds, meaning that at a range of 300 metres it had been neither a hit nor a faulty explosion at the end of the run, but a total mechanical failure. The only advantage was that U37 was now close enough to identify the target as the Swedish *Erik Frisell* of 5,066 GRT. Neutral or not, the ship was within the warzone. Although the crew abandoned ship, the master failed to take his papers with him. While alongside the lifeboat, the men in U37 discovered that two of the crew were still on board. Not sure if they had been forgotten in the heat of the moment or why the lifeboats didn't wait for them, Oehrn ordered the master back to pick them up and, at the same time, to bring his papers. From them Oehrn learnt that the ship was making for the United Kingdom with a load of cereals and was therefore a legitimate target. It was sunk with the 105mm quick-firing deck gun.

Following that, U37 spent much of the afternoon avoiding a number of fishing boats, but another radio warning of a U-boat in U37's position suggested that the lifeboats from *Erik Frisell* had been found. The fishing boats were rather suspicious. Four of them were sailing in line ahead; a manoeuvre favoured by the military but not by fishermen, who preferred to sail slightly to the side of the ship ahead to prevent a collision if the ship in front stopped or slowed down. The reason for this difference was that the navy kept a constant lookout but fishermen tended to meet so few other ships that they didn't bother and often there was no one keeping a permanent lookout. The skipper, who should have been controlling the ship, was often busy keeping an eye on the deck to see what the men and nets were doing, rather than peering at the empty seas in front of the bows.

By the time U37 was in the waters off the Scillies, Oehrn had become so irritated by groups of fishing boats that he felt like reducing their numbers, but didn't want to give his position away by doing so, so he delayed such drastic action until his presence had been advertised again. The next suitable target appeared on 22 May at 2130 hours, when it was still light in U37's longitude. It was obliging enough to zigzag into an ideal position for a submerged attack at a range of 1,200 metres. Lying nearly perfectly sideways on to U37, no one could have missed it, yet the torpedo just vanished without trace, without any result and without anyone on the target responding to it. Powerful words were called for. The second torpedo, discharged only a few minutes later, when the target was in an even better position, detonated most dramatically long before hitting anything. This woke up the men in the freighter. They stopped engines and used the remaining movement to turn away from U37. Oehrn immediately fired a third torpedo and, once again, missed. The fourth torpedo was discharged when he was only 500 metres away and it still missed. 'This is almost unbelievable' he remarked. He must have been incredibly frustrated and one wonders what the men down below were saying about the old man by the periscope inside the conning tower. Most of them were experienced men with a good vocabulary of delicate sailors' language.

You can't take your reputation with you when you start a new job and Oehrn's predecessor had been awarded the Knight's Cross of the Iron Cross shortly after Oehrn took command. Therefore the crew had been through more muck and high water than their new commander, who still had to prove himself. This wasn't easy because even the lords, the simple sailors, had the charisma to squash a commander who couldn't shoot properly. It happened more than once during the war that crews refused to put to sea with dummy officers and on most occasions the U-boat Command bowed to their wishes. Oehrn must have felt the 'loneliness of command' hit him especially hard during this desperate situation and there was nothing he could do about it, although the blow was softened slightly by the fact that the failures must have been at least partly due to faulty mechanics. Yet, whoever's fault it may have been, the old man of every outfit usually always gets the blame.

The ship quickly increased speed again and had withdrawn to a range of 3,000 metres by the time Oehrn ordered the gun crew on deck. He couldn't make out any guns on the freighter and although it was by now getting dark there were no illuminations, so he ordered the men to aim at the ship, instead of putting a shot across the bows. The first one hit, but the target was now pulling away so fast that further action was becoming increasingly difficult. Despite a calm sea and hardly any wind, it was no longer possible to guarantee hits with the 105mm quick-firing gun on the upper deck in front of the conning tower. Chasing the ship with the U-boat's gun crew on the upper deck was not an option. The waves from the bows would easily wash them off the boat.

Oehrn was still considering his options when the radio room reported a ship with the name *Dunster Grange* was sending SOS calls from close by. This had to be U37's target and confirmed that the men's estimation of 10,000 tons had been correct. On checking the register, they learned it had a size of 9,494 GRT. At about the same time, Oehrn identified a gun on the stern, which almost immediately afterwards put a shot across to U37. The aim wasn't terribly good and the shell missed by about 200 metres. The ship was now moving rapidly out of gun range and the night was too calm and too bright for a surface chase. In any case, Oehrn thought he wouldn't be able to creep up on the *Dunster Grange* again after the crew had been warned and while they were waiting for another approach. Prospects didn't look good. So, all he could do was to let it run away. His position had now been well advertised, so he sent a radio report back to base, reporting the disheartening failures of the torpedoes. Just to make life more miserable, at that particular moment in time there weren't any of those small fishing boats about to have a go at to relieve any pent-up anger.

Karl Dönitz, the Commander in Chief of the U-boat Arm was most disappointed. Since the beginning of the war he had been plagued with hundreds of such reports. At first he thought the faults lay with the men not carrying out correct firing procedures, but by the spring of 1940 he was sure it was a mechanical, not a human, problem. Things got as far as several internal enquiries and a court martial to get to the bottom of the failing torpedoes. When Victor Oehrn set out with U37, everybody had hoped that the faults had been rectified. Now Dönitz knew for certain that there were still serious gremlins inside the workings of his most important weapon and more action was urgently called for. He had personal and close-up experiences of similar incidents during the First World War, when the men reacted to their superiors by refusing to obey orders and the heavy-handed reaction of the leadership led merely to mutiny and open rioting. So Dönitz knew he was treading on a knife-edge and urgently needed to restore morale, which was rapidly being lost. He urgently needed successes.

Oehrn left his target and headed towards Cape Finisterre. Both the sea and the weather were brilliant, but those dreaded small fishing boats kept appearing too frequently. Every time they appeared in groups, which meant that having a go at one of them would mean being reported by others. It was infuriating. There were also aircraft out at sea, flimsy things with one wing above another and held together with string and canvass. None presented any great threat and could easily be avoided, but Oehrn can't have been terribly happy at this time of his life.

Shortly after lunch on the following day, while riding a slight swell with a force 3–4 south-westerly, Oehrn suddenly found himself confronted with a convoy. One has to bear in mind that such a conglomeration of ships could well be covering an area of several square kilometres and even when fully surfaced, the low position of the top of the conning tower did not provide an ideal platform from which to observe the exact composition of such a huge group. It could well be that a U-boat was unable to see the far side, making it extremely difficult to work out how many columns there were or how many ships there were in each column. On this occasion the weather was perfect for the convoy to spread out far across the water, making it impossible to inspect it at close quarters on the surface, especially as there was an aircraft circling over the top of it. There was also a destroyer and a modern minesweeper running along the sides and there could well have been more small fast warships that U37 had not yet spotted. The whole setup looked most confusing and disorganised, but there must have been some good order within the system. The ships didn't sail in a plain straight line, but instead the whole convoy appeared to be zigzagging slightly: each ship of each column would turn in succession, one after the other. This perplexing picture made it difficult to work out the exact direction the convoy was heading in and there were instances when Oehrn thought the ships were coming straight towards him. In his log he admitted to being too perplexed with the whole scene to form a reasonable plan of attack. He guessed that the most valuable target would be in the middle, rather than along the outside of the convoy, but he was too far away for a detailed inspection. In the end U37 dived deep and allowed the ships to pass over the top. A few far-off detonations of depth charges were heard, but nothing exciting happened and U37 returned to periscope depth once the deep-droned massed buzzing had separated again and individual ships could be distinguished once more. By that time more than four hours had passed since first making contact, but a few merchant ships appeared still to be in close proximity.

Although the angle of attack was now pretty difficult, Oehrn shot a torpedo at 1645 hours. Once again, he needn't have bothered. Nothing happened. There was no detonation, not even the sound of metal colliding with an iron hull. It was pretty disappointing and made more painful because it was the commander, and the commander alone, who sat by the periscope for such submerged attacks. Normally the first U-boat to sight a convoy should have reported the details to headquarters and shadowed it until more boats could move in for a combined attack at night, but on this occasion Oehrn knew he was alone, without anyone nearby who might make use of the juicy targets. Not only was this happening in the month of May, when the days are terribly long, but U37 was also lying to the west of the British Isles, meaning it was going to be light for some time to come. So, Oehrn attempted another submerged attack, but getting back into a favourable position was now proving rather difficult. The aircraft seen earlier to be flying low over the front of the convoy now turned its attention to the rear and forced U37 down on several occasions, pushing it too far away for another submerged attack. It was most infuriating, but gave the men some time to take a breather and wait until darkness fell to make another attack on the surface.

Just to make life difficult, the night was so terribly dark until the moon rose at around midnight that it was virtually impossible to make out what was going on. Oehrn had the impression that the convoy took that opportunity to split into two, but he couldn't be sure in the pitch-blackness of the night. Suddenly and without much warning a ship appeared from behind. This was ideal. U37 had been suffering from an uncomfortable balance for some time and losing 1½ tons from the rear would help the engineer officer a great deal in adjusting the balance of the boat. Now, imagine the situation, the waves were becoming calmer as the two dark shadows of the small U-boat and the big ship were slowly converging. The night was so clear that lookouts could even identify the silhouettes of two men standing by an impressive-looking gun on the stern. The gap between the ship and the U-boat continued to get smaller and then, at the critical moment when U37 turned in order to fire one of the two stern torpedoes, the ship changed direction as well. Someone probably made out the black shadow of the submarine, causing the target to turn drastically in the opposite direction. Oehrn still hoped to hit it and gave permission for the IWO to fire. Once more, he needn't have bothered. The torpedo missed, the target started sending a distress call and ships further away could be seen to be changing course and increasing speed. It felt like having disturbed a wasps' nest. To make matters worse someone even fired red Very lights towards the U-boat. These were a long way off, but still made the men on the top of the conning tower feel rather naked.

Oehrn had to do something and with the night still young thought about starting another run in at high speed to fire once more. This idea was quickly abandoned when he realised the escorts were also reacting by dashing wildly along the perimeter. So, in the end, he decided it would be better to tackle a straggler, observed earlier further towards the west. At least this took U37 away from the pursuers. The search lasted for a few hours, but it wasn't terribly difficult to spot the ship. It was fully illuminated. On closer inspection it was identified as the 5,728 GRT Greek freighter *George Embiricos* but post-war records suggest the correct name was *Kyma*. Whether it considered itself to have been neutral or not, it was sailing within a declared warzone and was sunk with a single torpedo. This time it worked!

The weather remained calm; U37 moved further away from potential hotspots and three days later, on 26 May, Oehrn used the opportunity to load the four torpedoes in the outside storage containers into the boat. This took four and a half hours and was not the easiest of operations. Oehrn remarked that the apparatus supplied for moving the heavy eels was clumsy and most difficult to use. He suggested that the people who invented it should be made to use it on the high seas. The torpedoes had to be pulled out of the sealed storage containers and then lowered down inclined rails into the torpedo compartments. Smaller, seagoing U-boats of Type VIIC carried two spare torpedoes this way and this larger ocean-going variety could accommodate four. The main torpedo hatches had to be opened so this heavy work could only be carried out during reasonably calm weather and even then, the boat's tanks had to be fully blown to raise it as high as possible above the water. The bow wave from a passing ship could easily wash enough water over the deck to flood the interior. Only a few months later the Atlantic became such a difficult hunting ground that U-boats could no longer risk carrying spares in these external tubes.

Later that same day U-boat Command sent a warning signal saying British auxiliary cruisers were suspected to be operating close to Spanish ports and within a couple of hours U37 was faced with one such suspicious ship. Getting close to it proved problematic and then, once U37 had got to it, the ship was virtually impossible to identify. It definitely had a gun on the stern and what looked like some anti-aircraft guns; there was also a strange structure covered in canvass, suggesting that it might be hiding more artillery. Although no longer in the warzone, Oehrn thought it was suspicious enough to sink with a torpedo. To everybody's surprise the eel worked and caused the target (the British 5,008 GRT freighter *Sheaf Mead*) to settle deeper in the water. Not long afterwards there was a most dramatic boiler explosion, and men with outstretched limbs could be seen hurling through the air. As shocking as the spectacle was, it did at least partially restore faith in the torpedoes.

Yet, the new high hopes were quickly dashed. The next torpedo didn't produce any results. The target ship, the Argentinean 3,425 GRT freighter *Uruguay*, didn't even notice that it had been attacked and several shots across the bows were necessary before it was brought to a halt. The ship's papers were inconclusive and without the normal proof of its destination. The men claimed they were making for neutral Ireland, but the Germans didn't believe them. Things didn't tally and the ship was too small to warrant another torpedo, so being in an unusual and isolated position, the men from U37 took their time and sunk it with scuttling charges.

The next target, big enough to warrant a spread of two torpedoes out of the rear tubes, presented itself at 0400 hours on 28 May. The result was incredible. A bright red flame interlaced most dramatically with white smoke appeared to engulf the ship and hide even the funnels. Amidst this most amazing scene, the men heard the detonation of the second torpedo. U37 left quickly and couldn't return until late afternoon when only a mass of small pieces of floating wreckage adorned the waves. Then, moving on, the troubling bane of a few days ago, the masses of small fishing boats, started making life difficult again. Eight hours later, U37 encountered one on its own with what turned out to be a French crew. It was sunk by gunfire. Oehrn remarked that sinking it was emotionally abhorrent. The ship was clean and well kept, and was probably the sailors' own property and their only means for earning a living. But, their government had declared war on Germany and therefore gave him no alternative other than to sink it.

The remarkable thing about what happened during the following days was that nothing remarkable happened. Oehrn operated his boat according to the commander's handbook and within the limitations imposed upon him by the Naval High Command. He didn't make any great efforts to find targets. They just kept coming. The weather was cooperative, making life not too hard and the main handicap came from a variety of mechanical failures. The engineers repaired these as best they could, but they did seriously hamper operations for long periods. The way things turned out, even these potential disasters weren't life threatening and hardly any of them hindered success. When one of the engines broke down for example, there was nothing around to make U37 want to go any faster than its temporary maximum of 11 knots. Even the arrival of targets was quite convenient. Hardly any turned up simultaneously and the timing between them allowed the men some rest before tackling the next serious confrontation. The men of the First World War's U35, under the most successful submarine commander of all time, Lothar von Arnauld de la Periére, managed to get their sinking rate into double figures on some days, meaning that there was hardly time to sleep or eat between sinkings.

U37's successes were certainly not straightforward and some almost got the better of the U-boat. One such incident occurred shortly after 2000 hours on 29 May, when smoke clouds advertised the arrival of another ship. While approaching it slowly, U37 got too close before the men realised that a massive winch on the stern was in fact a gun with a calibre of about 75mm. The first shots from it fell wide, but the gun crew were no dummies and detonations quickly crept closer. When they got within 20 metres of U37, Oehrn gave up and dived. The amazing point about this performance was that he had been running away from the ship for some time and there was already a gap of 9km. Although it was a valuable freighter with what appeared to be a single gun, the target was too small to warrant a torpedo and all the men could do was to remain deep until nightfall provided some cover for returning to the surface.

It was almost the end of the first day of June 1940 when the men of U37 were treated to a new experience with a G7a torpedo, the type that left a trail of bubbles. Oehrn attacked a small ship from a submerged position and he observed a perfect bubble trail leaving the U-boat, but not much else. When the stop clock told him it must have missed, he ordered the gun crew into action and surfaced to see the torpedo still running huge loops around the tiny target. The master of the Greek ship, the 950 GRT *Ioanna*, had been a submarine commander during the First World War and admitted that he was making for the United Kingdom and therefore expected to be sunk. Yet, despite his most desperate situation, he offered the Germans what was left of his provisions. Oehrn declined and dispatched another torpedo to sink the ship.

Another shadow had been spotted shortly before *Ioanna* went down and the following day, 2 June, was only a few minutes old when the lookouts confirmed there was more behind. This was the first sign of a convoy. Getting at it proved difficult. Conditions were not too good, but eventually U37 did get close enough to shoot another torpedo. It missed. Oehrn thought that they might have misjudged the course and position of the target. It didn't take too long to reach another advantageous firing position, but this torpedo missed as well, this time due to a sticky firing button on the top of the bridge. This type of problem occurred in many U-boats and many commanders modified the firing procedure so that they did not rely on the bridge's electric trigger. Instead the order to shoot was also shouted through the boat so that the torpedo mechanics by the tubes could press their manual triggers as well, just to make doubly sure the system worked. However, on this occasion Oehrn was in the predicament of having expended all torpedoes but still having a number of targets within range. It was most infuriating.

Despite the appalling torpedo failures, U37 had attacked and at least damaged eleven ships totalling more than 50,500 GRT. Bearing in mind that commanders who reached 100,000 tons were awarded the Knight's Cross, this one voyage brought Oehrn's personal bag pretty high. Without digging through wartime statistics this has got to be one of the (if not 'the') most successful war cruises up to that time. Victor Oehrn had commanded the small coastal boat, U14, for twenty-two months up to October 1937, but after that held a number of land-based positions and hardly stepped inside another U-boat until he took over U37 on 6 May 1940. So, when he set out for what was to become a fantastic, milestone voyage, he was still very much an inexperienced submarine commander.

In addition to these successes, U37 also brought home some vital intelligence suggesting that it was far easier to get close to convoys than had been anticipated. The escorts were nowhere near as sharp as they had been expected to be and attacks against the U-boat came over as vague, almost slovenly attempts to throw bombs. Nothing came close enough to annoy U37. Things looked easier than many people had imagined. The future looked bright.

5

SHORT-RANGE SURFACE ATTACKS AT NIGHT

Wolfgang Lüth was a remarkable character; one of only two U-boat commanders to have received the Knight's Cross with Oakleaves, Swords and Diamonds. (The other was Albrecht Brandi.) He also served in long-range boats to the Far East, but is probably best known for having been shot accidentally by his own guard a few days after the end of the war because he failed to reply to a challenge during a dark night. In September 1940 he was still a junior officer, who had seen some action as First Watch Officer of U38, an ocean-going Type IXA. At the end of his first war voyage he was moved to the U-boat School to become a commander. This was a massive step and those modern sources that claim that a watch officer could replace the commander if he was injured or ill are wide of the mark. Watch officers had an important and specific role inside U-boats, but their training stopped a long way short of commanding a submarine. Most important of all, they were not usually trained in how to attack. Thus this period of going back to the school bench was most important for Wolfgang Lüth.

Lüth's first command was very much the opposite of what he had been used to. Instead of a large, relatively comfortable boat, he commissioned U138, a small Type IID coastal submarine. This differed from its Type II predecessors inasmuch as it could accommodate more fuel, but the inside living space and the armament remained the same. There were only three bow torpedo tubes, one puny 20mm anti-aircraft gun and capacity for only five torpedoes. The crew was made up of four officers and twenty-one men, considerably fewer than the forty-four to fifty-six men required to take a Type VII or Type I to battle.

On 11 September 1940 the tiny U138 cast off in Kiel and tagged on behind the *Uckermark*. Known as *Altmark* at the beginning of the war, this supply ship had accompanied the pocket battleship *Admiral Graf Spee* into the South Atlantic, had escaped the dramatic scuttling in the Rio de la Plata estuary and was then attacked in Norwegian waters by men from the destroyer HMS *Cossack*. Now she was following a Sperrbrecher (barrier breaker or mine detonator) up the Kattegat to Norway. Once close to the coast there and separated from her U-boat tail, *Uckermark* made off with a couple of torpedo boats at high speed and left U138 to pass uncomfortably close to a drifting mine while on the way to call for a few hours at Kristiansand and then make for Cape Wrath on the north coast of Scotland.

A bright moon made the nights a little too light for surface attacks. Despite this, a ship approached at about 2100 hours on 16 September and U138 chased it until around midnight before it got close enough to launch an attack. The coming of darkness also brought a helpful haze and made it easy to approach incredibly close. Judging distances and size can be most confusing at sea. There are no landmarks for comparison and on this occasion all the men could make out was a vague shadow merging with the dark sea against a slightly lighter sky. So, imagine Lüth's surprise when he realised that he had got as close as 600 metres, but what he had estimated to be a large freighter turned out to be a small pot of no more than 700 tons. The torpedo ready for firing would probably have cost more than the target. Lüth, a professional naval officer, restrained himself at that last moment and called off the attack. Tackling a boat as small as this with only a 20mm anti-aircraft gun wasn't on either. It could well be that it had some-thing more impressive hidden on board. Larger sea and ocean–going U-boats at least had an 88mm or 105mm quick-firing gun to help them out of such embarrassing situations. All Lüth did was to laugh about the matter; something he later became famous for. As Otto Giese (who served with Lüth in U181 towards the end of the war) said, it was more embarrassing to be laughed at by the commander than being told off by him.

Astonishingly enough when lookouts sighted land later in the day, no one had any idea exactly where they were, other than they might just have sighted the northern tip of the Hebrides. The reason for this was that the sea had been whipped up by a fierce north-westerly for some time, making life in the tiny nutshell of submarine most uncomfortable and impossible to see the sun or stars. At the same time, the waves shook up everything that was not screwed down, including the contents of the fuel tanks. This would normally not have mattered, but they had already collected a thick layer of greasy sludge at the bottom, which was now so well mixed with the oil that it found its way into the engine room, where it blocked fuel pumps and induction jets.

Cleaning them took four hours, but this work was carried out down in the depths, a long way below the turbulence of the waves and thus gave the men a respite from the extreme rolling and pitching. Bearing in mind that this was the first war voyage for a large proportion of the crew, they must have welcomed the break from being seasick. Suffering with such dire feelings was not easy, especially as the men were not passengers who might take to their beds. The men had to continue with their duty no matter how bad they might have felt. One solution was to have a bucket with a little old engine oil standing by to be sick into. The filthy oil still floated on the top of whatever the men threw at it and its oily stench was a lot more amiable than that of partly digested last meal. Type II U-boats stood up well to depth charges and they were easy to manoeuvre. This lack of stability was a definite drawback during stormy weather. Even hardened sailors, who had been through the most appalling storms, found they had to re-learn how to cope with the constant and incredible motion of these small submarines.

The next target came into sight at lunchtime on 18 September and, having just passed St Kilda's Rock, this time the men in U138 knew exactly where they were. The problem was that the sludge was still finding its way into the interior fuel tank hanging from the ceiling of the engine room. This important tank held about a day's supply of fuel and was regularly filled from the deep-down storage bunkers to gravity feed into the engines with the help of some small pumps. The sludge was so light that it could not be detected inside this tank, but it blocked the filters and the induction jets all the same, bringing the engines to a sudden and unexpected halt. This could have made things a bit awkward if someone from the opposition was about to have a go at you. On this occasion the target turned out to be another one of those small fishing boats, not worth a torpedo and, once more, Lüth ran away from it.

It was shortly after breakfast on 20 September when a force 6 north-westerly made sure that the men of U138 were none too happy while eating and sighting the northern tip of Ireland. The faint outline of the land was nowhere near as attractive as smoke from a ship heading in a vague easterly direction. Its speed, a little too fast for the small U-boat, didn't put Lüth off attempting a chase. In doing so U138 accidentally ran into a most impressive convoy (OB216) heading in the opposite direction. This was obliging enough to be moving at a slightly slower speed than the other ship and there appeared to be only two escorts, running along the flanks. The big drawback was some constant activity in the air above the merchant ships. This meant the chase became more complicated, with U138 being constantly pushed under and thus making it impossible to get in front. Lüth had to contend himself with an approach from the side.

Rough seas made it difficult to see far through the periscope, so this was an ideal opportunity to use the sound detector. It would only work efficiently when the engines were not making too much noise and for much of the time U138 had been running at high speeds to maintain its position in relation to the merchant ships, making the sound detector of no use. Water gurgling past the hydrophones and the incredible din produced even by the comparatively small electric motors shielded any subtle sounds from far-off ships. Bursts of high speed could be kept up only for relatively short periods of a few hours before the batteries were exhausted, so there were ample opportunities to alternate between high speeds and going into slow silent drive to check on the position of the noise. Prolonged dives, to hide from persistent escorts, were still a feature of the future. Therefore it was reasonable for Lüth to take such a risk. For most of the time U-boats were forced under for only a few hours. In later years, when it was necessary to remain submerged for 12, 24 or even 36 hours, then it would have been suicidal to risk draining so much power from the batteries. Lüth also guessed that the biggest and best targets were likely to be some distance towards the middle of the convoy and therefore did not take the first opportunity to aim at whatever came into sight.

The superstructures of the nearest ships were clearly visible when the partly flooded boat dived in order to allow one column of merchant ships to pass over the top. It was shortly after 9 o'clock at night, still too light for a surface attack, when the first torpedo was fired from a range of 460 metres. Bearing in mind that the general submarine doctrine of the time was to attack from a distance of several miles and then shoot a salvo of two or three torpedoes; it is unlikely that any of the merchant lookouts would have searched for a periscope so close to them. The earlier wind with its choppy waves had subsided by this time, making it ideal to continue at periscope depth. The explosion which followed was considerably louder than the noise of a torpedo going off and Lüth thought that he must have hit the engine room and triggered an explosion inside one of the boilers. At the time of firing, he was so close that the target filled the entire vision of the periscope; even with it set at its smallest magnification.

Being in an ideal position inside the convoy, it took only seconds before Lüth was ready to fire his second torpedo. This ran for 19 seconds before detonating. Nine seconds faster than the first shot. The third torpedo ran for 24 seconds before creating another loud and impressive detonation. This third ship remained hanging on the surface for some time with what looked like a broken keel, but the first two had vanished from sight by the time U138 surfaced to inspect the damage.

The torpedoes, fired on 20 September 1940 at 2120, 2123 and 2126 hours against Convoy OB216 sank the tanker *New Sevilla* (13,801 GRT) and the freighters *Boka* (5,560 GRT) and *City of Simla* (10,138 GRT), meaning that Lüth had succeeded in inflicting the maximum damage he could on the convoy. He hit it again a few hours later with a spread of two torpedoes and sank the freighter *Empire Adventure* (5,145 GRT). The running time was an agonising 3 minutes and 7 seconds. Frustrations set in when Lüth noticed more targets presenting themselves at a time when he had run out of torpedoes. Again, nothing serious followed. There was no retaliation from the escorts and U138 could withdraw quietly while taking the time to make extensive notes on how the opposition had reacted. One ship had stopped to pick up survivors; others were shooting illumination rockets into the sky and some even used searchlights, but all to no avail. They didn't find the U-boat.

U138 headed in a southerly direction, to refuel in Lorient (France). There was plenty of activity in those Biscay waters with an abundance of fishing and sailing boats, making the return voyage somewhat hard going, but nowhere near as prickly as at 1152 hours on 26 September. Then, suddenly without warning, the rudder was ordered hard to starboard and the port engine full ahead while the starboard engine went into full speed in reverse. This sort of drastic action didn't happen often and caused several men to hold their breath while they watched a torpedo run into their side. Luckily their guardian angel had not taken a lunch break and the torpedo appeared again on the other side, having passed too deep under its target. A couple of minutes later, when the men counted not one, but four torpedo detonations, they realised this was indeed their lucky day. There was obviously another submarine about with hostile intentions. This hair-raising interlude was not the end of the day's excitement. Shortly afterwards an unidentified aircraft came close enough for the small 20mm gun to take some pot shots, but missed, just like the bigger guns firing at it from the coast.

It was 1335 hours when U138 made fast in Lorient for the men to make a run on French wine and beer. The two previous incidents were most annoying and illustrate how effective the Royal Navy Submarine Service and RAF Coastal Command could be. Germany never managed to prevent such intrusions. Later, huge bunkers were built along the French Atlantic coast, but neither the navy nor the Luftwaffe ever supplied the necessary support to get U-boats safely in and out of those volatile harbours.

Although this first war cruise by U138 is often quoted as an example of the unprecedented success of small coastal submarines against convoys, this was not the beginning of the story. Nor are many historical accounts correct in saying that aces such as Otto Kretschmer and Günther Prien were responsible for creating the formula that generated the successful period during the autumn of 1940. The successes during that period were not reaped by wolf packs as many historians claim, but by what the Germans called 'the short-range surface attack at night'. The trigger for this was Erich Topp and U57, another small Type IIC coastal submarine.

Topp was born in Hanover shortly before the end of the First World War and joined the navy in 1934. He served as First Watch Officer in U46 under Herbert Sohler until April 1940. Then he was sent to commanders' school and shortly afterwards Sohler became Chief of the 7th U-boat Flotilla, based for much of the war in St Nazaire. Topp's first war patrol with U57, where he sunk two ships, started and finished in Bergen, Norway. Then he took U57 south to Lorient, sinking one ship on the way. These results may sound meagre, but they were considerably better than a number of boats, which came home empty handed. The Supreme Commander in Chief of the U-boat Arm remarked in Topp's log that his operations were conducted with special guts, tenacity and skill. Very few men of the time seemed to have taken into account the fact that luck must also have played an important role.

The significant crunch and the model for shaping the future came in August 1940 when U57 put into Lorient for refuelling and for dealing with a number of repairs made necessary by an attacking aircraft. Fifteen hits were discovered; three in the bridge and six marking the conning tower fairing. So the men were lucky to have been on their way down into the depth when this happened. They were also lucky that many British aircraft were fitted with only small calibre weapons.

Leaving Lorient on 14 August, U57 ran into its first target five days later while lying to the west of Northern Ireland. This short period of time is important and a vital tool in the statistics when considering the war at sea. Later U-boats were at sea for several weeks before sighting targets. On this occasion it was early in the morning and although the freighter stopped for a while, it eventually turned away and moved out of range for the planned submerged attack. This had hardly been digested when U48 under Hans Rösing came close enough for Topp to suggest the bigger boat might be better for catching the illusive ship. U57's engines rattled out of their mounts at

10 knots and really strong words were required to drive the boat up to 12 knots. U48, a larger Type VIIB, had a top speed of 17 knots and could easily cruise at 11 knots.

Rösing's chase didn't get U48 close enough and eventually he gave up. In any case, he was hardly in charge. This was one of the few occasions where the commander, required because naval regulations stated that boats may not manoeuvre without one, was happy to go along as a passenger and let the old hands of U48 run their own show. One can judge the men's abilities by the fact that U48 became the most successful boat of the Second World War and it went to sea for a comparatively short period of twenty-one months before joining the training flotillas in July 1941. The First Watch Officer was the vibrant Teddy Suhren, about whom a number of books have been written, and the rest of the men were also well-known characters. It was Suhren who signed the boat's log during this voyage and who did most of the shooting. Their original commander, 'Vaddi' (Daddy) Schultze had been taken ill and admitted to hospital, Hans Rösing was on his way to France to become FdU (Flag Officer for U-boats West) and the U-boat Command needed a hard nut to cope with the men of U48. So the temporary combination worked very well. Heinrich 'Ajax' Bleichrodt, who took over from Rösing, described the men of U48 as an unusual bunch of wild characters with whom it was best not to mess. Both Rösing and Bleichrodt were thankful for the U48 experience in helping them to gain the Knight's Cross of the Iron Cross. Bleichrodt refused to accept his unless the IWO, Teddy Suhren, also received one. At first Dönitz (BdU – Supreme Commander-in-Chief U-boats) shot him down, saying that only commanders are awarded Knight's Crosses. Yet Bleichrodt persisted and put his request in writing, saying that it was the IWO who fired the torpedoes on the surface and Suhren had sunk more ships than anyone else. Dönitz then accepted the argument and awarded Suhren a Knight's Cross on 3 November 1940; ten days after Bleichrodt.

To return to the Atlantic on 22 August 1940, U57 received an incredible hammering from an aircraft instead of finding another target. This dropped four depth charges close enough to break glass and even put the starboard engine out of action. Most of the damage was repaired but one troublesome bolt made it impossible to isolate the cylinder to which it was attached. It also proved impossible to remove it in order to fit a replacement. The engine was out of action, without any hope of repairing it at sea. Many men would have given up and returned home, but Topp prepared to continue. His tenacity paid dividends. Two days later, less than an hour after midnight, U57 found itself on the surface in the middle of a convoy (OB202). The targets were so close together that all three torpedoes were shot in three minutes, hitting three ships. (*Cumberland* 10,939 GRT and *Saint Dunstan* 5,681 GRT were sunk while *Havidar* 5,407 GRT was damaged.)

This was the first time that the multiple attack method was used and although other commanders might not have managed to shoot as fast as U57, this became the order of the night attack. It was possible because the British submarine detection device, Asdic, didn't work when the target was on the surface and radar had not yet been put into successful production. The first success with this see-in-the-dark device came seven months later when U99 and U100 were sunk. Yet, unlike Wolfgang Lüth in U138, Topp had to pay a heavy price for his success. The moon illuminated the convoy just as the IWO was aiming at the first target and one of the escorts was already heading towards U57 by the time the third shot was made. A dozen or more depth charges came close enough to make life most uncomfortable and following that Topp remained submerged for twenty-two hours, suggesting that the men had to deal with considerable damage.

The following homeward journey was not without incident, but nothing serious happened until Topp was waiting in the Elbe estuary to enter the locks of the Kiel Canal at Brunsbüttel. Stopping in the strong tidal surge was relatively easy. It was going in the opposite direction to the U-boat, so the engines held the boat in a stationary position, but no one had warned Topp that he was waiting in the wrong position. It was a pitch-black night and a Norwegian freighter leaving the locks couldn't see the incredible turbulence in front until it ran clear of the canal's approach. At that moment the fierce current hit the ship with a vengeance and pushed it sideways so hard that it crashed into U57. The submarine filled with water in some 20–30 seconds. Most of the men managed to get out and some even stepped onto the deck of the small freighter, almost without getting their feet wet. Others were not so fortunate and seven were lost in the blackness of the night, despite the immediate and concerted rescue attempt. U57 was later raised, used as a training boat and later also for experiments with the new schnorkels.

The big problem at this time, when U57 was sunk, was not attacking, but finding targets. Karl Dönitz, the Commander-in-Chief of the U-boat Arm, kept urging U-boats to report convoys and then to keep shadowing them until a group attack could be mounted. These group attacks should not be confused with wolf packs or patrol lines. There was no close-knit group at sea; it was more a case of as many boats as possible getting close enough for a combined onslaught. The first two heavy group attacks against convoys were against HX72 in September and against SC7 in October 1940. Both were homeward-bound convoys from Halifax (Nova Scotia) to the United Kingdom. At this period a number of U-boat commanders complained that it seemed pointless joining such groups because they met so many attractive targets on the way and could never be sure whether or not they would reach the convoy in time.

During the late morning of 20 September 1940, U100 under Kptlt. Joachim Schepke intercepted a signal direct from U47 under Kptlt. Günther Prien saying he had sighted a convoy. (Both of these were seagoing boats of Type VIIB, built specially for the task of chasing convoys.) Schepke wasn't terribly interested at first because an attractive target happened to be passing. This was moving a bit too fast and U100 eventually headed towards the position given by U47. Conditions were good: a steady force 3 north-westerly was blowing over a slightly choppy sea, with clear skies and occasional showers. It was late the following afternoon when the Operations Room at U-boat Headquarters ordered U48, U65, U43, U99 and U100 to converge on U47's convoy. To make doubly sure that Prien wasn't going to start shooting before the other boats arrived the BdU (Commander-in-Chief) sent a signal to U47 ordering it to shadow the convoy and to send regular position reports.

Orders like this were more than essential. The Commander-in-Chief, Karl Dönitz, spent a great deal of time with his men. As a result he got to know many of them intimately and it was not unusual for even low-ranking seamen to discuss personal family matters with him. This meant he was well aware of what was going in the boats and more than one commander was sacked as a result of Dönitz talking to the lower ranks, rather than the officers. He also knew that two main themes for avid discussion inside U-boats were how to avoid becoming a convoy's shadow and how to avoid being detailed for weather reporting duties. Dönitz wouldn't have liked these jobs either, but they were important and he continuously hit hard that these vital duties were not deliberately avoided. The men at sea didn't like trailing convoys or using their radios. Otto Kretschmer, for example, acquired the nickname 'Silent Otto' not because he didn't speak, but because he transmitted radio messages as rarely as he could get away with. Many men were convinced that it was the best way of giving their position to the opposition's radio direction finders.

Yet more than twelve of such shadowing signals arrived from U47 during the next twelve hours and later there were also additional signals from 'Ajax' Bleichrodt, indicating that U48 had found the merchant ships as well. Despite an abundance of help from the two shadowing U-boats, U100 still didn't find the convoy. When such critical situations arose, it was common for U-boats to dive to use their listening gear. Various different systems were fitted to U-boats, but they all functioned along similar lines, with a set of sensitive underwater microphones (hydrophones) that could be adjusted to determine the direction that noises were coming from. This gear was sensitive enough to detect ships too far away for lookouts to see from the top of the conning tower, but once they had closed in it was not accurate enough for aiming torpedoes, which had to be aimed visually. The sound detection gear was affected by waves and did not function properly while boats were near the surface.

It was 2200 hours when U100 picked up the first sounds of what could only be a large conglomeration of ships. Schepke surfaced and had hardly run towards it for any length of time when he sighted the convoy's starboard wing. Shortly afterwards he counted some twenty targets. Without further thought and without hesitation he moved closer to locate the biggest. He was in such a position that he could have fired all four bow torpedo tubes more or less simultaneously, but took his time in finding the most lucrative ships. Then he turned and ordered the IWO to shoot the rear tube. One of the torpedoes vanished without apparently having hit anything, but all the others produced violent detonations. The longest distance to a target was 3,300 metes, so U100 was attacking from quite some distance before closing in. Things became so hectic and Schepke was so determined to shoot all his torpedoes that he didn't hang around to observe what was happening. This was something he was later reprimanded for by the BdU (C-in-C) who told him he should at least have ensured that the ships he had hit did sink. One wonders what would have happened to these convoys if the Germans had provided their U-boats with the type of armament found in foreign navies: six bow and two stern tubes. In all the cases mentioned so far, the sinking rates within the convoys would have been phenomenal.

Once all five torpedo tubes had been emptied, Schepke found himself in the middle of the convoy's second row. The detonations caused the merchant ships to squeeze tighter together, making it somewhat uncomfortable for U100 and the lack of space hemmed-in options for withdrawing. There were patchy clouds with the moon finding gaps to occasionally illuminate a slight swell but with hardly any significant waves. There were no signs of any aggressive military activity, probably because the escorts were busy searching along the outside of the convoy. So, with both the weather and the opposition calm, Schepke gave permission to reload torpedoes and by midnight three tubes were ready once more. It took only a matter of a few minutes before the IWO was back at the torpedo aimer on the top of the conning tower.

Some highly acclaimed books have stated that the commander was below, working a torpedo calculator during such surface attacks, which is a load of rubbish. He kept an eye on the general proceedings and told the IWO which target to aim at. This was necessary because the person aiming torpedoes could get so deeply involved with what he was doing, and he needed to concentrate on a variety of different numbers, that he could well lose touch with what was happening around him. The boat's own speed and direction were fed into a torpedo calculator located inside the conning tower. This was nicknamed the 'fruit machine' in the Royal Navy and was usually worked by an intelligent petty officer. The officer at the torpedo aimer would shout down the estimated distance to the target, its estimated speed and its estimated heading. The angle between the submarine and target was transmitted down automatically from the torpedo aimer on the bridge. At the beginning of the war, there were still a few U-boats without angle deflectors meaning that the entire boat had to be aimed at the target, but the majority could already hit ships running ahead of the torpedo tubes but a good distance to their sides. The glasses of these aimers, incidentally, did not have an aiming grind inside them. They were ordinary x7 or x8 binoculars with special armour so that they would not suffer in an emergency if the boat dived while they remained clipped in position.

The day of 22 September 1940 was only twenty minutes old when Schepke started his next attack, aiming first at a tanker and then at a large freighter. The tanker erupted into a most incredible ball of fire with its deck cracking so dramatically that large pieces flew up out of the flame. The other torpedo missed. The distance of 2,200 metres was probably a bit too much for a stored electric torpedo whose batteries had not been fully charged before firing, so Schepke had to pay the price for his hurried determination. The third torpedo, also an electric one, was shot from a slightly shorter range and managed to hit.

The weather conditions and the surface of the sea were becoming noticeably calmer as the night grew older, making it possible to constantly reload torpedoes without having to dive below the action of the waves. As a result U100 gained more opportunities for attack and, despite other failures, managed to reap an impressive total before the night came to an end. Unfortunately the conditions that gave rise to the calm sea were also responsible for removing the clouds and a bright moon started illuminating the scene, meaning it would have been wise to abandon surface attacks. However, with so little retaliation from small warships, Schepke took the risk and had another go with the bright moon immediately behind him.

The BdU (C-in-C) at U-boat Headquarters sent an order telling Schepke to remain shadowing the convoy. Schepke replied that he had been pushed away by destroyers, had lost contact and was already on his way to Lorient. He didn't get terribly far when the U-boat Command stopped him in his tracks with an SOS, saying an aircraft had been forced to make an emergency landing far out at sea and everybody in the area was to search for it. U100 headed towards some white lights from a signal pistol but found they had been shot by U138 under Wolfgang Lüth and the airmen were not found.

To sum up this set of attacks by U100 against Convoy HX72:

U100 left Lorient in France on 11 September 1940 and was back there on the 25th after its successful second war voyage. So the boat was at sea for only two weeks and reaped the following successes:

21 September:	2310 hrs: *Canonesa* 8,286 GRT: sunk
	2310 hrs: *Torinia* 10,364 GRT: sunk
	2311 hrs: missed
	2313 hrs: *Dalcairn* 4,608 GRT: sunk
22 September:	0022 hrs: *Empire Airman* 6,586 GRT: sunk
	0050 hrs: *Scholar* 3,940 GRT: sunk
	0152 hrs: *Frederick S Fales* 10,525 GRT: sunk
	0214 hrs: *Simla* 6,031 GRT: sunk

The commander of U100, Joachim Schepke, had already served as commander of the small coastal submarine U19, with which he sailed on five war voyages, sinking nine ships with a total of 35,000 tons. Following this he commissioned U100, a larger, seagoing boat of Type VIIB. A number of men from U19 were promoted and therefore went their separate ways to take them eventually to other boats, but a few accompanied Schepke to the new U100.

The fact that a number of inexperienced men were among the crew made itself plain during U100's first war voyage when it sailed from Kiel to Lorient. On 16 August 1940, Schepke sank the British freighter *Empire Merchant* (4,864 GRT) from a submerged position. Then he surfaced and while observing the scene the boat suddenly dived underneath him. There was just enough time to close the conning tower hatch, but not enough to also get inside, so Schepke was left clinging to the periscope support, hoping the engineer officer would correct whatever had gone wrong. Schepke received a good ducking before he could breathe freely again and the men in lifeboats must have had a good laugh, but it is unlikely that they would have known that they were watching the commander literally fight for his life.

What happened was that someone forgot to close the valve of a diving tank, which therefore started filling with water and had reached that critical mass just as Schepke was eyeing the men in the lifeboats.

In addition to U100 the following U-boats also attacked Convoy HX72:

U99 (Kptlt. Otto Kretschmer) torpedoed six ships
U48 (Kptlt. Heinrich 'Ajax' Bleichrodt) two ships
U47 (Kptlt. Günther Prien) one ship
U32 (Kptlt. Hans Jenisch) one ship

According to post-war records the total number of ships sunk added up to fourteen. The British freighter *Elmbank* was first hit by U99, then by U47 and then the coup de grace was delivered later by U99.

The short-range surface attack at night paid excellent dividends throughout the autumn of 1940 until the seasonal cold weather and mountainous seas curtailed the activities. It is amazing that these bold surface attacks against convoys incurred very little retaliation and hardly any losses. U102 vanished in July 1940; U32, from the above-mentioned group which attacked Convoy HX72, went down on 30 October; U31 went down on 2 November and U104 around the end of the month. There were a few other losses, but those were far enough away from the main focus not to have any had any connection with the all-important convoy war. There were no losses at all during December 1940, nor in January or February. Even today there are gaps in the knowledge as to what happened to some of the lost boats, but it would appear that none of them fell foul to attacking escorts at the moment of their short-range surface attack at night.

The Operations Room on land was quite well informed about what was going on at sea because boats usually maintained radio silence until they were about to start their run-in to attack. The first signal to go off was intended as a warning to other boats, to prevent them coming too close and to prevent a possible collision. Following this every radio operator usually had a small pile of messages lying ready for transmission, which they would then send all at once. The reason for this procedure was to avoid providing the British land-based radio direction finding systems with information about U-boat positions. The Germans knew of about forty such stations. These could determine the approximate position of any radio transmitter at sea, but they were not accurate enough to work out a U-boat's position in relation to a convoy. So, it was thought to be safe to transmit once the boat's position had become known or was about to be revealed.

U32 (Hans Jenisch) was the first of that loose-knit group to suffer from such serious retaliation that the boat had to be scuttled. U32 returned to Lorient from the attack against Convoy HX72 early in October, but set out again on the 24th of that month to be sunk by depth charges from HMS *Harvester* and HMS *Highlander* on 30 October. The commander Hans Jenisch and thirty-two men were picked up, but nine men lost their lives. Interestingly enough, U32 was hardly sending position reports nor tackling the convoy at the time shortly before the loss.

Looking at this sinking from the British point of view makes it more interesting than what might be considered as a simple sinking from the German side and U32 is a good example of something that happened on many occasions. The ships in convoys quickly needed to establish visual as well as radio connection with each other as soon as the first U-boat attacked. The big problem was that often it was impossible to determine exactly what was happening and escorts didn't always know that ships close to them were being torpedoed. These days we see the most dramatic visual effects in films, but in reality very often nothing significant happened and even people sleeping in a torpedoed ship weren't always woken by the noise of the explosion. Something obviously had to be done. An alarm system had to be created. Bearing in mind that Britain had not yet got around to supplying its merchant fleet with adequate lifesaving aids, it was going to take a while before an efficient set of warning systems was going to be created. At first, convoys developed a system of coloured lights shot from signal pistols to tell others what was going on and the direction from where an attack could be coming from.

The strange incident involving U32 started shortly after midday on 30 October 1940, when lookouts spotted the freighter *Balzac* (5,472 GRT) some 150 miles north-west of County Mayo in Ireland. The weather and sea conditions were not brilliant. Poor visibility in heavy rain showers dominated much of the day and low clouds made it easy for aircraft to surprise any U-boats. *Balzac* was zigzagging through an area where activity had been reported and was taking no chances. U32's attack on her followed a classic textbook pattern and went well for the Germans; except that this was the second time that the torpedoes malfunctioned. A few days earlier U32 had experienced similar problems while tackling the *Empress of Britain*. This huge passenger liner was then under tow as a result of damage sustained during an onslaught by aircraft. U32's attack on this slow-moving target required two torpedoes, one after the other. Now, during the attack on *Balzac*, the torpedo failures seemed to repeat themselves. The first torpedo vanished and, again, another torpedo had to be fired. This one detonated 50 yards beyond the target, creating an eruption from which a blue haze rose slowly into the air. The strange thing was that *Balzac* didn't recognise this as a torpedo attack, but assumed she was being shelled and sent a distress call to that effect.

Jenisch was referred to by the Royal Navy as 'the first star commander to be captured' and a person with a Knight's Cross was not easily put off by mechanical failure. Yet he had become extremely suspicious of his target, thinking *Balzac* could be a submarine trap of the type used during the First World War. So, instead of attempting another attack, he followed the freighter. While this was happening, HMS *Forester*, having picked up *Balzac's* distress signal, made off at a high speed of 25 knots towards it and sighted the freighter at 1740, some hours after U32's attack. *Balzac's* men guessed that the U-boat was still on its tail but didn't have any weapons for dealing with a submerged submarine. All they could do was to steer into every heavy rainsquall, but despite this, the U-boat continued to stick and couldn't be thrown off.

At this stage there are crass differences between the German and the British reports about what happened and it seems as if Jenisch was so intent on hitting the freighter that he didn't pay enough attention to the presence of the warship. Of course, the log from U32's last voyage went down with the boat and the information about its end comes from the memories of survivors. Whatever went on, at the critical moment Jenisch was sitting by the attack periscope inside the conning tower. The torpedo mechanic had just sent his last confirmation,

'Tubes Ready', the necessary information required before the order 'Fire' could be given. So, at that crucial stage, only seconds or minutes before Jenisch was going to shoot, propeller noises were heard in the boat. Jenisch responded by telling the engineer officer to go deep as quickly as possible. U32 dropped down to 140 metres, a depth it had never reached before. Men held their breath. Many of them knew that part of the hull near the engine room had been repaired with a patch welded onto the outside and now they wondered whether this was going to hold. The noises from the strain of water pressure pressing on the boat added to the tension as the men waited, many of them exhausted and frightened.

The first depth charge was not so serious but the second and third erupted immediately above the boat with the effect that it felt as if the whole ship was being pressed down by a huge hammer blow. It rose again almost immediately, but the eruption shattered glass, and most serious of all it fractured one of the rigid pipes containing compressed air. Luckily it was not clean break. It sounded like a valve had been removed from a car tyre, only the screeching was so loud that orders could not be heard. Despite the confusion, men were making emergency repairs in the dark. The lighting had failed. Unperturbed, Jenisch ordered the boat back to periscope depth, where he tried to attack the destroyer. By that time the compressed air in the bottles was so low that it was insufficient to push the torpedo out of its tube. This gave the men no alternative. With hardly any air for blowing the tanks and with almost all of it inside the interior of the boat, they had to surface or die. Once up top they found destroyers waiting for them.

Increases in pressure, although not pleasant, were nothing out of the ordinary in a submarine. The compressed air for ejecting torpedoes was always vented into the interior to prevent bubbles from rising to the surface, so men were used to varying pressure in their ears and sometimes it was so extreme that the man opening the hatch was sucked out with it. Luckily U32 surfaced right between the two destroyers, making it rather awkward for them to use their big guns without possibly hitting each other. Yet a good number of smaller calibres were brought to bear, but somehow these didn't prevent the men from abandoning ship. Both sets of hydroplanes had jammed and the rudder could not be moved to prevent the boat from turning in a tight circle to starboard. One of the destroyers attempted to ram, but couldn't turn tight enough and stopped to pick up men swimming in the water instead. In many ways this was rather a romantic scene of chivalry at sea. The Royal Navy men must have been pleased with their efforts as they fished the Germans out of the water. The last rays of the setting sun were still illuminating the upper atmosphere, making it an ideal scene for filming. The men from U32 said they were well treated, but some of them didn't like being locked up in solitary confinement in a Glasgow jail for a day until they were moved to other secure accommodation.

During the autumn of 1940, the losses of merchant ships as a result of groups of U-boats converging on convoys for short-range surface attacks at night were enormous. It reached a peak with every U-boat at sea sinking almost six ships per month. The loss of life was even more incredible. The British Monthly Anti-Submarine Reports from the Naval War Staff at the Admiralty tell us that Britain contributed to these dreadful losses by not providing adequate lifesaving aids for merchant seamen.

6

ON THE PERIPHERY OF ACTION.

The period of so-called 'Happy Time' in the autumn of 1940 was not successful for everybody. Some boats put to sea without ever coming close enough to hit anything. Obviously, with well over a thousand U-boats and even more commanders, there are bound to have been a few duds; there would be in any group that big, no matter how well it had been trained. It is possible to explore this deep pit of failures without embarrassing anyone who didn't come up to scratch. One of these, which didn't make it at first, was U58. Its commander, Hein Schonder became a Knight of the Iron Cross in 1942, indicating that he was no also-ran, but he wore that prestigious decoration for less than a year before being killed in action as commander of U200. In June 1940 he took command of U58, a small coastal Type IIC submarine of 291/435 tons with a crew of twenty-five, living in exceedingly cramped conditions. With it, he sailed to Lorient in France, where the following account starts as he was running into port at the end of his first war cruise as commander. The boat itself wasn't new, its keel had been laid down in 1937, a year after the Olympic games in Germany and it was launched the following year in October 1938. Schonder became the boat's second commander.

The voyage from Bergen had not been easy. For some time U58 had been trailing what looked like a thick black rope before spreading out into a wide tail in the wake. The exhausts were encrusted

with such a sticky residue that the engines had to be partly dismantled to scrape it out again. The men had hoped this might result in
unscheduled leave, but the French dockyard workers got the problem
sorted in a few days and it was exactly one week later, on 2 September
1940, when U58 set out for its second war voyage with Schonder
as commander. The all-important trim dive, to balance the boat for
underwater cruising, was conducted near Isle de Croix. This was followed by the usual tests and a practice crash dive before U58 headed
north-west, keeping the setting sun on the port beam.

It was a few minutes past 2200 hours that night, only a few hours
after they had left, when lookouts reported the first surprise: on the
port side, where the sun had been earlier, they now spotted a lurking submarine. It was difficult to work out its nationality. Although
the cool water was as smooth as a duck pond, it had an irritating
haze hanging over it, hiding any subtle distinguishing features. The
men knew that U38 (Heinrich Liebe) and U59 (Joachim Matz) were
on their way home with a good number of success pennants and
this shadow could be one of the two. A British boat so close to base
seemed unlikely at first, especially as this was the second time that the
men had stumbled upon such an unwelcome guest. The Royal Navy
had already greeted them while coming out of Bergen. After watching the submarine for a while, it was the boat's behaviour, rather than
its appearance, which made the men suspicious. The large hulk was
hardly making any headway and it was pointing in a northerly direction. That meant it wasn't making for Lorient or any of the other
German bases along the French Atlantic coast.

It didn't take long to conclude that it couldn't be German and
would therefore make an ideal target! Turning slowly towards it, the
lookouts found the submarine disappearing into an increasingly thick
pea soup of mist. This was rather a good opportunity. It meant that
U58 couldn't be seen either and it shouldn't be too difficult to get
closer. It looked as if U58 hadn't been spotted, so the diesel engines
were shut down in order to proceed on the much quieter electric
motors. Amazingly, the mist quickly turned into a full-blown fog,
making the submarine vanish like a magician's performance on stage.
Straining their ears, the men thought they heard some clanking, but
no one was sure whether there were faint sounds or whether their

imagination was playing tricks. The noises were hardly audible. Then, suddenly, as if Hollywood had produced the best possible dramatic effect, a black shadow loomed up out of the fog. It didn't even look real, more like a ghostly apparition. Despite the fantastic appearance, commanders were employed to act, not to observe semi-natural phenomena. It was only 500 metres away and this time heading straight towards U58. Schonder had to do something. It was too late for any action other than the quickest evasive manoeuvre to prevent being rammed. He had no alternative. The only practical choice was to swing U58 onto the same course as the giant. This put U58 some distance ahead and caused the huge hulk to rock gently in the German wake. What an opportunity! A sitting duck! The only problem was that all U58's torpedo tubes pointed forwards! The tiny coastal boat didn't have a sting in the tail.

By this time the distance between the two had closed down to 200 metres. Even a blind lookout should have noticed the disturbance from the other's bow waves and it quickly became obvious that U58 had been spotted. The huge 2,000-ton Clyde Class, towering above the tiny 300/400-ton U-boat turned, yet despite Schonder having calculated his chances of survival as 3:0 against him, there was nothing Goliath could do to harm little David. Being end-on now, the U-boat presented such a small target that every torpedo could easily miss. In any case, Schonder was more concerned about a huge, aggressive-looking deck gun, forward of the conning tower. It was fully enclosed and he had no way of knowing whether it was being manned or not. The prospects were not terribly promising. The combination of a dead calm sea and very close range meant that the first shot had to hit. The giant was also faster and a quick press on the gas pedal could easily squash the tiny fly in its path. Schonder knew he didn't have much time left to live and played his one and only trump card!

Alaaarm! He could dive in less than 30 seconds and there was no way that the giant could match him. What's more, once underwater he could run circles around his big opponent.

U58 had hardly left the surface when a massive detonation tossed the men out of their action stations. Now they knew for certain: it was definitely the opposition. The deafening blast from what could only have been a torpedo had hardly subsided and everybody's ears were still ringing with the after-effects when Schonder heard the sickening noise of propellers passing overhead. Those who realised that this had to be a submarine breathed the first sigh of relief. Had it been a destroyer with depth charges, they would all have been dead and gone.

Less than half an hour later U58 crept cautiously back to the surface, and Schonder peered around the empty blackness and then ordered tanks to be blown. The eerie wake of a periscope was spotted only about 80 metres away on their port side, but the murky night with the mist still blurred details and water lapping against the head lens made Schonder hope that it was too dark for them to be seen by the opposition. U58 had no tools with which to find a submerged submarine. Therefore he took the precautionary measure of continuing to expose the smallest possible silhouette and running away as quickly and as quietly as possible. The biggest fear during this escape was that Britain might have a good sound detection system for accurately locating the hammering of diesel engines. Despite extra lookouts towards the stern, it remained too murky to see approaching torpedoes, so it was unlikely that the submarine would get an accurate aim. U58 vanished into the black vastness. This proved that there were times when the emptiness of the restless Atlantic and even the troublesome Black Pit of Biscay could be most helpful.

The disturbing point about this brief, but rather frightening encounter was that it was not the first time! Earlier, off Norway, Schonder had been faced with an almost identical situation. There the submarine seemed to have been waiting some 25 miles off the coast, right in the middle of a German approach route. There was nothing Schonder could do to deal with such a target, other than satisfy himself with a curt comment in his log, saying it was high time that something was done to prevent such intrusions into vulnerable coastal waters.

Throughout the war, nine U-boats succeeded in sinking Allied submarines and some twenty-five Allied submarines managed to sink U-boats. There was only one case where both submarines were submerged at the time of the attack. In most other incidents it was a case of a submerged boat attacking one on the surface, usually as a result of one running into the sights of the other. The reason for the higher proportion of Allied successes was that their submarines were sent out with explicit orders to patrol the approaches to the German bases, while U-boats only attacked the opposition's submarines at accidental meetings. Freighters were far more important targets.

Two days after meeting the submarine, towards late afternoon, while being rocked by small waves, the lookouts sighted the south-west corner of Ireland and it was shortly after lunch on the following day when they checked their position on the north-west coast. So far nothing of significance had happened. Only the occasional fishing boat and about one aircraft per day had disturbed the passage. This changed dramatically on 6 September when the men realised there could be some co-operation between the tiny trawlers and the air force. This fear was confirmed by a trawler that didn't seem to be fishing or going anywhere specific but definitely had an aircraft circling low overhead. Once again, the opposition was too diverse and there wasn't anything Schonder could do other than hide and hope for the best. Two agile opponents were too much to cope with.

Soon after diving the men found that the boat started rolling and pitching down in the depths, suggesting that the weather up top was whipping up some deep-water movements. Later, when they surfaced into the blackness of the night, they found their suspicions confirmed by rougher waves and seriously reduced visibility. Their onboard weather forecast had been accurate. It seemed pointless to go further east into the North Channel. Targets would be difficult to spot and the vast open Atlantic felt considerably safer than the narrows of the British approaches. Somehow, the idea of sailing into the opponent's sea-lanes presented the men with a formidable mental barrier. The strong westerly also brought with it the eye of the storm, with the centre of the depression probably right above the U-boat. Any thoughts of engaging the weapons had to be discarded, so there was nothing to do other than consume the minimum of fuel and hope the next day would bring better conditions.

At this stage of the voyage, diving was presenting the engineer officer with more than the usual headache. The batteries should have been cleaned out during the recent spell in port, but the work hadn't been deemed important enough. Now they were clogged up so badly that the system was struggling to provide just over half of the usual power.

This meant diving for any prolonged period was not to be recommended. No one fancied the idea of being caught close to the British coast with an inability to hide for long periods. After all, that was the U-boat's only weapon against determined anti-submarine forces. So far these had not presented a significant threat. Evasion had usually been possible and only very few unlucky boats had fallen foul of British depth charges. Yet, despite the statistics being in U58's favour, no one fancied testing the opposition's determination.

A moderate gale, enough to make day-trippers profoundly seasick, was blowing when lookouts spotted the dark shadow of a freighter during the intense darkness of the early hours. Getting close enough, through an oncoming sea, was real punishment for the machinery and torture for the men. Those on the conning tower at least had the advantage of being able to chain themselves to their positions. Those working in the interior could only hope they would survive the ordeal without too many bruises or worse injuries. Finally Schonder ordered a spread of two torpedoes, both of them set to a depth of three metres, but none of them found their mark. The settings were checked, and double-checked again. Nothing! No error. Plain definite misses. Schonder could only curse that the sea wasn't calmer and that he didn't have a deck gun. He did not sacrifice the third torpedo still lying in the tubes and instead of pursuing his target went deep to reload.

He knew U58 was standing in the path of an anticipated eastbound convoy, reported earlier by U47 (Günther Prien) and radio signals kept flooding in, but there was an annoying disagreement about positions. Both U47 and U65 were supposedly pursuing the same groups of ships and both of them were providing positions with a difference of twenty miles in their reckoning. Two destroyers came past U58, oblivious to the U-boat in their path, but the sea was still too rough for such small, shallow draught and fast-moving targets. Schonder guessed the merchant ships were not far away, but nothing gave him any clue as to the direction in which they might be. At 0400 hours, he cursed. The seas were moderating, visibility improving, but still there were only empty seas with no sight of a convoy. Schonder argued that fifty ships sailing together had to cover a pretty big area and U58 had to be sitting right in their path. So, what could have gone wrong? The only plausible answer was that they had changed course.

The natural elements were not supporting the hopes and aspirations of U-boatmen that day and the coming of daylight brought with it higher seas and stronger winds. Frustration was running even higher than the mountainous waves. 'There was no point in consuming fuel,' cursed Schonder in his log. 'We have to wait, to ride out the storm.'

Three days after having fired their first two torpedoes the lookouts spotted another shadow. It was within five minutes of the time that they had seen that first freighter. This one, heading west, was more modern and larger, riding high and empty in the water. Schonder didn't want to sacrifice more than one torpedo. The weather was bound to improve and there would be fully laden targets for his remaining two electric eels. This decision wasn't good. He lost another torpedo without reward and all he and his men received was more punishment from the waves and winds. Later the Supreme Commander-in-Chief even added a mild reprimand, saying that the saving of torpedoes while there are targets at hand is not good policy.

It was during the last hours of daylight on the following day when lookouts reported a number of shadows on the port bow. All of them were too far away. In any case, there was no point in attempting a pursuit. One of the cooling pipes for the diesels had been giving trouble for some time. Excessive heat and too many vibrations were causing so many regular leaks that the mechanics and engineer officer were constantly standing by with repair materials to plug holes. It was not until six hours later that the hunt could be re-started. This time three potential targets were spotted, approaching slowly from the south. It wasn't possible to make out what they were, but the torrid belching smoke suggested they were not burning good quality fuel. For almost two hours U58 stalked the prey. The crew was ready for action, despite many men still feeling incredibly seasick. Then, when the funnel tops came into sight, it quickly became clear that these were not big ships. The last rays of daylight allowed the men to make out the unmistakable silhouettes of three small fishing boats steaming into Donegal Bay. They looked like neutrals and, in any case, they were too small for expensive torpedoes. The lookouts didn't know whether to laugh or cry. Whatever, it had been another one of those frustratingly tense moments followed by disillusioned tiredness; another one of those exasperating hunts with no result.

Three hours later, at exactly midnight, the Obersteuermann took his usual position fix from the stars. This time it was an easy matter. He didn't even have to look up at the magnificent starry sky, dominated by a bright full moon. Both the lights on Tory Island and at Rinrawros, in the Irish Republic, were illuminated to their usual pre-war intensity, making it dead easy to get an accurate fix. Surprisingly the hauntingly mysterious coast was otherwise lit by only a small number of isolated domestic lights. The peaceful serenity radiating from the land was, however, reflecting the wrong type of image. The air and water was constantly filled with muffled sounds of detonations. All of them were too far away to make out their exact locations, but close enough to remind everybody that the peaceful backdrop of Ireland was misleading them into a false sense of security. They were still surrounded by a large proportion of unforgiving war on a ferocious ocean. Finding that war was proving increasingly difficult and visions of returning home with those sought-after, self-made success pennants flying from the extended periscope were becoming an illusion of bitter disappointment.

The booming detonations continued clearly and star shells illuminated part of the northern sky, but nothing appeared. U48 was still constantly reporting the position of a convoy, but there were no targets for U58. The coming of daylight was accompanied by another one of those by now regular muffled thuds, followed immediately by a sharp cracking noise, indicating that another cylinder head had burned through. Bad visibility encouraged Schonder to seek out the safety and comforts of the deep to repair the damage. The next night, he started the homeward run. The bad weather during the last few days had been coming predominantly from the south-west and he wanted to keep enough fuel in reserve to battle against the seas and their accompanying winds.

Later, it appeared as if a possible target had been blown towards U58 by the dreadful weather. This was so bad that there was no point in even considering a chase. In any case, the engines were ruling the roost once again and U58 went deep into comparative safety to repair them once more. Drawing closer to the French coast brought back the memory of that massive monster from the Clyde class. Could there be another British submarine lurking in the approaches to Lorient? Schonder was not going to take any risks and allowed himself plenty of extra time for his estimated time of arrival in port. There was, of course, always the hope of surprising the bugger and hitting him with the last remaining torpedoes.

Eighteen days after it had left, U58 made fast next to the hulk of the *Isere* in Lorient. There was just over a week of recuperation and living on land while the boat was in dock for repairs before the next cruise drove them out to sea on 2 October 1940. This time the men found no lurking submarines, nor did enemy forces trouble them. U58's own machinery dictated the terms of engagement. After a day's worth of steaming, black acrid smoke started pouring from the port exhaust. Consequently the mechanics removed one of the pistons and replaced it with a spare. This had hardly been completed when another piston started displaying similar symptoms. The remains of the piston rings were discovered as little fragments at the bottom of the cylinder. It was 1600 hours on their second day at sea, and almost exactly the same time as they had cast off, when the radio operator reported a breakdown of the sound detection system. A large section was failing to amplify any sounds and just made a wildly irritating buzzing tone. The boat continued chugging along at moderate speed, running-in the new cylinders, when the engineering officer added to the problems by telling Schonder that he could only run the diesels at high speed for very short spells, otherwise he risked an exploding crankcase.

Retracing the early stages of the route U58 had taken on the previous occasion, Schonder felt adamant that he was not going to make for the Irish coast again. There was too much murky weather blowing up from the south-west. Instead, he chose to go further west, aiming for a spot where he had sunk two streamers on an earlier occasion. Arriving there, he was greeted by aircraft, rather than suitable targets. Frustration had already set in, and Schonder's frame of mind meant that he was likely to vent his anger on whatever appeared. U58 had been running on the starboard engine for some time. The other one was still spouting forth that irritating streaming cloud of black smoke. Some of this had also found its way into the interior of the engine room, where men were constantly coughing and choking. Things got so bad that they isolated one of the cylinders and continued running the engine without it. Schonder wrote that the state of the engine made him feel like a tired, mobile, moored mine. These comments didn't go down too well with the U-boat Command, when officers there later studied the report.

Despite the problems with the engines, by midnight on the fourth day at sea, U58 was standing in the approaches of the North Channel and a few hours later, just after dawn, a couple of mast tips came into sight. At the same time a flying boat headed directly towards the U-boat, forcing it below the waves. Luck seemed to be with U58. The estimated 6,000 tons didn't change course and kept approaching closer. Then, just as things started to look good, the ship suddenly turned and sped out of range. Schonder was in the process of deciding whether or not to risk his troublesome engines in a hunt when another aircraft made the decision for him. The aircraft didn't show interest in the U-boat, suggesting that U58 had not been sighted, but there was no way the small and somewhat slow U-boat could match the speedier performance of the freighter. So, there was no point in pursuing it. Aircraft remained thorough nuisances for the rest of the day and muffled detonations at half-hourly intervals suggested that U58 was not too far from the action hot spot. Yet finding the location of that spot was proving increasingly difficult.

Once again moderate seas gave way to a howling westerly, making the use of weapons impossible. There was nothing for it other than to sit out the rough storm and hopefully not consume too much fuel. Yet despite the deplorable weather, faint rumbling detonations could still be heard for much of the time while the boat lurked in the depths. The next target came into sight at about the same time as the weather was starting to show positive signs of improving and as it was early evening it put Schonder into a good position. He was going to wait until total darkness would cover a surface attack.

The first torpedo to leave the tube at 2131 hours turned out to be a direct hit, right between the bridge and funnel. For a brief period the ship disappeared behind a dramatic cloud of smoke and spray, but then everything settled back to how it had been before the blast. Consequently Schonder ordered his first watch officer to sacrifice another torpedo. Closing in to 600 metres of a stationary target guaranteed another hit. Once again the detonation produced dramatic effects, but fifteen minutes later everything looked just as peaceful as it had been before the attack. Schonder and the first officer cursed and then sacrificed another torpedo. This time there was no detonation at all, but the crunching noises of bulkheads breaking suggested that the pressure of water inside the floating wreck was too much for some of the walls. Slowly the hulk dropped lower in the water. The second watch officer brought a copy of Gröner's book on merchant shipping to the bridge with the hope of identifying the target. It hadn't used its radio and if there was a name on the bows, then it couldn't be read. It was thought to be a 7,000–8,000 tonner with seven hatches of the Clan Macarthur type. It was almost midnight before U58 left the scene. Parts of the wreck were still on the surface, but the men did not discover its name. (The ship was the SS *Confield* (4,956 GRT) from Convoy HX76.)

Having taken U58 to a safer position, Schonder gave the order to dive and for the remaining two torpedoes to be loaded into the tubes. This was quite a difficult and disruptive procedure, meaning everybody in the bow area had to either get out of the way or help with the arduous task. Reloading one tube usually took a minimum of half an hour if everything went smoothly. Often it went on much longer because items stored on top had to be moved out of the way before the torpedo could be moved.

This time U58 was in luck. The men must have positioned themselves in just the right location because they only had to wait until shortly after daybreak before the next target slowly appeared out of a bank of white mist. Everything was perfect. A tanker was heading towards the U-boat and it was only a case of running at high speed to get into a better attacking position. This time the weather was also in the U-boat's favour. A mist on the water's surface was hiding the conning tower. Diving in front of the tanker, it was a case of waiting for him to draw closer. This time Schonder had discarded thoughts about sacrificing more than one torpedo for an empty ship and fired a salvo of two.

So far everything had been going according to the rules taught at commanders' school, except that then something extraordinary happened. Just at that critical moment, shortly after the torpedoes had been fired, the tanker suddenly stopped engines and made a drastic change in course, before running away with definite short zigzags.

There was no way in which Schonder could observe his torpedoes through the periscope. What was more, it had been raised for such short periods of time during quite poor visibility that he thought it would have been impossible for the opponent to see the head lens protruding above the water. The only plausible assumption was that the shallow setting of the empty tanker had made the torpedoes break the surface. This trait had been reported by other commanders as well, saying shallow-set torpedoes behaved like agile dolphins by attempting to jump clear of the water. What else could have alarmed the men on the ship and caused this sudden change? The tanker had been observed for best part of an hour and seen to be sailing in a straight line until just that critical moment shortly after the torpedoes had been discharged.

Schonder had no choice other than to commence his homeward run. All of his torpedoes had been used up. The first three hours passed in relative calm, but then U58 was troubled by a large number of aircraft passing overhead. It felt as if the opposition was organising a deliberate hunt. Darkness finally put an end to the disturbance, leaving the tiny U-boat in peace to pursue its objective of running into Bergen (Norway). Schonder thought it would be good idea to take on board at least a couple of torpedoes for the run through the North Sea. The men were in luck and safely put into the base, but torpedoes and detonators were stored in two different locations and it was Sunday. The German Navy usually worked around the clock, but somehow Norway had shut down for the weekend, providing the men in U58 with an unexpected rest on land. What was more, a number of cars were made available for a tour of the Hardangerfjord area. As it turned out, U58 did not meet any other targets for the Norwegian torpedoes. Instead of action, the men had a calm voyage via Heligoland to Brunsbüttel and then on to Kiel for a well earned refit.

Dönitz, Commander-in-Chief for U-boats, wasn't pleased and told Schonder that it is the commander's responsibility to ensure that his boat is fully operational. Therefore he should not have put to sea with such rickety engines. Schonder felt somewhat hurt, as if he was being kicked for something that wasn't his fault. Was it a case of passing the buck? After all Admiral Dönitz had demanded full engagement. Everything had to go out to sea. Dönitz also didn't

accept Schonder's reasons for the third and failed shot at the stationary ship on 8 September and added the comment at the end of U58's
log that this had not been a fully satisfactory operation.

U58 had become fully operational at about the same time as the
war started and had seen constant action since then. Dönitz had always
demanded full engagement from his men and machines, giving them
very little rest. Now, when U58 was starting to pay the price for this
intensive action, Dönitz was blaming the commander for the failures,
saying he should have insisted more forcefully that the boat went into
dock for a thorough overhaul. Somehow, somewhere there appears
to have been a misunderstanding between seagoing commanders and
land-based staff officers. This was especially true as far as comparatively inexperienced men such as Schonder were concerned. These
days, more than half a century after the events, it is terribly difficult
to explain or understand these goings-on. Even that wonderful illu-
minator called hindsight doesn't help to shed light on understanding
these indifferences. All the staff officers in the Operations Department
were ex-U-boat commanders and they should have known and
understood the problems people like Schonder were facing. After all,
the majority of these officers were without any practical technical
education and one wonders why there was such an apparent shortage
of engineers in the bases.

Heinrich Schonder was promoted to become commander of the
bigger Type VIIC boat, U77. With this he undertook ten operational
voyages, attacking at least ten ships before taking on the command of
U200. U58 was withdrawn from active service to join the training
flotillas and its next commander was Hans-Joachim Rahmlow, who
later surrendered U570 to an aircraft in the mid-Atlantic.

7

HEADING FURTHER WEST TO THE EDGE OF THE ABYSS

U108's (Kptlt. Klaus Scholtz) First Operational Voyage

This ocean-going Type IXB giant set out with hopes of making a significant contribution to the U-boats' 'Successful Time', but the men didn't find the war and were lucky to have escaped the first serious massacre.

U108's commander completed his three-year officer training in 1930, three years before Hitler came to power, but his name is hardly known. It doesn't feature in many foreign books and it is doubtful whether even many naval enthusiasts in Germany have heard of Klaus Scholtz. Yet he became a Knight of the Iron Cross twice, gaining the first award on Boxing Day of 1941 and the Oakleaves less than nine months later.

The hot summer days of 1940, when the first tiny coastal dwarfs Type IIC and Type IID were being made ready in Lorient to operate in the Western Approaches off the North Channel, saw Scholtz occasionally cooling off on the sandy shores of the river Weser. Swimming at low tide was not a good option because the remaining water resembled black sludge due to the high volume of the industrial waste from Bremen that was mixed with it, but incoming tides supplied refreshingly clean seawater from the North Sea to provide magnificent free-swimming facilities.

Scholtz arrived in Bremen in July to literally watch his submarine being built at Deschimag AG Weser's shipyard. This was quite humbling for many naval officers because the scruffy codgers from the shipyard knew a good deal more about the workings of a submarine than the chaps in newly polished uniforms. Unlike sailors, these workers didn't respond to authoritarian barking and were likely to remind pretentious young officers that their uniforms were so clean because they hadn't done any work in them.

The climax came on 22 October 1940 when U108 was finally commissioned to go on her first sea trials. By this time most of the crew had been assembled and the key personnel was in place. When not on official duty, their radio was tuned to the Atlantic frequency for the latest news, and at that time there was no shortage of it. The sinking successes were coming in so fast and so frequently that Knight's Cross production had to increase. U-boats generally maintained radio silence for fear of being discovered by British monitoring stations, but now they were shooting so many torpedoes that their positions were constantly compromised and there was nothing stopping the flow of signals. Everybody could find out what was going on and the news was always most encouraging.

The following months seemed to drag by for the men in U108, despite trials and operational training having been cut down to much less than what experienced submarine commanders considered to be basic essentials. Everybody was itching to get out into the Western Approaches and to participate in the successes of the 'Happy Time'. This was a period when U-boats penetrated the outer defence rings of convoys to fire their torpedoes from within its ranks, often singling out the best targets at point-blank ranges. Instead of the conventional recommended attacking distance of 2–3 kilometres, they closed in to 500 metres on the surface at night. Consequently, every torpedo became a hit and often three, four, or five ships would go down in quick succession.

It was bitterly cold on 15 February 1941 when U108 nosed out of the gigantic sealocks in Wilhelmshaven to follow *Sperrbrecher 32* to Heligoland. This wasn't going to be a social call. The coastal waters were littered with ice floes, making a bow protection cap essential. Although the crew could jettison these heavy pieces of steel once the danger had passed, there was no way the men could get them on board and they were too valuable to throw away, so the cap was removed when the boat called on Heligoland.

The voyage towards the Faeroe Islands was uneventful and boring and only the duty lookouts saw anything of the empty skies and seas. It was too cold and wet for many smokers on the bridge. Enough fishing boats and the occasional aircraft were encountered to create a few diversions, but generally even these failed to bring any form of relief to the daily monotony. The first real tension came in the form of a mysterious curiosity rather than a dangerous threat. Dawn was breaking when Scholtz ordered the boat to submerge. The inconsistent light of daybreak and dusk could be beneficial for submarine hunters. Hours later, tables were still blocking the main passageway with dirty crockery from lunch when the sound detection operator reported a ship on their port quarter. The silence created by drowsiness after a filling meal appeared to become even quieter as Scholtz whispered the order to rise up to periscope depth. He wanted a quick look, but didn't see anything. It was still a long way away. The noise increased. As it came closer the sound also slowly faded and U108 dropped down to 40 metres, steering back on its original course. Once there, the noise returned to where it was first heard. This time Scholtz did not seek confirmation and turned the boat away from it. Again the sound slowly became quieter, but then, suddenly, it seemed to be coming back and sounded as if it was overtaking U108. It then faded once more, as if engines were slowing down and being shut off. What the bloody hell? Curiosity drove Scholtz to have another look through the periscope. Again he couldn't see anything.

Nothing at all!

Surface!

Still nothing! No ship. Just an empty sea.

What was it? So far no one has offered an explanation.

Scholtz was still peering with some confusion at the empty seas when the radio operator handed him a signal from the U-boat Command: 'TO U108. MAKE WAY VIA THE NORTH OF THE FAEROE ISLANDS. CARRY OUT A RECONNAISSANCE OF TRAFFIC RUNNING THROUGH THE COASTAL WATERS OFF REYKJAVIK IN ICELAND AND ATTACK SUITABLE TARGETS'. The next day Dönitz (Commander-in-Chief for

U-boats) told U46 (Engelbert Endrass) and U108 to report all con-voys, even when there were no other boats in their areas. Every U-boat commander knew that the recent gold had been struck in Britain's Western Approaches off the North Channel, fairly close to land. Not many U-boats had gone as far as the barren openness of vast Atlantic around Iceland, so the idea of investigating an island more than three quarters of the way to Greenland felt like having to go to the other side of the world. The only comforting thought was that Endrass was also in the vicinity. He was no beginner. Having been First Watch Officer aboard U47 under the already legendary Kptlt. Günther Prien, he had fired the torpedoes that sunk the battleship HMS *Royal Oak* inside the Royal Navy's anchorage at Scapa Flow.

Knowing that Endrass was close by didn't compensate for an irri-tating discovery. The sealed envelopes in the commander's cupboard didn't include any detailed charts of Iceland nor was there a sailing handbook with information about the coastal waters. The general naval chart told the men where Iceland was, but they knew it was rather rocky and could be uncomfortable if they bumped into the wrong parts. What was more, when they got there they discovered that the Icelanders weren't making life easy for lurking U-boats. Their fishing fleet was still at sea, making it difficult to remain unseen. Scholtz had a burning desire to eliminate some of these lone nui-sances, but orders prevented him from carrying out such radical forms of unrestricted warfare. He had to wait for obviously belliger-ent merchant shipping. Luckily for him, this wasn't long in coming.

It was late afternoon on 22 February 1941 when between excru-ciatingly cold snowstorms and intensely painful spray from waves, the lookouts spotted a column of smoke. Turning towards it, it soon became evident that there was a freighter with two masts and one funnel some 30 miles away. Despite the order of high speed bringing the boat up to 14 knots, U108 didn't seem to be getting any closer and it wasn't until well after darkness, at 2000 hours, that an attack looked possible. There were a few more knots left in the engines, but dragging these out would also have dramatically increased the fuel consumption and Scholtz thought patience was going to be the best aid on this occasion. It was almost two hours later before he ordered action stations and this already anticipated move was followed by another half hour of tenseness before the IWO snapped the order to fire. Although the men observed a dramatic hit in the freighter's aft section from a range of just over 2 kilometres the result was more than frustrating. It didn't stop the ship. Instead it increased speed and turned towards the coast. There was no response from the radio, but a Morse lamp was seen flashing towards the land. It being a clear night, visual communication was possible over quite vast distances.

Scholtz followed calmly, still controlled by his faithful partner, patience. Twenty minutes later frustration set in. Not having noticed any effects from the explosion, he ordered another shot. This detonated most dramatically a good way before getting anywhere near the target. The idea that it might have hit a piece of floating wreckage or even a lifeboat was discussed while a third eel was being made ready. This time there was another hit. Almost immediately the ship settled deeper in the water and finally it disappeared. It was the end of the Dutch steamer *Texelstroom*. This also demonstrated Scholtz's inability to estimate ship sizes. His reported 5,600 tons turned out to have been only 1,617 GRT. Far distant lights were seen heading towards the sinking spot before U108 made off for a day of unexpected peace below the turbulence of the waves.

It was just before 2100 hours the following night when Scholtz received another signal from the U-boat Command: 'TO U108. IMMEDIATELY MAKE TOWARDS THE CONVOY REPORTED BY U552. U97 DO SO LIKEWISE, IF THE POSITION CAN BE REACHED'. Scholtz just grinned, to which the radio operator answered in the negative, without waiting for the obvious question. The message didn't say where U552 (Erich Topp) was! It became obvious that Scholtz wasn't terribly perturbed and, once again, relied upon his patience. Three hours later someone at U-boat Command in France woke up and noticed the omission. Scholtz reacted to the next signal by merely pointing the boat in a different direction.

The men in U108 didn't have to wait long. Only it wasn't a convoy ahead that got them on their toes, but smoke astern. Thinking that the black mass was coming closer, Scholtz moved into the anticipated path and dived, turning the cat and mouse game into a test of agility. The eyepieces for the periscope were in the commander's control room inside the conning tower, while the engineer officer, controlling the boat's movements, was in the central control room immediately below it and the sound detector was by the radio compartment, some distance forward. Theoretically two watertight doors should have separated all three vital components from each other, but many commanders ignored such rules because communication through voice pipes was too remote and they preferred to commute between the three, even if it meant leaping about like a mad monkey.

Faintly whining propeller noises grew steadily louder until finally they could be heard by everybody in the boat without the need of the sensitive sound detecting gear. Taking a quick peep, Scholtz saw not one, but two ships. One was a short distance behind the other. Identifying them as small reconnaissance vessels, he did not take any action. There was no point advertising his presence and chasing away an entire convoy by having a go at two sentries. After all, this was the time of the multiple attacks and there were six torpedoes ready for firing. Scholtz wanted to reserve these for fat freighters. Slowly, as the noise subsided, U108 surfaced. Shortly afterwards another small ship came into sight. Could this also be part of a reconnaissance ring? Scholtz didn't take any risks and quickly dropped back into the depths. Once down, he was rewarded with a deep and heavy oscillating thumping. It had to be something big. The brute turned out to be so huge that it could be made out through the periscope at an estimated range of 8 kilometres. Once Scholtz had established the basic characteristics, the 12,000 tons vanished into a snow shower. This was an ideal opportunity for U108. Instantly, the boat shot to the surface, lookouts poured through the hatch and the hunt was on. It was too good a target and the convoy could wait.

The men on board the steamer knew full well that they were heading into U-boat-infested waters and didn't oblige by presenting themselves as easy prey. Taking advantage of the poor visibility, the freighter made a sharp 90° turn and all Scholtz could do was to curse. It meant running into an oncoming sea and the target was too fast for that. Reluctantly, U108 was swung back onto the course for the convoy. Two hours later, Scholtz received another unexpected hammering. This time it came in the form of a signal from U552, saying that contact with the convoy had been lost. Just a few hours earlier U108 was faced with the prospect of having two worthwhile targets. Now both of them had vanished into the vastness of the fierce Atlantic. Infuriating, but there was nothing anyone could do. Making matters even worse, the waves grew rougher, the temperature colder and intense snowstorms cut visibility down to almost nil. At the same time, waves, washing furiously over the deck and conning tower, prevented the men from making snowmen. Again, Scholtz cursed and took to the comforts of the deep to relax in the strong aroma of freshly made coffee.

Four hours of peaceful calm were followed by the old man's desire to have a look at daylight. It wasn't terribly encouraging. Rough seas still raged, drenching the lookouts before they could clip the chains of the safety harnesses in position. Scholtz obviously had slept long enough and wasn't going to provide more cellar comforts. Instead the boat slowly chugged through the turbulence. Once again, the remnants of lunch were still scattered around the interior, and a good proportion of smashed crockery was littering the corners, when the lookout infuriated everybody by spotting a ship. Action replaced the usual rest after lunch, not that anyone minded. Success was always better than sitting idly around in such uncomfortable conditions.

It turned out to be another small reconnaissance craft. Not even worth a torpedo. It appeared briefly and then vanished again into one of those regular snow squalls, without taking any notice of the U-boat. A short while later a massive passenger ship with three funnels put in an appearance. The officer on duty instantly identified it as an auxiliary cruiser and would have loved to have a go at it, but the weather had worsened to such an extent that there was no hope of engaging any weapons. The raging force 6–7 gale made it impossible to get in front of the giant and U108 was too far away for a torpedo.

Meanwhile U552 reported having made contact with the convoy again, but Erich Topp also added that the seas were too rough for attacking. Mountainous water, gales, snowstorms, ice encrusting the bridge and clothing and the nauseating lack of success continued for four cold, uncomfortable days. Nothing could destroy the harmonious life in the U-boat like the cold, the wet and storms. Men started getting on each other's nerves and tempers started running short.

Neither propaganda nor training had prepared any of them for such extended torture. One submariner once said that conditions like this can only be described to a person who has experience of such foul situations. It is much too much for a modern person to imagine.

Later, when things finally calmed down and a target came into sight, it did so at the most inappropriate time: it was broad daylight in the mid-afternoon and the blasted periscope was full of water! There was nothing for it but to wait for darkness and attempt a surface attack at night. Once it started getting dark, the quarry didn't show any lights and steered a predictable zigzag course. This was all rather suspicious, making it unnecessary for Scholtz to look for further evidence in order to decide whether he should attack or not. It definitely looked like a belligerent. The first torpedo from tube 2 jumped clear of the water before running some distance ahead of the target, causing the ship to slow down most dramatically. U108 was only about half a kilometre away and the lookouts must have spotted the U-boat, even if they missed the torpedo. Scholtz didn't fancy going any closer and ordered the IWO to get off another shot as quickly as possible.

'Bloody Hell!'

The IWO couldn't be that bad. Only 500 metres away from an almost stationary 6,461 GRT and he missed! Once again lookouts reported seeing the torpedo jump almost clear of the water, like a graceful dolphin. Following this, the torpedo probably nose-dived under the target. This confirmed that it probably wasn't the IWO's fault, but due to the damned machinery. In moments like this you need a scapegoat, you need someone to curse and you need another shot. At last there followed an incredible detonation, smoke and spray followed and the ship started broadcasting a distress call, under the name of *Effna*, saying she was fully laden and on her way east to Britain.

The crew had taken to the boats, but seeing nothing significant in the blackness of the night, one of the lifeboats was rowed back alongside. Lights were turned on. People carrying torches were seen running along the decks and then the radio room erupted into steady activity. There was nothing for it. Scholtz sacrificed another torpedo. Sadly this sealed the fate of those seamen who had climbed back on board. It appeared as if this torpedo also triggered an internal explosion. Perhaps too much pressure had built up in a boiler. Whatever, *Effna* dropped into the cold depths to be no more. First watch officers tended to get terribly irritable after such depressing experiences like missing with an almost full load of torpedoes. Consequently everybody's life is made sheer hell until the real culprit is found. Eventually the IWO could emerge from the black cloud of gloom hanging over him with the knowledge that some mechanical irregularities had been found inside the torpedo aimer and these were probably the cause of the trouble.

Adding insult to injury, the machinery had another go at U108. Having spent three hours reloading the torpedo tubes, the men in the bow compartment heard the definite noise of someone on the outside knocking hard to get in. Obviously they knew this was impossible and a quick investigation suggested the extraordinary noise was the external door of tube 1. It had worked loose during the storm and was now protesting most vigorously. Not only that, but the outside pressure doors had been bent, allowing water to flood into the tube. This put the men in rather a strange predicament. The torpedo already in the tube couldn't be fired, nor could it be withdrawn for loading into another tube. So, in an instant the mechanical hardware denied them the use of another torpedo. The men could curse loudly, but there was nothing any of them could do about it. The inert iron had won the day.

This infuriation hardly perturbed Scholtz, who merely pointed upwards at the weather. Everybody knew that it had turned back to being too rough for engagement anyway. Later, when calmness prevailed again, a ship did oblige by coming into sight, but massive neutrality markings indicated that the 10,000-ton tanker could not be attacked. Then U552 reported another convoy. This time the U-boat Command did not respond, leaving Scholtz in a quandary about what to do. He had a strange feeling that what ever decision he took, it was bound to be the wrong one. Not having anything better to do, he headed towards the ships without waiting for orders. The snag was that the position was not terribly clear, so U108 requested homing signals for confirmation. This worked quite well. At last a ship came into sight, although the men in U108 weren't sure whether it was part of U552's convoy or not. Being mid-afternoon, Scholtz decided to keep in visual contact until darkness allowed for a surface attack.

This time the efforts were frustrated by an order from the U-boat Command to form a patrol line some distance to the east. Again, Scholtz was placed in one of those peculiar predicaments. If he stayed to attack the ship he would be blamed for making a gap in the wolf pack, allowing the convoy to slip through. If he did join the patrol line, then Döntiz was bound to reprimand him for not sinking the ship. This time it would have been good to have a tactical commander at sea, rather than in a land-based control room a long way away. The U-boat Command ordered a speed of 10 knots and the sea was so rough that U108 could manage only 4 knots. By the time U108 took position in the patrol line, two thirds of the fuel supply had been used and it was another submarine, rather than a group of merchant ships, which came into sight. The weather was pretty appalling, making it difficult to see what was going on and impossible to get an accurate fix in order to determine one's position. Checking their navigation, the men in U108 thought the shadow was probably the next boat in the patrol line. This had hardly passed out of sight when another steamer with navigation lights appeared. It had to be neutral if it was passing along the edge of Germany's declared war area.

Later, shortly after Scholtz sent a message to the U-boat Command saying a shortage of fuel made it necessary to return home, a reconnaissance aircraft reported sighting a convoy of twenty-four ships, two heavy cruisers and four destroyers. These were excellent targets and in a most convenient position on the way home. Spirits rose instantly as the men realised that they might still find a few ships for the remaining five useable torpedoes. However, the expected convoy wasn't where it should have been. Instead of ships, U108 found empty seas with good visibility. The only consolation was that the weather had settled down to a moderately rocking sea instead of the incessant storm. Despite the respite from the elements and excellent prospects, the fuel situation was becoming critical and the engineer officer was wondering whether they had enough reserves to avoid possible attackers. It seemed likely that there wasn't enough left for chasing another illusive convoy. The only practical option was to make for France.

It was 12 March 1941 by the time U108 made fast in Lorient, after having been at sea for a total of twenty-five days. The men were pleased to be back in port, despite the lack of success. Sinking two ships was an exceedingly small bag compared with the masses of tonnage sunk by others during recent months. Although the men hardly knew it at the time, they had been rather lucky. U47 had probably already gone down and U70 had definitely been sunk. The aces Otto Kretschmer in U99 and Joachim Schepke in U100 were to follow in less than a week's time. Grim new events described in the next chapter were shaping the future of the convoy war. U108 had passed along the edge of an abyss and it is quite likely that had the lookouts found those fallacious convoys, the subsequent action could well have brought an abrupt end to the boat's long career.

8

SIXTY-FOUR DYNAMIC DAYS OF 1941: TWO METAMORPHIC MONTHS

Thirty-nine ships of Convoy OB290 were making 8 knots through calm seas on a moonless night, when shortly after midnight of 26 February 1941 the freighter *Kasongo* was hit by a torpedo. There was just enough time to send a distress signal before the 5,254 GRT freighter vanished, almost as if by magic. Everybody in the convoy had been on especially full alert for the past four hours, since receiving a signal saying there were indications that the westbound ships were probably being shadowed by at least one U-boat. Yet, despite the tension and extra vigilance, there was little anyone could do to help the stricken seamen. The horizon was hidden behind a veneer of mist and it was too dark to see anything as small as a submarine on the surface. In any case, none of the escorts were even aware of the attack until they received *Kasongo*'s distress signal. The slip of paper had not yet been handed to the duty watches on the bridges when two white rockets from the tanker *Diala* streaked into the starry sky. She was some distance ahead of the first victim, but no one would have known this as they gazed into the blackness of the night. The gap between each column was five cables and the convoy was made up of eight of these, so the merchant ships covered a distance of almost 4½ miles or just over 7 kilometres; much too far for anyone to keep an overall eye on. (One cable is 608 feet in the UK and 720 feet in the USA. So, in modern, metric measurements one UK cable is about 185 metres and about 220 metres in USA. Therefore in the UK 5 cables are almost 1 km and in USA just over 1 km. The Royal Navy recorded the cables mentioned here, so they are almost certainly British.)

None of the observers would have known who fired the U-boat warning flares. Torpedo detonations bore no resemblance to the impressive petrol flames shown in modern films and even a loud explosion was often dissipated by the weather into a dull thud, making it exceedingly difficult to know exactly what was going on. So it took a while before the convoy commodore, who was responsible for the merchant ships, and the senior officer of the escorts could take defensive action. Once alerted by the radio signal and by the rocket, the 1,085-ton converted yacht HMS *Enchantress* was detailed to turn out into the open waters beyond the convoy's port wing, but didn't see anything despite expending a good number of star shells to illuminate the darkness. The deep-seated tension created by the explosion turned into real pandemonium a few minutes later, when the convoy commodore, aboard SS *Samuel Bakke*, ordered an emergency turn to starboard (the right-hand side). Watching the resulting spectacle must have left him fuming with anger and frustration. The ships in the starboard columns maintained their courses while those on the other side of the convoy turned left instead of right. Cursing didn't help. The commodore didn't rattle his charges to make them comply with his order. Instead he had the good sense to change the instructions, to comply with the majority of ships turning left. However, the manoeuvre didn't throw off the U-boat. Two more explosions followed a few minutes later, shortly after the ships had settled on their new course.

The senior officer of the escorts reacted to the distress rockets by bringing his ship, HMS *Whitehall*, up to 20 knots, while star shells were shot to illuminate the sea. Nothing was seen, other than a Sunderland aircraft dropping flares, which helped to emphasise the vulnerability of the columns of merchant ships. The destroyer HMS *Whitehall* had been launched before the end of the First World War and did not provide the deep-seated confidence of being capable of coping with the rigours of modern warfare. Yet, she was by no means the oldest lady of the escort group. Two other destroyers,

HMS *Vanquisher* and HMS *Winchelsea*, were more than a year older, having been launched late in 1917.

In the meantime HMS *Enchantress* had almost run out of star shells and decided it might be better to go back to her position at the rear of the convoy, rather than search the empty waters. The year-old HMS *Pimpernel*, a flower-class corvette, was also searching empty seas when she was ordered back to her station around the merchant ships. She had hardly changed course when the instructions were countermanded, sending her to search for survivors instead. These were relatively easy to locate, since the last two torpedoed ships (SS *Rydboholm* and SS *Borgland*) didn't sink. Feverish activity kept them clinging desperately to the surface, although their precarious positions suggested that the crossing of the Atlantic would be expecting too much. The second target, the *Diala*, benefited from Germany's torpedo failure problem: magnetic pistols, which were supposed to detonate under the keel to break their target in half, had been too unreliable and therefore Günther Prien in U47 used contact detonators instead. This made a gaping hole in the side of the tanker, allowing its ballast to pour out and thus lift the hole higher in the water. Turning round, *Diala* eventually made it back to Britain.

Convoy OB290 was later confronted by Focke Wulf Kondor aircraft, but did not cross the path of another U-boat. Even the experienced Günther Prien failed to relocate it. However, three days later, on 28 February 1941, after the convoy had dispersed, he did sink the 4,223-ton freighter *Holmelea* with his 88mm quick-firing deck gun. Following this, the weather changed for the worst. This resulted in the escape of both the Swedish *Rydboholm* and Norwegian *Borgland* and kept Prien away from further action. Two weeks passed before U47 sighted her next convoy, this time the westbound OB293. What exactly happened next is difficult to determine, but it looks as if Prien sent his last sighting report at 0454 hours on 8 March, almost a day after having shot his last torpedoes against the 20,638 GRT British whaling ship with the Norwegian name of *Terje Viken*. Kptlt. Otto Kretschmer (U99) thought he delivered the coup de grace later the same day, but this action also failed to sink the monster. The unsalvageable wreck was finally put under on 14 March by gunfire from two British destroyers and a corvette.

Following the first attack on Convoy OB293, U47 vanished in a similar fashion to the first ship it had sunk from Convoy OB290: almost as if by magic. The U-boat Command, now located at Kernevel near Lorient in France, sent several requests for U47 to report its position, but there were no replies and a few days later it became clear that the famous ace, Günther Prien, was not going to come home. He was the man who had sunk the battleship HMS *Royal Oak* inside the Royal Navy's anchorage at Scapa Flow and the first person of the U-boat Arm to be awarded the Knight's Cross. He will probably remain one of the most famous submarine commanders of all time. It is not known what happened to him, but it looks most likely that the boat dropped silently into the depths as a result of either a human error or some type of mechanical failure. What is definite is that U47 never made it back to any port. This loss marked the first of a long series of particularly shattering losses for Germany, which became a critical turning point in the U-boat war.

This milestone in submarine history marks the beginning of a period when the U-boat offensive started slipping into depths from which it was never to resurface. During the autumn of 1940, every U-boat at sea had been sinking on average almost six ships per month. The best they ever achieved after Prien's loss was marginally more than two, during the early summer of 1942. The disappearance of U47 also marked a dramatic increase in the number of U-boats sunk. After the Norwegian Campaign of 1940, one or two U-boats were sunk every month and 1941 started with no losses at all during January and February. Then, suddenly, the following two months saw the total of lost U-boats rise to a staggering nine. Not only was this figure too dramatic to release to the media, but the list included a number of national heroes who had been worshipped in a similar manner to the way football and film celebrities are treated today. They included Fritz-Julius Lemp in U110, Joachim Schepke in U100 and Otto Kretschmer in U99.

The next boat to go down after Prien, U70 under Kptlt. Joachim Matz, was sunk during its first war cruise. Having left Kiel on 20 February 1941, U70 met a chain of encouraging successes in what was still regarded as a lucrative area off the North Channel. Reconstructing these today, without U70's log, is not easy especially as the majority of torpedoes missed by a wide enough margin for no one at the receiving end to have noticed them. Whatever happened during those early hours of 7 March 1941, U70's problems came with the third target of the night. The 7,493 GRT Dutch tanker *Mijdrecht* was brought to a standstill at 0725 hours, while the rest of Convoy OB293 moved on.

The blackness of the night was turning into an inhospitable grey dawn, making it possible for Matz to see what was happening and he quickly had a closer look at the drifting tanker. Since it was already light enough to be spotted on the surface, he gave the order to dive. This usually allowed for the U-boat to drop down to about 80 metres. Then, when the hydroplanes caught it at the correct depth, it would slowly glide upwards again to periscope depth. This was done by steering with the hydroplanes in a similar fashion to the way aircraft are controlled, without blowing air into the tanks. Once at a depth of 25 metres, the large, super-sensitive depth gauge came into play, to help the men with the delicate juggling act of stabilising the 1,070 tons of steel. Once at the correct depth, a few metres below the surface, a huge manometer was used to hold the boat steady. By the side of this large depth gauge and right in front of the hydroplane operators was a huge drawing of the conning tower with extended periscope and the liquid inside a 'U' tube indicated the position of the surface of the water. Thus it was possible to remain unseen in just the right depth, without the need of a window to see the surface of the water. However, this was a tricky undertaking at the best of times and something the hydroplane operators and the engineer officer would not have practiced too often. On this occasion they didn't get it quite right. So, when Matz raised the periscope, all he could see was water gurgling past the head lens. At the same time, everybody would have been aware of wave action and of a multitude of loud noises created by water washing around their boat.

The men in the stricken tanker must have been fully aware of their precarious position and were therefore keeping an extra sharp lookout. It seems highly likely that they spotted the hulk of the grey shark as it lurked in the impressive clearness of the North Atlantic. Again, we are not sure of the exact sequence of events, but at this critical moment the tanker managed to raise sufficient power to make headway. Running over the U-boat, it scraped a gaping hole into the conning tower fairing. The boat immediately dropped deeper, but the force of the impact did more than just damage the upper part, which could be shut off from the rest of the interior. With the boat still under control, but slowly filling with water, Matz decided the best course of action would be to remain silent in the depths until the cover of darkness provided an opportunity to surface and to survey the damage. The boat had been up top for most of the night, therefore the batteries were charged, the compressed air bottles full and the prospects looked good. The snag was that it was getting light, meaning that this was going to be a long wait.

To make matters worse, it was not long before the men realised their diving gauges were not functioning properly and it seemed likely that they were sinking deeper than what comfort allowed. In the end, the engineer officer, the 34-year-old Leutnant zur See Wall, could no longer maintain a safe depth with the hydroplanes alone and asked for permission to increase speed. This provided more leverage for the hydroplanes to make a greater impact. It was not long before his next request became more drastic. He needed to counterbalance the weight of the additional water by blowing a little air into the diving tanks. This was an incredibly difficult procedure if it was also necessary to remain submerged. The air in the tanks expands as the boat rises and the outside water pressure reduces. This means the speed at which the boat ascends increases and then comes a point where the tanks cannot be flooded quickly enough to maintain control. So, instead of remaining submerged, the boat broke the surface like a floundering whale, surrounded by a mass of bubbles escaping from the bottom of the diving tanks.

U70 was still in luck, low clouds and less than clear visibility provided a small amount of comfort for the lookouts, but at 0815 hours the approaching corvette *Camellia* spotted the submarine just where the tanker had suggested it might be. Despite the desperate situation, Matz and his men had things under control and another controlled dive took U70 into the depths. This left *Camellia* in an awkward situation because her Asdic wasn't working and all she could do was to drop depth charges with a variety of settings in the hope that they would at least annoy the opposition. They didn't. The men in U70 felt highly relieved as they realised their luck and that the detonations were way off their mark. The men thought there might be a leak in one of the high-pressure air pipes supplying the diving tanks, causing bubbles to rise to the surface and mark their position. Their big gamble was to hope that a ship on the surface might not notice the bubbles.

About an hour later the corvette *Arbutus*, with functioning Asdic, replaced the *Camellia*, which was detailed to escort the damaged tanker. Further attacks against U70 at 1013 hours, 1126, 1134 and 1212 hours didn't bring any results, despite a variety of depth settings on the charges. Unfortunately for the men in the submarine, it was becoming more and more difficult to control the water flooding into the boat. The ballast pump, designed to push the water out, was switched on for short periods only, when *Arbutus* was heard to run her engines to a high speed. Hopefully those were be loud enough for her hydrophone operator not to hear the ballast pump grinding down in the depths. It was shortly after *Arbutus's* seventh attack at 1244 hours that U70 surfaced.

The boat appeared as if it had been part of a conjurer's trick, with men on the corvette gaping in astonishment. The appearance seemed to have been a miracle because the last depth charges exploded immediately on top of the U-boat, so fatally close that they should have sunk it. U70 had, of course, surfaced earlier after the collision. Therefore Matz knew the damage to the conning tower wasn't going to prevent him from opening the hatch, but he was totally unprepared for what happened next. He and the lookouts waiting behind him were blown out by the high pressure that had built up inside the boat. The hatch was only just wide enough for a man to slide through and to be forced through at speed meant that the commander and the next six men were seriously hurt as they crashed against iron protrusions. Things were not much better down below. Men were pushed against bulkheads as the wind swept out through the tiny opening, like the discharge from an airgun.

U70 remained afloat for another half hour or so, but it was a case of every man for himself. Jumping into the cold Atlantic was the only practical option. The men in HMS *Arbutus* claim to have hit the conning tower with a 4-inch shell and pom-pom fire was directed at the men as they abandoned ship. As a result eighteen were lost, but

Matz and twenty-five survivors were saved. The commander of the corvette did his best to save the men in the water by dropping them a couple of Carley life rafts before going on to deal with the wreck they had escaped from. Closing in to ram the U-boat, HMS *Arbutus* changed course at the last minute with the hope of boarding the prize, but it was too late, U70 was finished.

Despite this success, there was no point in anyone in Convoy OB293 resting on their laurels; the radio had already warned them to expect more than one U-boat and firm evidence of this was not long in coming. Some twelve hours later a torpedo hit the 5,258 GRT freighter *Dunaff Head*. (Fired at 0109 on 8 March 1941 by UA under Hans Eckermann.) By this time the westbound convoy was some 30 miles south of Iceland, chugging through less than satisfactory conditions and with visibility down to less than 1 mile. This was ideal for U-boats. It provided good cover and the excellent sound detectors made it possible to locate the convoy with reasonable accuracy at ranges of about 15 nautical miles. Lookouts on the top of the conning tower would probably not have spotted ships over such a vast distance, even if they were tall vessels on the clearest of days. The destroyer HMS *Wolverine* should normally have turned away from the merchant ships to search for the U-boat by shooting star shells, but the experience of the previous night, when a vast number of such illuminants were expended and nothing was found, made her commanding officer, Lieutenant Commander J.M. Rowland, decide it would be better to remain where he was. This paid dividends. Just less than half an hour later his lookouts spotted what looked like a diesel exhaust lacing the mist. Men on the bridge had hardly focussed on it when the hydrophone operator reported a mechanical noise in the same direction as the smoke.

Rowland increased speed, signalled HMS *Verity* and told his men to load sharp ammunition instead of star shells. He was determined not to give his position away. Not long afterwards the men spotted what had to be the wake of something and this made Rowland run his engines up to top speed, in the hope that he would find the U-boat by chasing its bow wave. Rowland ordered silence and made sure none of his men got itchy trigger fingers. He realised that the natural conditions were now on his side and it would be possible to get close enough to surprise the U-boat. Then, amidst the tension of the night, the darkness was suddenly illuminated by a star shell from HMS *Verity* just in time to see the U-boat disappear below the waves.

For some inexplicable reason, the Asdic did not work, or at least there was no echo from what was known to be a definite target. To make matters worse, the swirling mist made it exceedingly difficult to pinpoint exactly where the U-boat had been. Reducing speed and going into a search routine, the Asdic suddenly produced an accurate enough response for *Wolverine* to plaster the estimated position with ten depth charges. Then, when the noisy detonations had died away, everything was just as calm as it had been before. *Wolverine* found herself alone, moving slowly through a grey curtain of mist. *Verity*, which had provided strong psychological support by being within sight, had vanished. On top of this, Asdic suggested there was nothing below the surface. All Rowland could do was to repeat the tedious search routine. The next twenty minutes appeared not only to have been exceedingly long, but also especially lonely. The men fell into the type of situation where they didn't believe their own judgement anymore. They realised that they were in a tricky predicament: the weather made them damp or even wet and an uncanny coldness crept through their bodies as they strained all senses to penetrate the loneliness of the black night. Of course they could not rule out becoming the U-boat's next target. It was not the most pleasant of feelings. Luckily for the men, it didn't last long and soon they were shaken by another pattern of eight depth charges. Following this, the procedure was repeated once more.

Wolverine was desperate to have *Verity's* support, but could not make contact with her, so Lt Cdr Rowland had no choice but to mount another attack on his own. Then, when *Verity* did reappear, Rowland immediately sent the details of his attack by radio and by signal lamp. The message had to get over quickly, if they were going to work as a team. However, communications were not at their best. Suddenly, without much warning, *Verity* vanished again, almost as if someone had closed the curtains. On top of this, it was virtually impossible to establish any position on the surface because both the waves and the swirling grey continuously changed pattern. Rowland resorted to marking the position where the Asdic had suggested the submarine might be with a flare and then turning to run in at high speed to drop depth charges in the right spot. *Verity* reappeared from behind the curtain, but radio contact could not be re-established. It really was a most inconvenient time for the wireless to break down.

The next set of depth charges had not yet been dropped when someone reported a strong smell of diesel oil. Turning round and examining what looked like a patch on the surface didn't yield any further evidence. The hydrophone still suggested there was something rather noisy deep down and not too far away. What was more, it seemed likely that the oil trail could have come from a torpedo. The merchant ships were too far away, so it looked as if *Wolverine* had been the likely target. Not a deeply calming thought during the cold of the night. Then, amidst a multitude of confusion and the absence of an Asdic echo, the men guessed that the submarine had probably surfaced. (Asdic could not detect surfaced submarines, only submerged ones.) *Wolverine* ran her engines to a high speed once more. This was not the easiest of undertakings: U-boats were known to outrun many of the old destroyers and there was a good chance of losing this one among the mist in the blackness of the night.

Once again, the men in HMS *Wolverine* found themselves in a hopeless situation, where many must have wondered whether it was worth continuing with what seemed to be becoming a hopeless search. There were no clues to suggest they were getting nearer to their target and it was even possible that they were sailing in totally the wrong direction. After all they had no positive indications where the U-boat might be and could rely only on their intuition. Then, suddenly, at 0415 hours something was spotted on the starboard bow. There followed a most remarkable chase where the U-boat remained on the surface. Yet it was more than difficult for *Wolverine* to get close enough to attack. Although her engines could bring her up to 20 knots, the ship had to slow down frequently to use hydrophones in order to confirm the position of the by-now dived U-boat.

In the end the hunt paid dividends by bringing the destroyer into a position where more depth charges could be dropped. Once again, the men were disappointed. There was no sign of any wreckage. *Wolverine* continued dropping depth charges at 0619 hours, 0633, 0656 and at 0755, but on each occasion the Asdic echo was slightly different to what had been earlier and then, when lookouts spotted porpoises, they realised they had not been hunting a U-boat. An orange light seen earlier in the darkness of the night could also not be accounted for. The men wondered for some time what this could have been and in the end put it down to possibly having come from a German life raft.

Following this long hunt, British intelligence officers learned from U-boat survivors that U47 with Günther Prien had not replied to calls from the U-boat Command and had probably vanished. Soon afterwards German radio confirmed that the boat would not be returning to port. This combination provided the British Admiralty with sufficient information to accredit the loss of U47 to HMS *Wolverine*, although there was no evidence that the long and frustrating hunt had been successful.

It seems incredibly strange that no one at the Admiralty checked the U-boat Command's log after the war. Had they done so, they would have realised that Günther Prien sent his last radio report with position and weather details at 0454 hours, shortly before HMS *Wolverine* had abandoned her hunt. Had Prien been the subject of such an intense chase, where he undoubtedly had suffered considerable damage, he would certainly have mentioned the matter. What is more, the average number of U-boats at sea during March was five and this dropped to two in April and the identity of each U-boat at sea, together with its position was given in the U-boat Command's war diary. So it would not have been too difficult to work out who had received a considerable plastering on the night when HMS *Wolverine* participated in this most dramatic hunt. The unfortunate victim was UA under Hans Eckermann. This boat had been built before the war for export to Turkey, but was never delivered and was commissioned into the German Navy instead. Being a large, ocean-going type, it was pitched against convoys and later even engaged as emergency supply boat. Despite serious damage, the boat made it back to Lorient, making fast there on 18 March 1941.

The most significant happening of this time took place during the early hours of 17 March 1940 while a group of Knights Cross holders were attacking the eastbound convoy HX112. Kptlt. Otto Kretschmer, the most successful commander of the Second World

War, was lying on his bunk when the alarm bells shrilled and the watch officer dropped down from the top of the conning tower to report a destroyer approaching at high speed. This in itself was nothing new; many U-boats had sleepy lookouts, but it was so significant on this occasion that novelists would even describe it as sinister. It marks the beginning of 'the' major turning point of the war at sea. The ship on the surface, HMS *Walker* under Commander Donald MacIntyre, dropped its last two depth charges so accurately that even the experienced crew of U99 could not catch the boat until it dropped down to below 200 metres. Water flooding into the interior, mixed with a foul concoction of dirt and oil from the bilges, started washing around the men's feet, giving Kretschmer no alternative other than to abandon ship. Volkmar König, an ensign on board to gain his first experiences of the Atlantic, recounted how things were happening relatively slowly. There was time to send a sinking report back to base and Kretschmer ordered a signal to be flashed in English by Morse lamp to the destroyer, asking for his men to be picked up. Even once the majority had got off and plenty of water was washing in through the open deck hatches, there was still no sign of U99 sinking, so the engineer officer, Oblt.z.S. Schröder, returned from the relative safety of the top of the conning tower to the clammy interior to open the diving vents. This caused the boat to drop so rapidly that it took him with it. The rest of the men were all saved except for two seamen who somehow perished during the last darkness of the early morning.

Not far away was U100 under Kptlt. Joachim Schepke, another Knight of the Iron Cross. An escort had surprised the U-boat as well and was homing in at high speed when the men first spotted it. Once underwater the men didn't need the highly sensitive sound detection gear to hear the frightening whine of the small, fast ship on the surface, stopping occasionally to get good bearings with its Asdic. The depth charges were so accurate, reported Siegfried Flister, a trainee commander, that the men assumed the destroyer seemed to know not only the direction of the avoiding manoeuvre but also its exact depth. U100 also dropped far too deep for comfort before the men could catch it, allowing far too much water to flood in. Despite frantic repairs, the depth charges had done their job and it was only going to be a matter of time before the water seeping into the interior was going to sink the boat. Even with ballast pumps working at full speed, the water level continued to rise, giving Schepke no alterative other than to surface. What happened there is well known. HMS *Vanoc* (Lt Cdr J.G.W Deneys) had already turned and rammed U100, squashing Schepke and locking Flister in place on the top of the conning tower. Flister was to lucky to have been released from his clamp-like hold when the ship pulled back, and even luckier to be picked up with only five other men. The rest went down with U100.

The significant and, for novelists, sinister, element of these happenings is that this was not only the first time that a U-boat had been detected by radar but also the first occasion where radar had led to the sinking of a U-boat. This combination of being able to see surfaced U-boats during dark nights, to force them under and then use Asdic to accurately drop depth charges put a sudden and most dramatic end to the U-boats' successful period. Never again were U-boats going to reap the fantastic harvest they had been gathering during the autumn of 1940.

To appreciate how the events leading to the end of U99 and U100 unfolded, it is necessary to step from the conning tower onto the convoy escorts' bridges and this can be done by consulting Anti-Submarine Warfare accounts prepared shortly after the war by the historical section of the Admiralty War Staff. The astonishing point about this sinking was that the two victims were not alone and the Admiralty regretted that the other U-boats were not sunk as well. In those days radar was still known as ASV – a term derived from Air to Surface, but for this account it might be better to use the better-known non-technical version.

So, to return to Convoy HX112, Kptlt. Fritz-Julius Lemp, who had earlier commanded U30 and sunk the liner *Athenia* on the first day of the war and seriously damaged the 6,207 GRT tanker *Erodona* shortly after midnight on 16 March, causing it to erupt into such a brilliant sheet of flame that no one in the convoy could have missed it. Even with everybody on the alert, U99 managed to get in shortly after this to torpedo another six ships. Bearing in mind that the U-boat had only five torpedo tubes, it is clear that the radar wasn't being terribly helpful on this occasion. There are several explanations for this. First, the tops of waves would have produced a mass of back-echoes, making it exceedingly difficult to differentiate between these and the tiny response from a conning tower. Secondly, the ships within the convoy also produced a considerable amount of interference on the radar screen, making it difficult to distinguish small objects near them.

Vanoc and HMS *Volunteer* immediately followed their counter-measures procedure but failed to find the U-boat. However, *Volunteer* did attend to a couple of stragglers, helping them to re-join the convoy but was herself without radar and failed to find the convoy again. A shortage of fuel then caused her to return to Britain. Shortly before daybreak on 16 March, when HMS *Walker* turned to investigate a white rocket, she learned that the Dutch tanker *Ocana* had been attacked, but although the torpedo hit the ship, it didn't explode. At first the escort officers thought this could have been an imaginary attack sparked off by the ship colliding with some floating wreckage. However, a little while later, shortly after first light, it became apparent that the ship had probably been hit by a torpedo which didn't explode. Four other ships were missing, but at that time no one knew what had happened to them. They could have got lost during the night and be straggling on behind. In fact three of them were with HMS *Volunteer*, some 30 kilometres in front of the convoy, so they had obviously been going a little faster than the rest during the darkness of the night. Of course, the necessity to keep radio silence meant the men at sea were not aware of what was going on around them. Yet, there had been enough activity to suggest at least one U-boat was still in contact and a Sunderland aircraft appeared later in the day to search the surrounding seas, especially at the rear where the shadow was thought to be lurking. Just to make life a little more uncomfortable, several floating mines, sighted throughout the day, had to be made safe by sinking them with gunfire.

It was early evening of the 16th when lookouts in HMS *Scimitar* sighted a U-boat on the surface, this time without any input from any radar. Both HMS *Walker* and HMS *Scimitar* approached at high speed and HMS *Vanoc* was also ordered to join the hunt, but despite searching until shortly after 2100, nothing was found and the ships rejoined the convoy. *Walker* was still slightly astern of the convoy when another ship was torpedoed and another three followed shortly afterwards. This must have been the major attack by U99. At midnight the commodore ordered a sharp emergency turn to the right and an hour later the ships returned to their original heading. At that stage, at about 0100 hours, a submarine was sighted at a range of about 1 kilometre and *Walker* went into high sped to ram it. The U-boat lookouts must have been a little sleepy because the approaching destroyer got to within 100 metres before the boat dived into the depths. Ten depth charges were dropped. They produced some dramatic detonations with an orange coloured flame, but no evidence of having hit the submarine. Searches and attacks continued for well over an hour.

In the meantime, the clock had moved on to 0200 of 17 March and HMS *Walker* was cruising at 15 knots after another series of attacks, when the radar operator picked up a positive echo in the range of about 1 kilometre. Immediately afterwards the submarine was sighted as well. *Vanoc* ran towards it, ramming it at right angles and squashing Schepke on the top of the conning tower. This happened so fast that the men racing to man *Vanoc*'s gun had not yet got into position by the time the bows sliced through U100. After that there followed one of those almost hilarious situations where neither ship could open fire on the submarine without possibly hitting the other ship as well. Some careful manoeuvring was called for. This almost ended with both of them ramming each other, but mishaps were avoided and things turned out well for the Royal Navy. HMS *Walker* was picking up men from U100 when radar indicated another small vessel closing in on the surface. U99 might still have escaped had the watch officer not panicked and run away fast on the surface rather than diving in to the depth charge cauldron. This small action may have gone under in far more dramatic hunts of the period, but it was most significant. It was the first step in beating U-boats on the high seas.

9

FROM THE WILD ATLANTIC TO THE CALM MEDITERRANEAN

U96, one of the early seagoing Type VIIC boats, experienced violent storms in the North Atlantic and found that the area to the west of Ireland had become a poor hunting ground for U-boats. While still riding out the atrocious weather, the men received an unexpected surprise. Instead of returning home, the boat was ordered to refuel in Spain and then make its way into the Mediterranean.

It was mid-September 1941 when two young officers stood to attention in front of their commander, something they didn't do very often because formality wasn't part of the boat's daily routine. Everybody had an important role in the team and the Old Man already had a Knight's Cross, making it unnecessary for him to demand the stiffness of officialdom from his men. This time the two youngsters stood to attention because they had come to say their farewells. One of them was Oblt.z.S. Hans Stock, who was to die less than two years later as commander of U659. The other, Oblt.z.S. Friedrich Steinhoff was also a remarkable character who survived the horrors of war to be killed while a prisoner of war in America. When the war ended, he made the fatal error of being one of the first U-boat commanders to obey his Grand Admiral and surrender to United States forces. After arriving in Boston, he was handcuffed and led through the streets to be humiliated by screaming masses demanding to see a 'Nazi' at close quarters. It seems highly likely that the guards did not appreciate a proud, upright officer and therefore severely battered him with sticks to assure he staggered, rather than walked, through the torturous proceedings. We are told that the beatings Steinhoff received were so severe that he later eased the pain by cutting the arteries in wrists with fragments of glass from his sunglasses. Yet members of his crew who witnessed his end told a different story. They said that his guards dealt the final blows. It was a sad end for an emphatic young man, who had done more than his duty for his country.

That day in mid-September, when the two were saying their farewells from U96, they were standing in front of Heinrich Lehmann-Willenbrock, a humanitarian commander and most able seaman. Naval High Command hadn't cut him out to become a submariner. Before the war he held the post of first officer of the sail training ship *Horst Wessel*, a prestigious position which could have taken him on to become a cruiser commander. But Lehmann-Willenbrock was a seaman who did not enjoy the pomp and circumstance that such positions demanded and he chose to join the unorthodox U-boat Arm. He was still training when the war started, but men of his calibre were rare and he quickly found himself commanding U8, one of the small coastal submarines, to learn the tricks of the trade.

U96 was a seagoing boat of Type VIIC. Strangely enough she had been commissioned exactly one year before Stock and Steinhoff left her for places at the submarine commanders' school. In that short period of time they had seen so much action that a major overhaul was necessary. Therefore it was the end of October 1941 before the boat was ready again. It was round about this time that a large number of new faces appeared. The acquisition of new men was one of the disadvantages of being a highly respected U-boat commander who trained his crew well. Consequently many of them found well-earned promotion in other fields and now U96 was going to put to sea with a good number of inexperienced characters. One of these, a young lieutenant, was not a sailor but a war correspondent by the name of Lothar-Günther Buchheim.

Many years after the war, he stunned people with a sensational novel that became the foundation for one of the most spine-chilling films ever made. *Das Boot*, with its haunting theme tune, became a household name in Europe and America. This sensational film was modelled on U96 and Lehmann-Willenbrock, and based on Buchheim's first experience of sailing in an operational U-boat. It is essential to bear in mind that *Das Boot* was written as a novel to describe U-boat life, it was not intended as a piece of history. Therefore, the events in the film bear some resemblance to what happened during the forthcoming voyage, but Buchheim also incorporated the characters of two other commanders and events from other boats into his story.

The question, which is frequently asked, is: does the film portray an accurate picture of U-boat life? Ex-U-boat men are divided somewhere along the middle about the first scenes on land, with half of them saying that such wild goings-on never happened and the other half agreeing that they participated in such events. Obviously any writer of fiction is going to incorporate maximum drama into his scenes and Buchheim has done this to the fullest, without falling into the trap of going entirely over the top. For most of the time nothing happened in a U-boat and the majority of commanders didn't even give verbal orders. The men knew what to do and small personal signals from the officers were often enough. An audience would get lost in extreme boredom if a film portrayed accurate submarine scenes and then, when something did happen, the audience would never know what was going on. So any film has got to be a compromise of fabricated happenings with explanations, none of which would ever be necessary in a real submarine.

It was 27 October 1941 when the new engineering officer, Oblt.z.S.(Ing.) Dengel and Lt.z.S. Buchheim stepped on board. Exactly twelve minutes later, the ropes were cast off and U96 reversed out of the massive submarine bunker in St Nazaire, passed through the sea locks and nosed out into the Atlantic, just as it is depicted in the film. The only difference is that the scene was filmed in La Rochelle, not St Nazaire. Although the men quickly settled into a monotonous routine, much of their action could not be anticipated and Lehmann-Willenbrock made sure that the men were constantly faced with the unexpected. This paid dividends in the form of helping the men to survive longer inside the U-boat. There were plenty of practice runs for everything the men would need to know during the next few weeks. It was essential that the newcomers fitted into the moulds left by their predecessors.

On average, U96 laid back some 200–250 nautical miles per day, bringing her quickly into the British convoy routes, but the men were still faced with a full day's sailing when Erich Topp in U552, with a drawing of a red devil on the conning tower, announced the position of a convoy. Lehmann-Willenbrock didn't have to make a decision himself: almost instantly he received orders from U-boat Command to make for the convoy. This was easy because Topp was also transmitting regular signals for the radio detection finder. However, nothing is that straightforward at sea, and when the first ships came into sight, it was difficult to work out whether they were a convoy or a submarine search group. It was just one of those days when everybody could have cursed. Visibility had been pretty good and at this critical moment, when it would have been advantageous to see for a long way, a thick haze came down, giving Lehmann-Willenbrock no alternative other than to run in the same general direction as the ships on the horizon. As with so many things, the haze vanished as quickly as it had come and an hour later the lookouts could make out four columns of merchant ships. They were part of Convoy OS10, running from the United Kingdom to Freetown in Sierra Leone.

Lehmann-Willenbrock now had the choice of either going in for a submerged attack, which could bring him one, perhaps two, targets within the periscope's sights before the considerably faster merchant ships passed out of range, or he could wait for nightfall and try a surface attack. The latter was the more attractive and a thick column of smoke and diesel exhaust fumes hanging low over the water from the convoy provided excellent cover for running with the opposition. It was shortly after 2000 hours when one single solitary flare was seen shooting up from somewhere close by. Lehmann-Willenbrock cursed quietly. He guessed what it meant. It was a visual signal for a change of course. What he didn't know was when it would take place or the new direction the ships would take. These minute details were probably worked out by convoy commanders shortly before sailing and did not follow a standard procedure pattern.

The surface attack at night turned into a right pain. The earlier clouds had lifted, exposing a wonderful starry sky and a brilliant moon with a huge reflection of shimmering white on an almost motionless sea, making it highly unlikely that anyone could approach anything unseen.

The other alternative of running ahead of the merchant ships and waiting for a submerged attack was no longer possible because by now it was too dark to see anything of significance through the periscope. It had to be a surface attack or the idea had to be postponed until the following night, but there were no guarantees that this would bring better conditions. Making maximum use of a few clouds to approach from the darkest horizon, U96 soon found targets for four individually aimed shots. Two of them were hits. One hit a passenger ship and the other a 5,000-ton freighter. Yet, as with so many things, the unexpected happened. Today it is possible to see the funny side of the event, although at the time it was incredibly infuriating. One of these torpedoes ran so slowly that U96 nearly caught up with it and almost bumped into its propellers. Blast it! Someone, somewhere was responsible for a blunder. Checking and double-checking the settings, the men came to the conclusion that it wasn't anyone in U96. It had to have been a fault built-in by the factory.

The torpedo was still running ahead of U96 when an escort noticed the surfaced U-boat and started shooting with a deck gun. Lehmann-Willenbrock estimated something in the region of 88mm. Not only was it shooting wildly, but the shots fell so far wide of their target that the men in U96 would have loved to retaliate, but the old man knew that it was safer down in the cellar. So U96 slipped down to 70 metres. There followed what the logbook describes as eighteen rather inferior depth charge detonations. Yet they were sufficient to make the newcomers sweat. Being anywhere at the receiving end of a depth charge attack is not a pleasant experience. Gus Britton, from the Royal Navy's Submarine Museum, participated in a sponsored parachute jump at the age of about sixty, when people predicted he would be scared out of his pants. Returning to earth, he merely stood up, smiled and told his onlookers that nothing would ever be as frightening as being on the receiving end of a depth charge attack. He added that there is no way that one can describe such horrors with words.

It was almost exactly twenty-four hours after Convoy OS10 had first been sighted when a number of small fast warships came into sight. U-boats would usually have avoided them, but on this occasion there were a number of bigger escorts, making an attack worthwhile.

As with all things, it was a case of making up one's mind in ten seconds, which is not a lot of time in which to make life or death decisions. Three men were seen high up in the mastheads, suggesting that they were lookouts for a submarine hunt. However, the ships were comparatively fast and their hulls didn't lie deep in the water, making them difficult targets at the best of times, and their zigzagging nature made them even more problematic. Just trying to get within shooting range was a problem and no worthwhile opportunity presented itself, so Lehmann-Willenbrock had to settle on being the hunted and hope that the depth charges did not become too aggressive. He was in luck. There followed a most lethargic assault. Lehmann-Willenbrock thought that the ships must be experiencing some problem with their Asdic because they seemed to be dropping depth charges in pairs in the area where the boat had dived, without making a concerted effort to find its exact location.

Evading the hunt occupied best part of the afternoon and there was no sign of any merchant shipping by the time U96 resurfaced shortly after dark. Yet those irksome small warships were still present, with one of them running towards the darkened horizon. Perhaps the convoy was in that direction? The search proved fruitless. For hours U96 cruised as fast as conditions allowed, charging batteries with one engine and driving the propeller with the other. At the same time the boat had been trimmed so that most of the bows were below the surface of the water. Not an ideal way of making progress, but the small silhouette this presented was brilliant for a situation where the bright night made it possible to spot the boat from considerable distances. The lookouts in U96 preferred to put up with frequent drenching from the waves rather than make life easy for the men in crows' nests.

U96's lookouts spotted a light rocket, several star shells and the occasional escort, but nothing resembling merchant ships. The whole search had become a cat and mouse game with everybody contributing his pfennig's worth in the hope of meeting with some success. Daylight brought with it very much the same pattern as before, but no merchant ships. The Operations Room at U-boat Command in France also made desperate suggestions by forming, disbanding and reforming a number of patrol lines, but none of them brought any form of success. The only variation in the general situation was

A seagoing Type VII ploughing through moderate seas with the upper deck awash. It was possible to raise the boat higher in the water, but then it would have taken much longer to dive and for most of the time boats travelled so that they were ready to dive in 25 seconds. The heavy deck gun for use against surface targets has a calibre of 88mm.

Left: Each tap of this trimming panel, with which the engineer officer balanced the boat, had a slightly different handle so it could still be identified when the boat was plunged into total darkness.

Below: An aircraft attacking a U-boat with gunfire and depth charges. The 37mm gun on the lower (rear platform and two twin 20mm anti-aircraft gun on the upper winter garden suggest that this picture was taken during the latter part of the war. It looks as this shows that critical moment when the gun crew had abandoned their positions but had not yet got below for the boat to dive.

The wide deck of a supply U-boat with a fuel pipe in the background. Transferring goods at sea was not easy and required considerable muscle. The German Navy never developed any hard-bottom boats for ferrying awkward packages over choppy seas and outboard motors were still in their unreliable infancy.

One of those painful moments after the crew had abandoned their sinking merchant ship and the U-boat closed in to interrogate the men in the lifeboats. This was also such a frightening and heartbreaking experience for submariners that many commanders would allow only older, mature members of the crew on deck during such traumatic occasions.

Above left: The conning tower of a small Type II with circular radio direction finder aerial and a foghorn to its right. The 20mm gun has not been attached to its support in the foreground.

Above right: A Type VIIC with an 88mm deck gun. Servicing these guns at sea was a major undertaking made worse on this occasion by the rough condition. These guns had some eighty oiling points, all of which needed a shot or two from a grease gun to keep the parts functioning properly.

An early Type IX conning tower with a single 20mm anti-aircraft gun. A number of success pennants are flying from a rope attached to the top of the extended periscope.

One might be tempted to think that this shows lookouts at sea, but gold edging on the caps of the two men on the right indicate that they are both commissioned officers and the men are wearing life jackets rather than lookout safety harnesses. This suggests that they might be ready to work on the upper deck. The binoculars clipped on to the torpedo aimer could also be used for taking bearings. Machine guns were introduced towards the end of the war, when aircraft often attacked boats in coastal waters and the beards indicate that the boat is running into port after having been at sea for some time.

U505, an ocean-going Type IXC, with severe damage, photographed long before the boat was captured by United States forces. The top of the pressure hull is roughly in line with the surface of the water and this damage to the fairing is not life threatening to the men. The core of the conning tower also consisted of a pressure-resistant cylinder and the damage here is only to the fairing around it, meaning that the boat was still capable of diving, despite this heavy damage.

Loading a practice torpedo with its characteristic red-and-white-striped head into a Type II boat. The deck was narrow and the inside so restricted that torpedoes had to be lowered backwards before they could be pushed into one of the three bow tubes. The net cutter towards the left of the picture was a leftover from the First World War and no longer served any practical purpose.

The comparatively narrow bows of a seagoing Type VIIC during a refuelling operation. The large number of men was necessary for hauling heavy pipes and cumbersome inflatables from the supply boat. The rope running over the gun is suspended from the jumping wire by a couple of lookout safety harnesses.

A small, seagoing Type II conning tower seen from the stern. The absence of lookouts suggests that the boat is in safe waters. The hatch is open and the attack periscope, with a small head lens, is partly raised.

Lookouts wearing light rubber coats with sou'westers. Boats also carried heavier rain gear for when conditions got worse. Each watch usually consisted of four lookouts and one officer. The object in the foreground, towards the right, is a magnetic sighting compass in gimbals.

A U-boat's front door – the conning tower hatch. The lid had a huge spring in the hinge to lift it without a great deal of effort and it was closed again by pulling on the locking wheel seen by the man's hand. There were two of these wheels on each hatch, so that it could be opened and closed from both sides. The shoulder straps indicate that this is almost certainly the Obersteuermann or navigator, who doubled up as third watch officer. His golden shoulder straps indicate that he is a warrant officer (or non-commissioned officer), who had been promoted from the ranks rather than having joined as an officer candidate.

Lookouts with partly raised attack periscope and fully raised circular radio direction finder aerial. These aerials were fixed to the outside of small conning towers but could be retracted into the conning tower wall on larger boats. Lookouts usually stood a four-hour-long watch, no matter what conditions prevailed at the time.

The early Type VIIC conning tower with a single 20mm anti-aircraft gun. The bulge at the forward base of the conning tower housed a magnetic compass, which could be viewed by the helmsman in the central control room through an illuminated periscope. The partly raised attack periscope with small head lens is also visible.

Above left: A torpedo hit against a stationary target.

Above right: An early version of a Type VIIC conning tower with the upward curving lip of the wind deflector at the top edge. The lower lip, about halfway up the tower, was known as the spray deflector. There is an intake for the radio aerial above the spray deflector and a circular foghorn below it. The watertight tampion in the barrel of the 88mm quick-firing gun had to be removed before shooting. At least two gunners were required, one to rotate the gun and the other to raise or lower it. The bracket for supporting the men's waists were usually turned inwards as seen on the right and rotated to face outwards (as can be seen on the left) when shooting.

U37 an early ocean-going Type IXA with two different sound-detector heads on the bows, forward of the hydraulic capstan. Most of the guardrails and the numbers on the side of the conning tower were removed once the war started.

A Type VIIC with early conning tower design on the River Elbe in Hamburg. The circle with bar above it, forward of the horseshoe-like life ring, is an identification for training and indicates that the boat was built at Stülken Werft. Boats from Howaltswerke in Hamburg used the same design but in white. The bulge at the base on the forward edge of the conning tower housed a magnetic compass. The square with a cross welded upon it indicates that there is also an emergency connection for blowing the tanks of a sunken submarine. The other emergency connection, for blowing air into the interior of the pressure hull, was marked with a cross inside a circle. These marks were welded on so that divers could find them by feel in muddy waters.

Boats like this Type VII, seen here with an early type of conning tower, carried the main burden of the battle in the Atlantic. The absence of the brass number plate on the bows suggests that this photo was taken after the start of the war but before the end of 1940, when the last net cutters were removed.

A torpedo hit against a merchant ship.

The stern of a supply U-boat with fuel pipe being pulled over to another submarine. The idea of supplying fuel from the stern of the tanker to the bows of the receiver had been thought up by experts at the Naval Command but they failed to supply a mechanical capstan on the stern of the supply boat for retrieving the cumbersome oil pipes and men often had to haul them back manually.

U4, a small seagoing Type IIA.

U56, a small Type IIC. These boats were fitted with only three bow torpedo tubes and a single 20mm anti-aircraft gun, yet at least one of them was given the order by radio to 'sink shipping either with torpedoes or with artillery' despite such a small calibre hardly having any impact against even small ships. The brass number plate on the bows and the white number on the conning tower were removed at the start of the war.

U1, a small seagoing Type IIA, was the first U-boat to be commissioned after the end of the First World War.

Above: U40, an ocean-going Type IXA with an early conning tower design. The protrusions on the deck, forward of the gun, are: (from left to right) a red-and-white-striped rescue buoy with light and telephone on the top, the hydraulic capstan, a 'T'-shaped, rotatable sound detector and another straight sound detector just aft of the net cutter. The insulators in the jumping wire and the radio aerial connection running into the conning tower are just visible.

Left: An ocean-going Type IXC with success pennants flying from the extended attack periscope with the small head lens.

U755, a seagoing Type VIIC, with rotatable sound detector head on the bows. A capstan, visible in some other photos, was detachable and fitted only when required for hauling heavy ropes. The hatch on the deck was the top of a watertight ammunition container and the brackets for supporting the side gunner are turned inwards so as not to block off the narrow deck space. The gun had two sets of controls and could be aimed and fired either from the left or right. Optical sights would have been clipped in place when shooting and the wheel above the breech altered the angle to compensate for distance and speed.

U32, a seagoing Type VIIA, with capstan in position on the bows. The original description states that the condition of the sea is 3. One wonders what it must have been like in even rougher conditions. The bulges in the jumping wire were insulators to prevent the long cable shortening with the hull when it was being used as radio aerial.

a considerable change in the weather, with a force 6 south-easterly starting to add to life's difficulties. Many men in U96 were astonished by Buchheim's performance. They had expected him to retire to his bunk and concentrate on being seasick, but instead he donned raingear and joined the men on the bridge to take action photographs. Sadly some of these suffered rather badly from the weather, but a number of dramatic water-damaged pictures showing this moment of the storm have been published by him.

Later, when a merchant ship did come into sight, it was found to be battling against the sea and there was no way the tiny U96 could match the performance of the massive ocean giant. It was a case of everybody on the conning tower getting exceptionally wet and cold, the engines blowing their guts out and the boat hardly making any headway. During moments like these, everybody wished they had chosen a more comfortable way of serving their country. Despite the storm, U-boat Command tried to establish another patrol line, but nobody knew whether the long chain of lookouts was complete. It was only when one U-boat sighted another that the men realised there must be some terrific gaps elsewhere. The idea was for the boats to be so far apart that ships could not slip between them. Now, the storm obviously frustrated this simple idea because it was very difficult to get an accurate fix on stars or sun, making it virtually impossible to navigate with such demanding precision. Yet there was always the hope of running into something and thus easing the pain of the search.

Things started looking more promising when a long-range Kondor aircraft from the newly established reconnaissance squadron broadcast a convoy sighting, but also advertised its incompetence by failing to give the convoy's direction and position. It was not until U572 succeeded in getting a bearing with their radio direction finder on the aircraft that prospects started to look really good. U572 was commanded by a rather interesting and somewhat mysterious character, Kptlt. Heinz Hirsacker, who remained in command until the end of 1942, when he was moved on to become First Officer of the destroyer Z10 (*Hans Lody*). Four months later he was sentenced to death by court martial and shot for cowardice in front of the enemy. Sadly, once again, the authorities slipped back to their rudimentary First World War methods and stole a man's life because of a person's shortcomings.

The search for convoys continued, continued and continued. New patrol lines were formed; their directions changed, but nothing came past. The seas eased a little – that was about all there was to write home about. Only standing orders prevented boats from using their radios while part of a patrol line, so there was no way of informing U-boat Command of the easing weather. This is not to say that the men were not kept busy. Lehmann-Willenbrock insisted that his men reacted naturally to any order or situation. Ideally submariners should not need to wait for orders; they should know what is going on and react accordingly. To this end a number of training exercises continued throughout the voyage. U96 was in the process of concentrating on practicing depth keeping and steering the boat at the same time. The idea was to throw the boat onto a drastically different course without raising or dropping it in the water. It was an important skill that might one day make the difference between life and death.

Despite keeping the men on their toes, three full weeks of almost aimless drifting around the Atlantic dug a huge hole in morale. At that time, although the men didn't know it yet, the lack of targets and increase in disturbances by small fast warships was gaining momentum. The sinking successes that had been anticipated never occurred again: they were a feature of the past. With the despondency created by a lack of success and life in incredibly uncomfortable and wet conditions settling in, everybody started looking forward to the homeward-bound voyage. Knowing that there was not enough fuel for a prolonged chase meant that the men expected the old man to make the decision at any moment, but just at that critical time as the crew eagerly awaited a change of course, the unexpected happened.

Not only was it unexpected, but it was also a first for U96. The radio operator was decoding the usual set of messages when a confusing mass of jumbled letters made him think he was tinkering with a signal intended for another boat. Instead of producing a legible message, the code writer produced another batch of meaningless letters, but definitely addressed to U96 for officers only.

Radio messages transmitted in Morse code had to be typed into a gadget that looked something like a sophisticated typewriter. Each time a key was pressed a letter illuminated on a panel above the keyboard and this usually produced a message in plain language. This time, however, the radio operator handed the entire contraption over to the first watch officer, who displayed considerable irritation and needed some help to set up the machine. Although he carried a list of settings, he had hardly used a code writer since learning about its intricacies during a crash course many months earlier. First he had to check a vast number of sockets at the front, making sure that they were connected in the correct manner. Then three (later four) wheels from a choice of five had to be selected and set into special starting positions. These wheels were obviously not the same as those used earlier by the radio operator, so some juggling was necessary. Finally, with help, he produced another set of meaningless words. Again it was addressed to U96 but with the heading 'for commander only'. Now it was the old man's turn to struggle with the machine. He had the same problem and gratefully accepted a little help in adjusting the initial settings before typing the scrambled jumble of letters into the machine.

Despite the clandestine arrival, the gist of the message didn't remain secret for long. There is nowhere in a U-boat where officers could discuss anything without being overheard, so there was no need to play a cloak and dagger game. People who have seen the film *Das Boot* or read the book will know the subject of the message. U96 was ordered to refuel in Spain before going on into the Mediterranean. However, the despondency that this triggered off in the film and the drama associated with the so-called 'Mousetrap of Gibraltar', was the director adding excitement for his audience. In reality U96 was one of the first boats to be sent through the Strait of Gibraltar and the majority of men were blissfully ignorant of the problems they were likely to encounter there. Even the thought of approaching close to a British naval base at the foot of the rock didn't worry them a great deal. They had heard ample stories of how U-boats had approached British harbours without interference. So, at this moment in time the men were looking forward to the warmer conditions of the Mediterranean, rather than being terrified by the prospects of passing close to Gibraltar.

Having been a true sailor aboard sailing ships, Lehmann-Willenbrock was one of the few who knew of the currents around Gibraltar, but he didn't let it be known that the undertaking was going to be highly complicated. For the time being he was more concerned with the practicalities of the order. Was he in a position to carry it out? Theoretically there should still be 28.5 cubic metres of fuel in the bunkers. Therefore, if the refuelling in Spain did not work out, would U96 then still have enough oil to get back to France? When the engineer officer explained that they could go to Spain and still get back to France by sailing at the slowest and most economical speed, the other officers felt a little more relieved. At least they had the option of aborting the refuelling in Vigo (Spain), which was then considered to be far more complicated than sailing into the Mediterranean.

The war correspondent Buchheim must by this time have been approaching the end of his tether, having exhausted U96 for stories. He had been looking forward to reporting successes, but instead he went out with one of the best commanders to spend an apparently endless period of four weeks seeing newcomers being seasick and the boat achieving virtually nothing. The radio signal asking for charts of the Mediterranean also included a request for Buchheim to be set ashore in Spain, something that U-boat Command turned down without even considering the matter. The Commander-in-Chief had a dislike of all types of passengers, whether they were established war correspondents or not, and there was no way that he was going to allow a mass of undeveloped film to pass through a neutral country or give the opposition the opportunity to capture someone who might talk about U-boats.

The first indication that U96 was closing in on the Spanish coast came before land was sighted. During the early evening of 26 November a small fishing boat was sighted on the horizon. Later the men's correct navigation was confirmed by the lighthouse on Cape Finisterre, the westernmost point of Spain, which was sighted shortly before first light on the following day. From there it was a case of carefully creeping up on a Spanish freighter, *Castillo Pernafiel*, displaying the correct light pattern on the side to help guide the boat into port. Then, shortly after daybreak, U96 dropped below the waves, but still headed towards the Island of Oms. It was a case of waiting patiently until the coming night, when the men could approach the neutral Spanish harbour under cover of darkness. Loading stores was going to be hard physical work and Lehmann-Willenbrock wanted every man fully awake, with his concentration at maximum. The landward side of this refuelling operation at least knew that U96 was on its way; therefore everything should be ready for a quick turnaround. Yet the schedule was too tight for allowing the boat to rest on the bottom and U96 continued crawling towards the northern harbour entrance, hoping nothing was coming overhead that could locate it down in the depths. It was mid-afternoon before the old man was satisfied that they could go no further and finally allowed U96 to gently drop onto the seabed. The Obersteuermann (navigation officer, who was a warrant officer rather than one with a commission) calculated that they had covered some 5,279 nautical miles (About 9,800 kilometres or just over 6,000 land miles) during thirty-two days at sea and wondered how many more they would have to cover before reaching a home port. During this period the boat used 123 cubic metres of fuel oil, 3,470 kilograms of lubricating oil and 2,840 litres of water. All of this was now running critically low. For all that expenditure the men succeeded in sinking two ships. One of them was the 5,998 GRT Dutch freighter *Bennekom*, but the other target has not yet been identified.

As things turned out, there were no problems in finding the German freighter *Bessel*. U96 surfaced at 2000 hours, approached the harbour on the surface, made fast just half an hour later and left again at 0400, to put some distance behind her before first light. What happened next was documented in the film *Das Boot*; only the bitter end was different. U96 was so seriously damaged that Lehmann-Willenbrock broke off the attempt to break into the Mediterranean and limped back to France. It was more than three years later, while lying at anchor in Wilhelmshaven, that the boat was sunk during an air raid on the city. By that time Lehmann-Willenbrock was no longer her commander, having left U96 four months after the refuelling in Vigo to become chief of the 9th U-Flotilla based in Brest, where he remained until August 1944. He was one of the few to have survived the war and much later became the master of Germany's first atom-powered merchant ship, *Otto Hahn*.

10

WILD WATERS TO THE WEST OF GIBRALTAR

Faced with continuously dwindling successes throughout 1941, U-boat Command attempted to establish patrol lines or wolf packs at right angles across known traffic routes. The idea was to catch and shadow convoys so that as many U-boats as possible could be called together for a massive group attack. U96, mentioned in the previous chapter, had been part of such a patrol line, but the weather some 800 miles west of Ireland was so atrocious that weapons could not have been engaged even if merchant ships had come within shooting range.

U108 (Type IXB) under Kptlt. Klaus Scholtz was completing its overhaul in Lorient when a massive Japanese force attacked the United States anchorage at Pearl Harbor. The boat cast off for its fourth war cruise on 9 December 1941, only two days before Germany declared war on the United States. The general instructions were to make for the west of Gibraltar. The war at sea was changing rapidly and it took so long to reach far-off destinations that boats were dispatched to general areas. Once there, they were given more detailed, up-to-date instructions by radio. At sea, the usual sequence of diving tests and training exercises to get the crew back into shape after their leave were interrupted with the unusual news that HM Submarine *Regent* was likely to pass close to *U-Hansmann*, *U-Baumann* and *U-Scholtz*. All three were told to report their positions and to converge on an interception course.

U-boat numbers had been secret since the beginning of the war and boats were usually identified by the name of their commanders, rather than by their numbers.

In this case U108 was accompanied by U127 under Kptlt. Bruno Hansmann and U131 under Fregkpt. Arend Baumann. Neither of them had long to live. U127 was depth charged less than a week later on 15 December 1941 by HMS *Nestor*, part of Convoy HG76's escort screen. This happened during a routine search instigated as a result of intelligence suggesting that there was a concentration of U-boats building up to the west of Gibraltar. There were no survivors. Two days later, U131 was marginally luckier inasmuch that everybody got off before the boat had to be scuttled. Having first been sighted by a Martlet flown off the escort carrier HMS *Audacity*, another aircraft appeared, later to be shot down while attempting an attack. During this moment of confusion and hectic action, surface craft closed in to plaster the unfortunate submarine with intense gunfire. At least one of the shots penetrated the pressure hull, meaning that it could no longer dive. Seeing that he had no alternative other than to prolong the agony of living, Baumann ordered his men to abandon ship while the plug was pulled to make it sink quickly.

HM Submarine *Regent* missed the reception being prepared for her and the tense action anticipated aboard U108 dissolved into more days of boring routine. U108 finally reached her allocated operations area as darkness was setting in. Having been moving at fast cruising speed, Scholtz ordered the boat to slow down and sail back and forth along north to south courses at the most economical cruising speed. This was kept up for almost twenty-four hours before the lookouts were rewarded with a column of smoke behind them. Turning the boat, they discovered a freighter steering a north–easterly course. There were a few more hours of daylight before U108 could approach any closer; therefore Scholtz remained at a respectful distance until darkness could cover a closer inspection.

A brilliant red sky still illuminated the western horizon over a dead calm sea when the Commander-in-Chief for U-boats ordered a new patrol line of the name of Seeräuber (Sea Robber). Scholtz checked his watch. There was enough time to attend to the freighter before the chain of U-boats had to be in place and until then he was free to do what he liked. It took another three hours to get close enough for action stations. By that time it was totally dark and the lookouts noticed that the target had illuminated its navigation lights. This was a bad omen. It suggested that the freighter was a neutral, meaning that the hunt had been in vain. However, Scholtz had enough experience to know that the opposition would make maximum use of all opportunities and a closer investigation failed to reveal a flag or neutrality markings. The situation was still tricky. It would be too easy to end up with rather a lot of egg on one's face as a result of sinking someone not involved in the war. Standing orders prevented ships being stopped at night, therefore Scholtz could not ask for the ship's papers to be brought over and if he attacked a neutral then he could face court martial. In the end he ordered action stations. It was impossible to make out the freighter's nationality and there were no obvious neutrality markings.

Although two torpedoes left at the same time, there was only one detonation. This time it was definitely a faulty detonator. About ten seconds before the detonation everybody on the conning tower heard an unmistakable metallic clang of the other torpedo hitting the target. Slowly the stern of the ship settled deeper in the water, one by one lights went out, two lifeboats were lowered and then, as if my magic, everything reverted to how it had been before the attack, only the lifeboats were now pulling away. Scholtz waited for developments, but nothing happened and after a while he sacrificed a third torpedo. This produced more dramatic results. The freighter must have had a large quantity of petrol or something equally volatile on board as a magnificent flash of yellow flame leapt high into the sky and then continued to burn on the surface of the water. No wonder the crew was in such a hurry to leave. The ship had not sent a distress signal, therefore Scholtz assumed that his position had not been compromised, but still there wasn't time for a close inspection. A year earlier he would have considered sending a distress signal or seeing to the safety of the men in lifeboats, but now, war had hardened everybody. Life was now a matter of life and death and U108 turned to obey the orders from U-boat Command to join the patrol line. (The target was the Portuguese ship SS *Cassequel* of 4,751 GRT, sunk at 2157 hours on 14 December 1941.)

Group Seeräuber was made up of U107 (Harald Gelhaus, who two weeks earlier had taken over from Günter Hessler, the Commander-in-Chief's son-in-law); U127 (Bruno Hansmann); U574 (Dietrich Gengelbach who was killed less than a week later); U131 (Arend Baumann); U67 (Günther Müller-Stöckheim) and, on the extreme eastern flank, U108.

U108 was hardly in position when a column of smoke piqued the men's curiosity. Despite promising prospects, Scholtz chose to investigate what it was before making the rest of the patrol line nervous with possibly misleading news. Just as well. Once a bit closer, he discovered a lone freighter instead of a convoy. Everything was perfect, a gentle sea, good visibility, the midday sun was high in the sky. U108 could hit the target without much trouble, but just at that critical moment as Scholtz made the decision to attack someone screamed, 'Alaaarm!'. An aircraft was approaching and U108 tumbled down into the depths. It had been spotted as a tiny dot near the horizon and no one knew whether it had also seen the U-boat or whether the observers up in the sky had focussed their entire attention on the freighter. Whatever was going on, Scholtz was not the type to be put off his objective and instead of floundering, he prepared for a submerged chase. Despite also having plenty of patience and waiting for half an hour, the sound detector couldn't focus on the characteristic thumping of merchant ship engines. It looked as if the ship had been heading straight for U108, but now there was no indication of it coming any closer. Perhaps the aircraft had seen the U-boat and there had been a drastic change of course. Even with a burst of high speed on the surface, the freighter remained out of sight. Then it dawned on the men that it was probably sailing alone because its high speed made it such a difficult target. Whatever, this was another one of those disturbing hunts which had to be called off. There was nothing anyone in U108 could do about it.

Turning round, U108 plodded back at economical cruising speed to take its place on the eastern wing of the patrol line. After supper the boat was in position to continue with the monotonous routine of sailing back and forth at 10 knots on north to south courses. Each leg was 20 nautical miles long or two hours' sailing. This was kept up all evening long, but nothing happened. Exactly at midnight, U108 changed course to make for a new position previously ordered by U-boat Command. Twelve hours later things were just the same. Reasonably warm air and a calm sea made life fairly enjoyable for lookouts. The men joked that it was very much like being on holiday and a great change from the winter storms of the colder latitudes. Nobody aboard U108 had much idea of what was going on and the next set of instruction didn't clarify the matter. The message from U-boat Command merely ordered all boats from Group Seeräuber to change onto a heading of 170° at fastest cruising speed.

The first sign of success came shortly after a leisurely lunch. A lone aircraft on the horizon ahead suggested that U108 might at last be drawing closer to the convoy. Obviously U-boat Command in France knew more than the boats at sea because Gengelbach, Baumann, Müller and Scholtz were told to go to top speed while the others were released to do whatever they fancied in their prearranged operations area. It was late afternoon when the aroma of coffee down below coincided with the sighting of another aircraft. This was indeed a splendid coincidence. It meant the boat had to dive and the men could enjoy a few minutes' peace and quiet with a welcome cup down in the safer depths. But this anticipated relaxation evaporated very quickly. U108 had hardly levelled off when the sound detector reported a high-pitched propeller whine. Not the deep droning thumping from a merchant ship, but a fast turbine. Damn the coffee – action was called for. They surfaced. The mast tips of a destroyer could just be made out beyond the horizon. Even more interestingly, far behind them were clouds of smoke. Masses of individual columns were rising high into the sky. There was nothing for it. Slow speed and transmit a sighting report. The destroyer was a pain, but a number of aircraft over the merchant ships looked worse: they could turn out to be disastrous.

Lookouts also spotted another U-boat, probably U67, before U108 dropped back into the cellar due to an approaching aircraft. Had this aircraft also seen U108? It was flying from the setting sun in the west into a darker horizon in the east, so there was hope. The destroyer was also getting closer, but no one was terribly alarmed because none of the lookouts had reported an increase in its speed. So it seemed highly likely that it was still unaware of the U-boat. Scholtz found himself in one of those agonising situations. The distance of 5 kilometres to the destroyer was a little too much for aiming a torpedo at a fast-moving shallow-draught vessel. It would be too easy to miss. It was also highly likely that the opposition would see torpedoes in the water. Common sense told Scholtz that an attack wasn't worth the risk. Instead he waited. Surfacing a few minutes later, he was faced with empty seas and with the mast tips disappearing below the northern horizon, meaning that the attack had to start from the beginning again. Heading north-west at high speed, Scholtz hoped to catch up, but instead of sighting those welcoming columns of smoke, another escort appeared to force U108 into the cellar once more. The only plus point was that the opposition seemed to be totally oblivious to the U-boat's presence, but this didn't prevent a reoccurrence of the frustration of possibly losing the convoy again.

The search continued long into an exceptionally dark night. Low clouds blurred the sharp line of the horizon and made it virtually impossible to spot smoke or mastheads. It was long after midnight before a shadow was seen to be approaching. It came pretty close. Too close for comfort. It was a sitting duck, but one with prickly guns, definitely not a merchant ship. Scholtz decided against attacking in the hope that it might lead him to the merchant ships, but following the destroyer didn't yield any results. Nor did a sighting report from U131. It was frustrating. Bloody frustrating. U108 was so close and yet so far away. Escorts galore, but nowhere the slightest sign of a convoy.

At 0500 hours U108 was running at high speed towards a position suggested by U131, when the duty officer shouted down the open hatch that an unidentified submarine had been sighted. By the time Scholtz got to the top of the conning tower, he found his boat already turning away, exposing the smallest possible silhouette to the opponent. Catching just a glimpse before the far-off boat vanished into a foggy darkness made it impossible to determine the submarine's nationality. It seemed unlikely to have been German, but the British protruding periscope supports high up on the superstructure weren't visible either. In the end Scholtz agreed with the men on duty that turning away was the best move. This had hardly been digested when U-boat Command instructed every boat to proceed at their highest speed to get into an attacking position before first light. Scholtz just shrugged his shoulders in desperation. What was the point of running at high speed if no one could tell him where the convoy was?

The warmth of the rising sun was making itself felt when the lookouts once more sighted that telltale series of smoke columns. Again, U108 was in a most advantageous position, exactly between the rising sun and the ships, making it unlikely that they could see him in the intense glare. Taking every opportunity, Scholtz put on a spurt to get ahead of the merchant ships, while broadcasting details. Two and a half hours later, men inside the boat heard some ten to twelve depth charges, but they were far enough away to prevent U108 deviating from its westerly course. By mid-afternoon, lookouts had counted thirteen ships and two escorts as well as a flying boat. Manoeuvring was good and shortly after nightfall U108 was sailing on a collision course with the convoy. At last the smell of success was in the air.

It was just a few minutes before 0900 when Scholtz ordered his men to action stations. In a way this was just a formality. He knew that everything was in good order and it was just a case of pressing the firing button. Twenty minutes later the first ships were only some 3 kilometres away. The situation was tense, and Scholtz was unable to concentrate on the firing process. He didn't even dare to cast an eye on the values being called out by the new first watch officer. With escorts behind him and several columns of ships in front, there was no way he could allow his attention to be taken away from the general situation. The commander's most important job was to juggle the constantly changing scenario and prevent any mishaps. On this occasion U108 was sailing into what could well turn out to be an inescapable trap and it was important to jump out before it snapped shut. Everybody on the bridge felt the judder as compressed air ejected torpedoes, but no detonation followed. The torpedoes must have missed. Trying to gain maximum advantage, Scholtz turned the back towards the next set of ships and ordered the rear tubes to be emptied. This time both the new first watch officer and a trainee commander watched the effects of a massive detonation rising high into the dark sky, but there was no time for formalities or to watch the sinking.

U108 was already running at high speed. The engines were making far too much noise to hear anything with the sound detector, so it wasn't even manned. Gliding past an escort, U108 went north to reload. The sea was mirror smooth meaning there was no need to dive. The big danger was that a later alarm could prove fatal if they had to dive while two torpedoes were hanging in their derricks. Shooting newly reloaded torpedoes from the surface was one thing, but trying the same trick from a submerged position was a good deal more difficult and could easily lead to an irreversible disaster. One man walking from one end of the boat to the other could upset the delicate balance of a submerged boat, so moving a number of 1½-ton torpedoes from their resting places to the torpedo tubes would make a drastic difference to the trim or balance. It could be virtually impossible to keep such an unbalanced boat at periscope depth. Therefore it was necessary to dive and wait for the engineer officer to play with the mass of wheels in the central control room in order to move the ballast into the right positions. The later trim dive following this reload took only about twenty minutes, but during that brief spell the men counted forty-six depth charges, suggesting that one of their number was having rather a rough time. The men didn't know it at the time, but they were listening to the end of U434 (Kptlt. Wolfgang Heyda). U131 (Korvkpt. Arend Baumann) had gone down the previous day and U574 (Kptlt. Dietrich Gengelbach) was sunk a few hours later. It was indeed a hard time for U-boats and U108's guardian angel was working overtime.

On this occasion U108 accepted the challenge and remained on the surface to reload the torpedoes, but stayed well out of the way of any action. Despite this, the process took two hours. Two frustrating hours. The torpedo mechanic had hardly reported the job complete before U108 was again at full speed to catch up with the convoy. Once again U108 was in luck, U107's reported position and course suggested that U108 was on a collision course. Yet the men searched in vain. The sun rose for another beautifully clear and empty day. U-boat Command emphasised the importance of the chase by sending a signal saying that the hunt must continue, even in daylight.

Everything went well until mid-afternoon on the following day when the port cooling pump burst, effectively reducing the top speed to 11 knots. There was nothing for it other than to report the damage. U108 could not take its place in the patrol line until the problem had been rectified. Later, the patterns of the previous days started to repeat themselves. Escorts, probably working in pairs, were sighted and despite shadowing them, it was impossible to find what the men were looking for. Then, later, following a whole night's worth of searching, the convoy had just come into sight when a tanker carrying highly volatile fuel erupted with such high flames that the darkness almost turned into daylight. Depth charge detonations, automatic gunfire and the whirling screech of torpedoes were heard inside the boat. It was an incredible display. Had this brilliant illumination and noisy commotion come a little earlier, U108 could have saved itself a long frustrating hunt. With the convoy clearly visible, it looked as if the escorts had withdrawn into a tight circle around the merchant ships and were shooting a multitude of flares into the sky. Obviously they guessed that the responsible U-boat could be somewhere close by and were making every effort to find it. As it happened, all this special illumination helped the men of U108 to discover that they were standing in an ideal attack position, right in the path of the convoy.

Despite daylight coming any minute, Scholtz grabbed the opportunity to get off as many shots as the time allowed. Two hits were observed before the entire scene erupted into pandemonium once again and the remaining darkness was illuminated with more flares. There was nothing for it but to go deep, down to 70 metres, to avoid the retaliation. That allowed for plenty of space underneath if depth charges forced the boat even deeper. During this process the hydrophones picked up the groaning sounds of two sinking ships and this was followed by something most unexpected: nothing! No depth charges and no high-pitched whines from warship propellers. Nothing. Periscope depth! Surface. Bloody hell. A miracle. All clear. There was no one around offering a chase, but plenty of searchlights were still illuminating the sky. U-boat Command added to the intensity of the moment by broadcasting messages saying boats were to maintain contact at all cost, but U108 couldn't oblige. The port cooling pump was giving them trouble again, meaning that speed had to be reduced to a maximum of 11 knots; repairs were more urgent than struggling along on one engine.

It was four days before Christmas 1941 when U108 almost compromised itself in a somewhat embarrassing situation. Having sighted the convoy just before lunch, Scholtz tried running ahead of it with a view to maintaining contact until the coming night, when he hoped several other boats could converge for more surface attacks. However, two aircraft forced him down before the merchant ships changed course towards him. This would have been rather convenient for a daylight submerged attack, but Dönitz would have been rather annoyed had the convoy been lost in the process. What was even more irritating was that all torpedoes had now been expended and all U108 could do was to keep shadowing ships in order to draw in other boats. Remaining submerged until they had passed overhead was not viable because that would have placed the U-boat too far back to keep up during the coming night. The idea was to maintain contact by running ahead of the merchant ships, rather than tagging on behind. U108 succeeded in reaching the surface undetected and the afternoon's irritation came from small aircraft with wheels, which could only have flown off an aircraft carrier. This was not good news, as finding the offensive carrier was going to be a good deal more difficult than being forced under by its aircraft.

Today we know that the aircraft came from the escort carrier HMS *Audacity* guarding Convoy HG76 and that her presence made a significant contribution to the Allied success. Not only did these tiny bees keep U-boats at bay, they were also instrumental in sinking a good number. They certainly made this convoy attack one of the blackest in U-boat history. A whole day was devoted to cursing. There were plenty of irritations and U108 had to keep up a constant up and down act. Yet, despite the persistency from the air, U108 managed to get along unseen and succeeded in maintaining the correct contact with the convoy. It was shortly before nightfall that the gremlins threw a major spanner into the works. U108 had to remain submerged for a long time to repair the controls for one of the diving valves and by the time the men were back on the surface, the convoy had made a drastic change of course.

It was several hours before U108 sighted the targets again. This time the U-boat was spotted by an aircraft, which must have called over a number of warships. These criss-crossed over the top of the submerged boat for what seemed to have been eternity, but without causing too much trouble and without dropping depth charges.

By this time everybody had recognised that the irritation of the aircraft carrier had become a real threat and U-boat Command sent a signal saying that the boats from Group Seeräuber must make the destruction of the carrier their main aim. This was easily said, but finding the ship was going to be most challenging. The convoy could well be covering a larger area of sea than the U-boat lookouts' field of vision and identifying which one of those ships might be an aircraft carrier was not at all easy, even if one were to witness a landing or take off.

As luck would have it, it was a few hours before first light on 22 December when U751 (Kptlt. Gerhard Bigalk) reported probably having sunk the carrier with three torpedoes. Dönitz replied quickly with the one word. 'Bravo'. The men in U108 also took a deep breath of relief, but they were more interested in the second part of the message, which told them to come home at once. Despite the sinking of the *Audacity*, aircraft continued to be severe nuisances throughout the homeward-bound voyage. It was impossible to relax because the alarm bells shrilled every two to three hours. Only Christmas Eve was more peaceful. The whole day passed without incident. Had the Royal Air Force called a truce for the festivities? Whatever, U108 was in Lorient in time for Christmas lunch and on this occasion the men were especially elated because their commander, Klaus Scholtz, had been awarded the Knight's Cross. There was absolutely nothing stopping them from getting sloshed on beer and good French wine. It was even warm enough not to have the urge to dilute the wine with hot water for making grog or Glühwein.

U751 (Kptlt. Gerhard Bigalk) had left St Nazaire on 16 December 1941 and by the 21st there had been no opportunity to obtain an astronomical fix for establishing an exact position, so when the boat was ordered to join the Seeräuber group, the men needed help with radio direction signals. Each U-boat had a circular radio direction finder aerial with which the men could determine the direction that radio signals were coming from. Homing signals consisted of a prearranged Morse message, consisting usually of only one or two letters. As it happened U751 had already made good progress and was therefore not too far away. The first indications that the boat was closing in were those irritating little aircraft with wheels instead of floats. They started making a nuisance of themselves before Bigalk had gone very far and they could only have come from a carrier: the location was too far away from land for such small planes. As luck would have it, U751 spotted the ship shortly afterwards, but took it to be a tanker with a long, flat deck and hardly any superstructure. It looked weird, almost like something from a science fiction film. It certainly didn't look like a standard tanker or a classic aircraft carrier. Yet it was big and definitely part of the convoy, so Bigalk sacrificed a spread of four torpedoes. By the time he fired, he was fairly certain that the tanker was indeed an aircraft carrier and it was well worth expending the four torpedoes.

The reason for Bigalk not recognising the strange hulk at first was because it had only recently been modified into an escort carrier. HMS *Audacity* was the German ship *Hannover* that had been captured by the Royal Navy earlier in the year. It was first used as a freighter and then had its superstructure modified and a flat flight deck added over the top. Officially called escort carriers, ships like this were to play an increasingly important role in the Battle of the Atlantic. U-boat operations near them were more or less impossible and they became the most sought-after targets. Life aboard the first ones must have been awful. The early ones were without undercover accommodation for their light and flimsy aircraft and all maintenance work had to be carried out in the open, on a constantly rolling and pitching flight deck. That couldn't have been much fun in the ferocity of the North Atlantic.

11

THE UNITED STATES AND RUSSIA JOIN THE WAR:TOO FAR, TOO COLD AND TOO HOT

The sixty-four dynamic days around March were not the only metamorphic periods for Germany in 1941. Later in the spring, intelligence indicated that massive Russian forces were being assembled along the Polish border. As a result, on 22 June 1941, Germany felt that it was necessary to declare war on the Soviet Union and launched Operation Barbarossa. About six months later, on 11 December, following the Japanese attack on the American anchorage at Pearl Harbor, Germany declared war on the United States. U-boats were then hurriedly made ready to cross the Atlantic, while others were already operating against Russia in the cold Polar Seas.

Too Far

Ten days before Christmas 1941, a 26-year-old with the two pips on the plain epaulettes of his coat indicating that he was a Kapitänleutnant (or lieutenant commander), struggled through the busy activity of the shipyard in Lorient to take command of U125. Ulrich Folkers was then, and still is today, an almost unknown character who gave his life to his country during the Black May of 1943, just a couple of months after he had been awarded the Knight's Cross. This shows that he was no dummy. Less than 10 per cent of U-boat commanders received such a prestigious medal. Among other things, it allowed them free travel on public transport and exempted them from having to pay income tax. Those steps through the shipyard were taken during a momentous time in history. The world was still shocked by the news of the Japanese attack on Pearl Harbor and then the German declaration of war against the United States came over as an even more horrific turn of events for the still comparatively small U-boat Arm. This tiny force was so insignificant that it could muster only five boats for the first attack against the all-powerful USA and U125 was one of those five. It was an ocean-going Type IXC, commissioned nine months earlier by Günther Kuhnke, who also became a Knight of the Iron Cross.

The crew had taken turns to travel the long distance on the U-boat special train to Germany, returning in time for the obligatory medical with the flotilla's own naval doctors. A few repairs were finished off, the boat was provisioned and armed and then cast off at around teatime on 18 December 1941 to follow U502 into the Bay of Biscay. It was no secret among the crew that they were part of the first thrust against what was becoming the most powerful nation on earth. Although their exit route out of France had already been called the 'Black Pit' of Biscay, it was still inhabited by a multitude of fishing boats. These had to be avoided and the knowledge that British submarines were also lurking in the harbour approaches made Folkers steer a deliberate zigzag course.

A cold breeze was blowing gently from the north-west over a relatively calm sea while the lookouts were treated to a most spectacular phosphorescence as the water crashed over their bows, but nothing came to prevent them steering a general westerly course of 254° at 12 knots throughout the night. Shortly before daylight, U125 dropped into the cellar. Folkers wanted to check the work done in the dockyard and took the boat deep to test that there were no hidden leaks, then, following a leisurely morning he returned to the surface at lunchtime to ventilate the interior before returning into the depths to continue with the voyage below the waves. This was starting to become common practice in this most dangerous area dominated by aggressive planes from the British Coastal Command. Once it was dark again, the boat surfaced to continue at its much faster and more economical surface cruising speed. Even the surface speed was so slow that it could hold up hurried cyclists. There were two ways of making progress with a U-boat, either to tootle along at economical speed of about 7–12 knots or to run in high economy mode of a diesel-electric run with a maximum of about 6 knots. This amounts to 11 kilometres per hour (less than 7 miles per hour) and is an excruciatingly slow speed for crossing such a wide stretch of water. Just for comparison, the distance from Southampton to New York is about 3,080 miles and a little mathematics would suggest that a cyclist would need more than two weeks of non-stop effort to get there. On this occasion only the Bay of Biscay had become a threat and it wasn't long before U125 was in the air gap of the mid-Atlantic where it could continue at a more leisurely pace without the newly introduced precautions to avoid dangerous nuisances in the sky.

U125 was already well to the west of Ireland when both aircraft and smoke on the horizon started dominating events. The smoke was too intense to ignore and a convoy sighting was immediately radioed back to headquarters. Only smoke and the occasional tops of masts were visible, making it difficult to work out both the speed and the direction of the merchant ships. U125 turned towards them, but found that aircraft over the top made the approach difficult and forced the boat into the cellar on several occasions. Yet this was the first time that a convoy had come to Folkers and he was determined not to waste the opportunity. Most puzzling of all was one approaching aircraft that had its navigation lights fully illuminated, making the men in U125 wonder what it was up to. The phosphorescence experienced earlier now started to become more annoying than the aircraft. It looked as if the boat was trailing a huge luminous rope. Since this brilliant display increased with speed, there was nothing for it other than to approach the convoy as slowly as possible.

Things would have been considerably easier had Folkers received a signal from U-boat headquarters ordering him to ignore the convoy and continue with his westward voyage. As it happened, an aircraft forced him away from the surface just as the first transmission of that order was on the way and he didn't receive the news until the radio operator picked up a repeat at 0700 hours the following morning. U125 was still nowhere near close enough to launch an attack when

Asdic pings became so loud that they could be heard in the conning tower without the amplifiers from the sound detecting gear. What was more, the people up top weren't playing with their submarine detection gear and it was not long before depth charges made life more than just unpleasant. The blasts were terrifying, seemingly shattering both men and machinery. Lights went out, glass cracked, the depth gauges shattered; more and more damage reports flooded into the central control room. It was utter chaos, dark, oil had squirted onto some machinery, frightening jets of water terrified the men and persistent dripping could be heard in addition to groaning men. There were no life-threatening injuries, but enough small wounds to draw blood and produce colourful bruises. Even some of the sturdy electrical trigger gear for the torpedo tubes was smashed and switches fell off the wall, making the interior look like the kind of pandemonium usually only seen in films.

The men worked feverishly to repair the damage. Following that, Christmas was spent in relative calm without disturbances other than a few test dives to check that the hull was not leaking. So far the weather had been very variable, without any serious quirks to make life too uncomfortable. This changed during the day before New Year's Eve, when U125 found itself battering into an increasingly ferocious sea. Waves hitting the conning tower were strong enough for men on the inside to hear and feel the incredible shattering as they crashed against the steel. The noise on the surface was deafening, even on the inside. Lookouts had to be chained in position to prevent them from being washed into the raging sea as it dropped onto the top of the tower before washing out again over the gun platform towards the stern. Just to add a little excitement to life, one of the two net deflectors on the stern snapped. These thick steel cables, running from the stern and bows to the top of the conning tower, doubled up as radio aerials and as attachments for safety harnesses for men working on the upper deck. Luckily a length of eight metres or so, attached to the stern, got jammed in the deck and therefore could not trail backwards into the sea where it might easily have wrapped itself around one of the propellers.

At this stage of the proceedings it would appear that U-boat Command became concerned with the possibility of U125 arriving on the eastern seaboard of the United States before the rest of Operation Paukenschlag and thereby triggering off a violent reaction from defensive forces. On 29 December Folkers received an order not to go too far west until the rest of the boats had reported their presence on the American side of the Atlantic. U123 under Reinhard Hardegen left Lorient on 23 December 1941 (five days after U125) and the other boats were also struggling through the atrocious weather and force 11 gales and at times were making hardly any progress over the ground. All the engines could manage was to prevent the boats from being blown backwards to where they had come from. Deck plates were ripped off and the force of the gale even damaged strong gun mounts. One of the torpedo tubes on U125 could not be fully opened or completely closed and the weather remained far too rough to send a diver down to inspect the damage. Even when it improved, there was no opportunity to make repairs and Folkers continued with the tube flooded and the outside door partly open. This meant that he couldn't even withdraw the eel into the interior to shoot it out through another tube. The external damage was not life threatening, but looked awful and gave the men a scratchy feeling as they prepared to face the United States in Operation Paukenschlag with what looked like a wrecked boat. 'Paukenschlag' has often been translated as Operation Drumbeat, which has hardly the same meaning. A Pauke is the biggest drum and a beat on it is something special, more than a mere drumbeat.

Folkers was still contemplating his mechanical problems and avoiding the occasional aircraft or small boat when U123 (Kptlt. Reinhard Hardegen) launched Operation Paukenschlag by sinking the SS *Cyclops* to the south of Halifax on 12 January 1942. The first target worth expending a torpedo on for U125 appeared on 14 January with full illuminations and obvious Spanish markings. Germany was not at war with Spain, so Folkers observed it for a while but didn't attack. The following day U-boat Command asked all boats to include details of their fuel reserves the next time they used the radio. This desire to know more about the fuel situation came as an additional bonus as the long journey across the Atlantic had used considerably less fuel than had been calculated. This was ample evidence that German submarines on long runs were more economical than had previously been imagined. In fact these figures were so good that even smaller boats, the seagoing Type VIICs, were later sent across the ocean to operate along its western extremities.

On 18 January 1942, U125 established its exact position via the Nantucket lightship with its lights at normal pre-war intensity. The lights from the coast were unbelievable, with illuminations all along the seafront. Some U-boats even found that these could be used for detecting blacked-out targets passing between lookouts and the coast. The American seaboard became an intensive hunting ground with virtually no opposition for some U-boats, but not for U125. On 20 January Folkers remarked in his log that he had now been in his allocated operations area for one week and spotted only one smoke cloud and the neutral Spanish freighter with passenger accommodation. It was 23 January before Folkers sent his men to their action stations to tackle a 7,000-ton tanker. Torpedo tube 4 could not be opened at all and tube 2 had been out of action with that inoperable outer door since that punishing gale some two weeks earlier. So the men had to content themselves with only two serviceable bow tubes. Both of these were discharged against the same target and both missed, or at least they didn't produce any significant results and the ship didn't even notice that it was within the sights of a U-boat. Turning and using the two stern tubes didn't work on this occasion. The target was already too far away, so U125 would have to start another attack with a new run-in to move ahead of the tanker. This was frustrated by a shadow that was identified as a destroyer. The tanker had disappeared by the time the destroyer was out of sight and the following four hours didn't bring U125 any nearer to the lucrative target. At midnight Folkers gave up the chase. Frustrations continued unabated, although Folkers did eventually manage to sink two ships before commencing his homeward run to Lorient. On 28 January 1942, with 90 cubic metres of fuel in the bunkers, U125 turned to head back home. The outward journey had indicated that at least 79 of those would definitely be required to get back.

It was 1100 hours on 22 February when U125 finally made fast in Lorient. The boat had been at sea for sixty-five days since it left on 18 December 1941. Historians have led us to believe that this was such a successful period for U-boats that they called it their 'Second Happy

Time', but the average sinking per U-boat at sea had dropped dramatically from almost six during the autumn of 1940 to a maximum of just two. So operations in American waters may have been successful for some boats, but even these massive successes could hardly screw the statistics any higher. It was already obvious that the war at sea had long been lost and it is remarkable that so many men volunteered to continue with the bitter battle on this unrelentingly hostile ocean. Historians have also led us to believe that most of the U-boat crews were made up of inexperienced youngsters, but statistics show the exact opposite: the average age of the crews got older as the war progressed. So the volunteers were not the suicidal zombies many have led us to believe.

U-boat Command was not terribly pleased with the results of U125's voyage and listed a number of shortcomings. In doing so Karl Dönitz (Commander-in-Chief) also remarked that the commander had not demonstrated a great deal of skill and this was probably due to a lack of experience. However, despite many U-boats coming home without having sunk anything, it would appear that not much was done to improve the intensity of wartime submarine training. Kptlt. Claus Korth, a Knight of the Iron Cross and one of the more senior officers for testing whether crews were ready to go to war said the best thing he could do for the good crews was to fail them, so that they would receive more training and therefore stand some chance of surviving against the heavy odds.

Walter Hartmann, a Torpedogefreiter (ordinary seaman), left a most fascinating document in the German U-boat Museum, elucidating some of the human problems as U162 under Jürgen Wattenberg crossed the Atlantic in April 1942. Getting into the Atlantic from Kiel entailed going via Norway before refuelling in Lorient and then heading west. Everybody on board was already violently seasick when U162 left Norwegian waters and again on leaving France, but the majority adjusted to the constant unpredictable motion, although this sickness became so bad that there were times when men could no longer cope with their duties and several tricks had to be tried out in order to survive. Some of the cheating was so bad that the men would have been court-martialled had their misdemeanours been discovered. For example, they pulled torpedoes out of the tubes but felt so ill that they could not service them. Later they pushed them back into the tubes and reported that they had been seen to.

Even when the bad weather subsided, the waves remained bigger than the boat. While travelling on the surface men were allowed on top of the conning tower to smoke and relieve themselves. In addition to this it was possible for three or four to squeeze into the commander's control room in the conning tower for a smoke by standing behind the helmsman. Wolfgang Hirschfeld, the radio operator of U109 and U234 started the war as a non-smoker, but took up the habit because that was the only excuse to breathe fresh air on the outside. Someone had even built an electric cigarette lighter in U125's conning tower room to save matches. The problem was that waves often washed over the top of the conning tower, making the upstairs space outside a little unpleasant and the cigarettes so soggy that they went out. (Smaller seagoing boats of Type VII did not have room for a helmsman inside the conning tower and such boats could be steered only from the central control room. Some of the tiny coastal Type II boats had an additional steering wheel on the top of the conning tower.)

The huge lead/acid batteries, located under the accommodation areas of U-boats, gave off a highly explosive mixture of hydrogen and oxygen. This was vented into the interior of the boat and an open fire there could easily have triggered off an explosion. Diesel engines were big enough to fill the entire space from keel to ceiling, so there were no batteries under that compartment. In addition to that, the engine room was well ventilated by a special air duct leading down from the top of the conning tower wall. Therefore, there were no problems when the diesel mechanic opened taps on the top of the cylinders, allowing a flame to shoot out. This was done at regular intervals to check that each section of the engine was firing properly. Each cylinder also had its own thermometer and usually there was an additional one for taking the temperature of the exhaust, but the fire test was quicker and more positive than waiting for cylinders to run hot.

In January 1942, when Operation Paukenschlag, the attack against the United States, started, there were on average forty-two U-boats at sea every day. This figure climbed steadily to reach sixty-one in May and 100 in September. Yet each of these boats was sinking less than one ship per month and at the beginning of 1943 this figure dropped even further, to about half. In other words two U-boats were required to be at sea for a whole month in order to sink one ship. During the autumn of 1940, the short-range attack at night was reaping almost six ships sunk per month per U-boat at sea. There are masses of logs with similar experiences to that had by U125 under Ulrich Folkers, where boats were at sea without even sighting the enemy. In addition to finding hardly any targets, many U-boats found themselves not only turned away by escorts or aircraft but also having to crawl home with serious damage. So life wasn't just a simple case of cruising across the Atlantic at the speed of a pedal cyclist; technical tenacity to cope with seriously damaged machinery was also a vital part of the survival equation.

Too Hot

Another boat to make one of the early crossings to America was U502, an ocean-going Type IXC, commanded by Kptlt. Jürgen von Rosenstiel. It was one of five boats to form the Neuland group for a combined attack on the oil installations of the Caribbean. (The name 'Neuland' was used for several different operations and cropped up again later in the war.) The boat left Kiel for a wide sweep through the North Atlantic shipping routes followed by refuelling in Lorient. It then set out from there for its second war voyage on 18 December 1941. Four days later it was back in port, dragging what looked like a massive oil tail behind it. This should have been repaired, but was somehow overlooked. As things turned out, there were a number of other minor problems and it was 19 January 1942 before U502 finally put to sea to battle against a brisk westerly force 4 wind and choppy seas. This made it possible to cover an average of about 130 nautical miles (240 kilometres) per day on the surface and it was only necessary to dive occasionally, usually for less than 10 miles (18 kilometres). Once this subsided, U502 increased its daily total to 160 nautical miles and on some good days even managed almost 200 nautical miles (370 kilometres). Commanders had considerable freedom in how they conducted their own daily affairs and this method for crossing the Bay of Biscay was different to how U125 tackled this part of the voyage.

This progress came to a most dramatic climax a few hours before the start of the New Year, when the engines were run up to high speed to blow soot deposits out of the exhaust. On this occasion a brilliant shower of sparks accompanied the anticipated black cloud. The startling display was considerably better than any fireworks back home. The annoying thing was that they didn't subside, but continued, even after a burst at high speed for over fifteen minutes. This was not ideal if they wanted to run away and hide from a pursuer. Even if there had been some bushes around, they wouldn't have hidden the brilliant display. It was not only the commander who started cursing and it was not long before everybody on board knew that this was the result of a major fault that had been reported at the end of the first war cruise, but obviously not rectified while in dock. One wonders why von Rosenstiel didn't test this before going such a long way from base.

The usual procedure for dealing with faults was for the engineer officer to report them to the flotilla engineer, who would then sanction repairs. There were many times when dockyards were too busy to deal with everything. Matters were then graded according to their urgency and some boats had to leave with minor faults. U134 (mentioned later) provides a good example of having had its hydroplanes damaged by another boat in Kirkenes, but leaving for a war voyage despite only being able to move them 10° either way. Dealing with them would have entailed a journey to Trondheim or Bergen or even further south to where a dry dock was available, so the men of U134 had to cope with the damage as best they could.

Von Rosenstiel had been hoping to meet the famous Trade Winds airstream, but although the men had learned of this famous airstream while still at school, nature refused to cooperate. Instead of steady north-easterlies, U502 kept encountering stark winds from the west, slowing down progress considerably. This was further aggravated on 5 January when the giro compass stopped working and the helmsman had to rely solely on the magnetic compass. This was located on a bulge at the base of the conning tower and could be viewed through an illuminated periscope from the central control below it.

The conning tower itself was made from non-magnetic phosphorous bronze and therefore didn't affect the compass.

The north-easterly trade winds were finally reached on 6 January. By that time von Rosenstiel knew that at least three other boats of the Neuland group were nearby. There was no need for him to know exactly what they were up to. Each one had a different objective and the only important point of cooperation was that all boats should start their attack simultaneously. The reason for this was not so much to make a dramatic impact upon the opposition, but to prevent one boat running into unexpected retaliation sparked off by an attack from another. At this period of time U-boat Command was still anticipating strong and highly aggressive anti-submarine forces in the far western waters.

As U502 approached the Caribbean and the waters became clearer and smoother, von Rosenstiel ordered another detailed series of tests and exercises. The men rehearsed every conceivable manoeuvre they might have to undertake and then checked that the oil trail from earlier had definitely been dealt with. Aircraft were sighted regularly as the boat approached land and there were even a few lucrative targets, but these were left in peace so as not to give away the boat's presence in western waters. It was 12 February when U502 entered the Caribbean after having passed through the Sargasso Sea and the Anegada Passage between the Virgin Islands and the Dutch Antilles. Two days later, at 0700 hours on 14 February, lookouts obtained a brilliant fix – the Colorado lighthouse on Aruba – and following the positive confirmation of their position the men started a detailed reconnaissance of the area. So far U502 had spotted several tankers, some empty and some fully laden, but no one at U-boat Command knew a great about the general situation regarding traffic or sea defences in that area, so an especially careful inspection was called for.

The following day, while still within sight of La Macolla light, U502 received a signal from headquarters reminding the Commander that ships, especially tankers should be their main targets and if these were not available then they should consider shelling land installations. Once U502 was free to start offensive action, there were no targets in sight and von Rosenstiel had to content himself with a 1,500 GRT tanker, which was attacked with a torpedo at around 0900 hours on 16 February. (This turned out to have been the 2,395 GRT *Tia Juana*.) The next few hours saw two more sinkings: by lunchtime the men had sunk the 2,650 GRT *Monagasa* and the 2,391-GRT *San Nicholas*. The effort put in to achieve these sinkings confirmed that artillery action during daylight was not a viable proposition due to the abundance of aircraft overhead. These would be presented with too good a target if they surprised a U-boat with the gun crew on deck. Getting the men back inside would take too long; they had to negotiate a slippery deck by squeezing past the sides of the conning tower, climb up the back and then down from the hatch on the top. The rush to get back inside could easily be obstructed by a chain of men passing heavy shells from the magazine below the radio room to the large gun.

A signal from U-boat headquarters arrived the following day, emphasising the need to attack land-based oil installations with artillery, but this wasn't as easy as the big bosses back home had imagined. Not all the waters around the islands were deep enough for submarine operations and U502 did, on at least one occasion, temporarily run aground. Although the incident was not life threatening, it was more than just uncomfortable and the lack of really worthwhile targets added to the men's frustrations. Navigation was not easy either. Despite being close to land, there were not all that many suitable landmarks and trying to identify oil installations from the sea was unexpectedly difficult. Rather than following the European principle of that era, where industrial plants were built without regard to the countryside, the installations in the Caribbean blended in well with their natural surroundings. This made it tricky to spot even something as obvious as a huge oil tank and U-boats often failed to identify targets for their incendiary shells.

It is important to bear in mind that U502 had left a European winter to operate in hot tropical waters and the men found the general living conditions considerably worse than they had imagined when setting out. The Caribbean might be a favoured holiday destination with good weather almost guaranteed as long as one avoids the hurricane seasons, but the men in U-boats found the area overbearingly hot. Inside the U-boats it felt like having driven into hell itself. Walls, bulkheads, machinery, everything dripped with so much condensation and perspiration that there were hardly any dry places left. Everybody stood, sat or slept in constantly dripping sweat, which created a number of major skin irritations. Food went bad very quickly and many of the provisions had to be thrown overboard because mould encased them more quickly than the men could consume them. Potatoes needed constant sorting to throw them out before they became a sickening sludge. Bread turned soggy and even rubbing the mould off didn't help. Instead of going hard, it turned mushy. Dried meat and smoked sausages did reasonably well as long as everything was frequently washed with salt water, although at times it seemed as if this only added another layer of diesel oil flavour to the outside.

American submarines were provided with soda and ice machines to keep the crew in reasonably refreshed condition, but in German U-boats there was even a shortage of drinking water, so this often had to be rationed in the tropics. The torpedo mechanics could ille- gally withdraw small quantities of distilled water from their hydraulic system as long as no one noticed, but this tasted so awful that honey or something had to be added to make it drinkable, even under those horrific thirsty conditions. Temperatures in the interior frequently reached 45 degrees Celsius or more when submerged and later in the year, when aircraft became even more of a problem, men had to remain incarcerated in their iron tube for long periods without being able to surface to ventilate the stuffiness.

U502 found that bombarding shore installations proved more dif- ficult than imagined as well. At first the sea was too rough, then on another occasion it was too difficult to spot any suitable targets, and then on the third occasion there was too much activity in the air, making the use of the guns suicidal because of the amount of time it would take to get the gun crew back inside. U-boat Command tried to coax the Caribbean commanders into action by telling them that the best time for shore bombardments was at dusk and at dawn. The almost total absence of any worthwhile targets made life sig- nificantly more difficult for U502. The radio monitoring service back home, B-Dienst, had decoded enough messages to suggest that this was a temporary setback and the traffic would re-emerge, but the men of U502 couldn't agree and disregarded any forthcoming advice. Yet they did torpedo three more ships, each of about 9,000 tons, to come home with a reasonable bag, but by the time they put into Lorient again on 16 March 1942, they had been at sea for fifty-five days (almost two months) and there was no way that such a performance was going to even keep pace with the ever escalating war.

It seems that U502 was faced with far more detrimental incidents than positive ones and even their shelling experience, one of the basic reasons for forming the Neuland group, almost cost the men their lives. Just before 24 February came to an end, tension rose in U502 as the word spread that the old man had started to chase a freighter. The artillery crew was ready to man the 105mm quick-firing gun in front of the conning tower and the hatch leading to the magazine below the radio room was opened in anticipation. As happened so often, although everything was checked and double-checked, the submerged approach didn't bring U502 any closer to the target and in the end the boat had to surface in order to spot the ship again. The freighter was zigzagging in short tacks and with the moon behind the U-boat, everything was just as it should be according to the rulebook. The target was in the best possible light, the range was reasonable and the next tack was going to bring it into a perfect position for an artillery attack. The first three shots sailed clearly over the top of the bridge and the fourth hit the water some distance ahead of the bows, not terribly impressive for a large target making about 14 knots at a range of only 2.5 kilometres. The noise of the shells passing overhead probably woke up the crew; the ship turned away and the seventh shot might have hit, but it was difficult to observe and no one was sure. Eventually, after the fourteenth shot, U502 gave up, still not sure why the gun crew was missing the target. Retaliation from a gun on its stern was pretty low-key, missing U502 by some considerable distance. So the situation still looked as if it was in the U-boat's favour, but von Rosenstiel thought that chasing the ship would not be worth it because it seemed unlikely that he was going to get close enough to hit it, especially now that its defences must now have been fully manned. He didn't want to get within range of some of the smaller weapons seen on the ship's superstructure. So, he gave up, turned away and headed back to Europe.

Too Cold

The following account looks at another comparatively successful boat, which was pitched against Russian forces in the bitterly cold Arctic.

U134 under Kptlt. Rudolf Schendel, a standard seagoing boat of Type VIIC left Kirkenes in northern Norway on Christmas Eve of 1941 and returned to Kirkenes on 20 January, after having joined the Ulan group against Convoy PQ7A. These convoys to north Russia must have been sheer hell for merchant seamen and even worse for the poorly equipped escorts. Many of the escorts, especially the anti-submarine corvettes, had their main accommodation area forward and the galley towards the rear, but without an internal connection between the two. This made something as mundane as collecting hot food an incredibly difficult obstacle course. To make matters worse, small warships struggled into Murmansk and Archangel (Russia) after the most inhospitable conditions and with serious losses from U-boats to find that the goods delivered a few months earlier with their previous convoy, were still lying on the quay and gently rotting in the cold Arctic weather.

Kirkenes was too far off the beaten track to have a torpedo store, so Schendel could only acquire two new ones. One of these came from U454 (Kptlt. Burkhard Hackländer) and the other one from U134's own outside storage container between the upper deck and the pressure hull. Type VIIC boats had one of these in the bows and another in the stern. They were pure storage boxes and the torpedoes had to be pulled out and lowered into the torpedo compartments before being able to discharge them. The stern tube had leaked and filled with water, so on opening the hatch at one end, the men found a solid block of ice with the torpedo embedded inside it and with temperatures well below freezing there was no hope of extracting the cold lump. So only one torpedo could be loaded.

Christmas Day proved to be a most memorable one. In order to comply with orders, it was necessary to run at 12–13 knots against a northerly force 8 wind and with the state of the sea rough enough for breakers to thunder over the top of the conning tower. With air temperatures as low as -15 degrees Celsius without taking the wind-chill factor into account, the sea turned to ice as soon as it had drenched the lookouts. There was ice on the metal, on the men's clothing, in their beards and in their hair. U134 could manage no more than 9 nautical miles over the ground and this was reduced even further when one of the engines gave up and needed to be shut down for repairs. Progress cannot be described as merely uncomfortable; it was exceptionally painful, even for the men in the slightly warmer interior.

Arctic boats didn't have special heaters to cope with extreme temperatures. In fact U-boats were without an adequate ventilation system and the extremities at both ends often got terribly stuffy. There were some hot water pipes running out of the diesel engines, but these couldn't cope with normal European winters, so portable electric heaters were supplied for colder weather. The problem was that these used so much power that they drained the batteries too quickly and often had to be switched off once the boat left port. Walter Hartmann, one of the torpedo mechanics in U162, explained how once at sea the men had to rely entirely on the little heat from the diesel engines. Even in warmer, more southerly latitudes the interior of the boat never got above 10–12 degrees Celsius. The men wore thick underwear under a warm tracksuit and then put their working clothes on top of that. U-boat leathers were pulled over the top as well and lookouts were also provided with special raingear. This was supplied to the boat and did not form part of the men's personal clothing. When sleeping, men stripped off as far as the tracksuit, but underwear was hardly ever removed unless one was going to put on a new set.

At 1120 hours of 29 December 1941, Bear Island came into sight and not long afterwards U134 reached its position in the ordered patrol line to await further orders. With water temperatures a few degrees below freezing, condensation on the inside of the boat froze to encrust the interior cold surfaces with a layer of ice. On the outside there were 5cm-thick ice floes near the island. In this cold hell, U134 did actually attempt an attack against a freighter battling its way eastwards, but both torpedoes – one fired some time after the other – failed. Astonishingly the third one hit, sinking the British 5,135-ton freighter *Waziristan*. Yet this only brought the balance back to zero because on 9 December U134 had sunk the German freighter *Steinbek* (2,185 GRT) by mistake. The convoy, which U134 had been directed towards, vanished in the Arctic mists and U-boat Command gave both U134 and U454 the freedom to operate where they wanted to. Instead of targets both boats found their lives dominated by aircraft rather than ships. The only positive advantage was that they appeared to be Russians who were not yet as determined or as efficient as the British Coastal Command in the Bay of Biscay. Yet, the one that attacked U134 did drop a depth charge a long way off.

Lt.z.S.(Ing.) Ullrich, the engineer officer, added some fascinating problems to the end of U134's log. He explained that due to the sea temperature being just a few degrees below zero, there was hardly any fresh water aboard U134 and all washing water in external tanks had frozen solid. In addition to this, the inside of the conning tower, the central control room below it, the bow torpedo room and the rear compartment including the electro-motor controls had a cover-ing of ice up to 1 centimetre thick. Various pipes, vents and valves all suffered from being frozen and it was necessary to wash these by run-ning through the salt water before many could be operated. Diving cells in particular jammed and had to be de-iced before their valves would move. This de-icing process of running a partly submerged boat through the marginally warmer sea had to be carried out at frequent intervals to ensure that it could dive when required to do so. The boat would be submerged slightly while it sped through the water and the ballast pumps hopefully removed any water that poured in through the jammed valves.

Hydraulic systems were still in their infancy and boats in the extremely cold latitudes discovered that thin, runny oil was not the best medium for making these work. Runny oil became thicker and even turned into a grease-like substance at such low temperatures. Some of the men of U134 thought that this thickening of the oil also contributed to their torpedo failures, as it required more effort to make things work; periscopes, the rod aerial and other such devices consumed considerably more electricity to operate them.

The problem with the northerly latitudes was that they were not terribly hospitable and often there was no respite from extreme con-ditions. It was a case of moving from one state of purgatory to another.

Luckily, on this occasion, the storm did not last terribly long but was followed by such crystal-clear visibility that the moonlight was bright enough to read on top of the conning tower. There was no way anyone could mount a surface attack under such brilliant conditions. The snag was that a target did present itself at the most inconvenient time. At first no one could make out what it was against the stark reflections of the moon, but they were hoping that it was a significant freighter. It didn't take long before the men were immersed in the horrible feeling of seeing a destroyer head-on, coming straight towards them. It seemed obvious that it had already had detected the U-boat and was now coming in for the kill.

Schendel dived to get out of the way and it was only later, when the destroyer approached that he realised it wasn't moving anywhere near fast enough to be chasing anything: it was moving at too leisurely a pace. So, instead of hiding, Schendel opted for the offensive and attempted to attack it, but the destroyer was already past the optimum position to do so. As it happened, nothing happened. The torpedo ran but didn't do anything and there was not even the slightest reaction from the opposition. It seemed as though the sound detection gear in the destroyer wasn't manned; otherwise the men would have heard the high-pitched whine of the torpedo running towards it. The night was too light for attempting another surface attack and the destroyer's speed too fast to pursue even with the fastest submerged speed. So there was nothing for it, the torpedo had missed. The men in U134 continued wondering for some time why the destroyer's lookouts hadn't seen the U-boat on the surface. The destroyer was clearly visible without the need of binoculars and one could make out individual features with the naked eye. How did the destroyer miss seeing the U-boat and why did the torpedo not sink it? The men of U134 thought the whole incident was rather weird.

U134 had been heading east from Bear Island and then south until the first Russian land came into sight. These islands and headlands are still so remote today that their names from the naval charts hardly feature on any western atlases. Modern Internet maps suggest that even the Russians who were stationed there during the war have long abandoned those inhospitable outposts. Yet, although nothing but desolation and wrecks from the past occupy the barren land today, way back in 1942 it was a vital link between east and west and was important enough for the Admiral Polar Seas to send a reminder to U134 saying that the sinking of even small boats was important.

Astonishingly enough, many Germans venturing into these remote stations agreed with Schendel when he wrote that the Russians were on full alert and ready and waiting for the German intrusion. There were only a few isolated lights and most of the coast remained wrapped in what appeared to be an almost otherworldly blackness. Despite the stark contrast of dark sea and the snow-white land, a haze often made it difficult to distinguish the point where the land met the water. The feeling of being lost in the vast emptiness was made worse by spotting a number of unidentified navigation lights. It was not until conditions got better and the sky allowed for an accurate fix on the stars that the men realised they had made a navigation error of some 25 miles. The isolated settlement they were looking for was somewhere else. This was not a happy operation and the men were pleased to get back to Kirkenes. One has to bear in mind that U134 was one of the boats that managed to sink shipping in those Polar Seas and many more came home empty handed. Success was hard to come by, even in the remote Russian convoy routes.

12

FIRST OPERATIONS WITH A PURPOSE-BUILT SUPPLY SUBMARINE

Towards the beginning of 1942, when U-boats started venturing into far-off waters, it became essential to supply them at sea, but the days of surface supply ships were long over. Around June 1941, when the battleship *Bismarck* attempted her ill-fated breakout, no less than ten supply ships were lost in a matter of a few days. Yet, despite these losses, the German Navy had developed such excellent purpose-built surface supply ships that two of them continued to be used after the war. One sailed under a British flag and the other under the Stars and Stripes. (*Nordmark*, also known as *Westerwald* became HMS *Bulawayo* and *Dithmarschen* became USS *Conecuh*.) Submarine supply ships, also designed before the war, were not placed high on the list of priorities and the first ones were not ready until some time after the United States had joined the war. At first the U-boat Arm hastily converted UA, almost as large as a Type IX, to be used as an emergency supply submarine. Shortly after that, the first large Type XB minelayers were converted and used successfully as well. The following is an account of the first purpose-built supply submarine of Type XIV to see operational service.

Kapitänleutnant Georg von Wilamowitz-Moellendorf stood out from a crowd of active submariners by his broad shoulders and by his age. At a few weeks short of forty-eight, he was much older than other U-boat commanders and even noticeably more mature than the dashing flotilla commanders with their flashy Knights' Crosses. Rucks Willi (Willi the Puller), the ferryman in Pillau, often wondered how this massive frame fitted into those small coastal submarines. Wilamowitz, as he was known in naval circles, had been a regular ferry passenger during the past fourteen months while commanding the training boat U2. Willi often told his passengers how he shuddered at the thought of being locked up inside such a tin can where you couldn't see the sky or feel the weather beating against your face, and he couldn't understand what made Wilamowitz keen enough to volunteer for such arduous duty twice in his life. Wasn't fighting in one world war enough? Yet, looking at it from the other angle, the majority of sailors in training couldn't see how Willy, a wiry old man, enjoyed being out in his ferry punt in all weathers, even when most people preferred to shelter indoors.

Wilamowitz, or the Wild Moritz as he was sometimes called, started his naval career way back in 1912, two years before the First World War, and wandered from torpedo boats to submarines during August 1917, when he served as watch officer in U46 and in several other boats. Although Rucks Willi was himself one of the old eccentrics left over from the time of the Emperor, he regarded Wilamowitz as an unconventional youngster and admired people like him for their audacity. During a chilly October evening in 1941, Rucks Willi took the opportunity of saying his farewells. There had been no official announcements, but, like the barbers in town, he was aware of most military secrets and knew he was unlikely to see Wilamowitz again in a sober state. This was his last run to town before moving on to a new, bigger boat in Kiel.

The move west could not have been more dramatic. When Wilamowitz stepped out of the station at Germany's largest naval base, he found himself confronted with the shattering reminders of war. Pillau, in the far eastern Baltic and far out of the enemies' reach, could have been on a different planet. There was still no shortage of anything in Pillau, but everything was different in Kiel. Shop windows looked depleted and almost ragged. There was also considerable evidence of air raid precautions and at night everybody had to suffer an inconvenient blackout, meaning there were a good number of obstacles between the bars in town and one's bunk. There were even a few signs of bombs having fallen, although the damage was more of an irritating nuisance rather than life-threatening destruction.

The hive of activity in the harbour had changed considerably since Wilamowitz first smelt the oily sea air, shortly after the turn of the century. In those days the huge smoking monstrosities that were coal-burning warships were often outnumbered by masses of smaller sailing barges, plying their coastal trade along the tide-less Baltic. Much of the romantic evidence of that bygone age had now vanished, but one could not help but be impressed by the massive glasshouse across the water at the Krupp Germania Works. It was full of submarines instead of those nimble coastal torpedo boats and destroyers that were being built there the first time Wilamowitz gazed at this impressive hive of activity. The size of the hangar was still awe-inspiring, even to an old man. His new boat, U459, the first purpose-built supply submarine, was already lying in the water in front of it, feverishly being finished off for its commissioning on Saturday, 15 November 1941.

When the U-boat Arm was re-founded way back in 1935, the naval hierarchy hadn't seen the need for supply submarines; even now, with the war more than two years old, it was still difficult for some quarters to appreciate the necessity for such specialised craft. The men working on this first batch of the special Type XIV gave the impression that they were plodding along at a comfortable pace, rather than scurrying to get things done quickly. The sometimes ridiculous military sharpness was definitely absent in this civilian shipyard. People talked to their superiors in plain, everyday language, without any trace of the elaborate formality demanded by the navy. This industrial enclave gave the impression of being just as far removed from the war as Pillau and when crossing the water to the amusement quarter of Kiel one found the bars doing a brisk business despite their thick blackout shutters. Yes, there may have been a war on somewhere, but even in Kiel it was still well camouflaged. Nothing, not even all the military offices, were running anywhere near to what was later called 'total war production'. Life was still cosy. No wonder: the invasion of France and the Low Countries had settled into an uneasy truce and news from the eastern front had also been frozen by the extreme cold of the coming winter.

The other important front, the Atlantic, seemed equally as remote. No one would have known there was anything going on at all, had it not been for the Supreme Military Command interrupting normal radio programmes with stirring fanfares. Only a few men in the frontline command centres were any the wiser that the majority of U-boats were having a hard time finding targets in the vastness of the ocean. Three weeks later, all this changed most dramatically. U459 was out training in the Baltic when the icy wind was suddenly heated up with news of Japanese forces having attacked Pearl Harbor. A few days later the United States of America joined the war on the Allied side and even the dimmest of the crew realised how important this new supply submarine was going to be. If U-boats were going to conduct any form of efficient campaign in the far western reaches of the Atlantic, they would need big supporting mothers to bring them the necessities of life; otherwise they would have to devote all their time to sailing backwards and forwards without much fuel or food left for hunting along the American coast.

The frightening news injected wild fervour into the peaceful pace of life inherited from Germania Works, and the men from U459 found themselves receiving priority treatment wherever they went. They could jump queues and even land-based officers reacted with exceptional speed to requests from the lowly 'lords' of this new boat. Unfortunately there was not much time for anyone to enjoy the change in status: everybody was kept hard at it and preparations lasted long into each night. Training schedules had already been curtailed by the presence of thick ice reaching far out into the Baltic and the news resulted in many more corners being cut. There wasn't even time to try out some of the new innovations, such as the deep freeze. These are now common household items, but in those dark days of early 1942 they were revolutionary new inventions found in only in a few large commercial undertakings.

Ice, of the variety that floated on top of the salty water in the harbour, was still very much a problem when U459 finally cast off from the Tirpitz Pier in Kiel on 21 March 1942 to follow a Sperrbrecher through a rockery-like Kiel Canal. Three other U-boats joined the group and a floating anti-aircraft battery followed on behind, but this need not have bothered. The journey was uneventful except for the roaring cheers from the girls at the Colonial School in Rendsburg, where tradition had it that salutes from warships were answered with wild cheers, no matter what lessons might be interrupted or what time of day it may have been. Ice conditions had improved significantly by the time U459 made fast on Heligoland, but the planned sonar tests with U702 under Kptlt. Wolf-Rüdiger von Rabenau, were postponed due to excessive fog making such trials too dangerous. This was just as well because several cylinder heads of one of the diesel engines developed serious cracks and needed to be replaced, meaning that feverish activity was required. A few days later, when the sonar tests did get underway, the men of U459 were more concerned with the discovery of a massive oil trail in their wake. This was serious enough for the resident engineer officer on Heligoland to suggest that U459 should return to the dockyard in Kiel. But when making such a decision he did not reckon with the strength of mind of the old skipper, who had not gained the nickname 'The Wild Moritz' for nothing. It may have been a play on his name, but the engineer quickly realised that you didn't mess with this old man, even if he was your junior in rank. Knowing a number of U-boats in American waters were relying on him turning up at the right moment, Wilamowitz was determined to put to sea. Therefore the problems were going to be rectified there and then, even if it meant a few senior officials losing sleep. Strangely enough, this leak, together with the cracked cylinder heads, were the only major mechanical failures of the whole voyage and the bad omen of going out in a dustbin full of mechanical disasters quickly evaporated.

The journey westwards was uneventful. A few depth charges were heard, but they were far enough away not to be troublesome and the aircraft that flew past were too small for anyone to distinguish their nationality. On top of this, the weather was reasonably calm with nothing more than a few brief force 7 blasts upsetting the cramped comfort of the boat. But even the moderate weather was sufficient to show up a few defects in the design. The old emergency diving trick of driving the boat as fast as possible before flooding the tanks didn't work at all; as soon as the diesels shut off and the electric motors took over, the boat came almost to a shuddering standstill. There was certainly not enough power to push it very fast against an oncoming sea;

even the diesels were not powerful enough to battle against a head-on storm and at one stage the engineer officer calculated that they were losing three quarters of their calculated performance due to a heavy head wind. There were times when it was necessary to run the engines at a fast, fuel-guzzling speed to make any progress at all and occasionally the course had to be changed to hit the wind slightly sideways on so as to prevent U459 being blown backwards over the ground. Wilamowitz didn't seem unduly perturbed. He had been in the navy long enough to realise that there was no point in getting frustrated with the inefficiency of machinery. You just make the best of what you have.

Although Wilamowitz knew where he was making for, he had no idea who he was going to meet or the exact position where refuelling was going to take place. All the last-minute arrangements were due to come by radio. To make life easier for the men in U459, Germany had changed the operational U-boat code on 1 February 1942, meaning the British cryptanalysts at Bletchley Park could not read this vital information. The messages were still being intercepted and intelligence was good enough to guess that refuelling operations were taking place, but it was impossible to determine the exact positions and Britain did not have the resources to hunt a few U-boats in such far-off isolated regions. As a result the first operational refuelling experiments took place in relative safety and without interruption, although it was still damn hard work. This was made even worse by a high proportion of the U-boat crews never having practiced refuelling at sea. Such undertakings had not featured in the training schedules and Wilamowitz was driven wild by several U-boats making a real hash of the proceedings. In the past, a few U-boats had been supplied from surface ships and surplus provisions had been passed from a homeward-bound boat to an outgoing one, meaning that the U-boat Arm had a little experience with replenishment at sea, but generally U459 was embarking on a completely new activity that no one had done before. So most of the detrimental quirks of the process were still waiting to be discovered the hard way.

The first customer was announced on 14 April 1942 in an isolated spot some 1,000 miles east of New York. This immediately brought the onboard bakery into full production to create some eighty fresh loaves at a rate of about a dozen per hour. Although operational boats were fitted with ovens, they hardly had the facilities for baking and used tinned bread or hard tack once their fresh supplies ran out. So, this new innovation of having fresh bread during the middle of a long voyage was indeed a terrifically welcome morale booster. The first customer, U108 under Kptlt. Klaus Scholtz, was sighted at 0100 hours of 19 April in a moderately calm wind of force 4. The other expected shopper, U333 under Kptlt. 'Ali' Cremer, was nowhere in sight, but no one was terribly worried at this early stage. With conditions improving rapidly towards daybreak, every effort was made to get the refuelling process underway as soon as it was light enough to see. The passing of a pipeline was no easy matter and was made even more difficult by none of the recipients carrying the tools necessary for connecting it to their tanks. So, a kitbag with the necessary hardware had to be passed over first. To encourage the interchange of news and to keep the signalmen busy, Wilamowitz offered to send over a team of specialists to polish Scholtz's new Knights Cross, which he had received in Lorient a few months earlier, after his fourth war cruise.

The idea was for U108 to sail behind and slightly to one side of U459 while a thick manila hawser was secured with two hosepipes attached. Unfortunately, the towing hook kept slipping out of its eye, meaning that considerable manoeuvring and a good deal of technical naval language was necessary to make the whole process run smoothly. In the end it took some ten hours of cursing before the full amount of fuel and lubricating oil was transferred. The idea of passing solid goods over in a large 6-metre long inflatable did not go down too well either. Even force 4 winds were too rough for the huge dinghy. To make matters even more difficult, the dinghy must have been sliding about inside its storage container for the rubber to have worn dangerously thin in several places. This was repairable but added a nauseating interruption to an already precarious undertaking.

Having trailed the refuelling contraption out, it was eventually necessary to retrieve it again. The men were doing this from the aft deck of U459 to the bows of U108, but the only capstan to pull the heavy pipe was forward of the conning tower, adding just a little complication to the process of getting it back. The supply boat could have done with a rope puller on the stern as well. The pipes were

165 metres long, meaning there was a lot of rubber clogging up the upper deck waiting to be stowed in boxes, and coordinating this was not at all easy. To make things more difficult, it was now 0200 hours the following day, meaning the operation had to be carried out in total darkness and the men did not dare to show lights, despite having chosen an unfrequented part of the Atlantic. As earlier training exercises had already suggested, stowing the pipe was a good deal more difficult than running it out. The theory was straightforward enough, but the heavy lids of the storage boxes hinged upwards, meaning that they offered considerable resistance to water washing over the deck and were often slammed shut at inappropriate times, which resulted in many cries of pain from men caught in between.

Coping with the huge 6-metre long inflatable dinghy presented an additional problem. It was floating in the water attached by its painter when this retrieval operation started. The men hauled in the rope until they came to definite frayed end with nothing beyond it. The dinghy was nowhere to be seen. The frayed bit of the rope suggested it had made off on its own in the darkness and even a three-hour long search did not bring any happy results. The men had to contend themselves with the thought that the blasted thing wasn't much use anyway and they could do without it. This was quite good in one way because the men discovered that the passing of goods with a small, one-man air force style life raft was much better than the heavy naval monstrosity. Rowing in such comparatively heavy seas was very difficult, so the men took to pulling it with a long rope from one boat to the other. This made it possible for both boats to run at a speed of 2–3 knots in order to maintain steerage. Moving the inflatable from one boat to the other was not too much of a problem, but the difficulties arose when it came to loading and unloading. The hulls of submarines were definitely not designed for small boats to come alongside and a good number of packages as well as men went overboard. The men could swim, but the majority of packages were too heavy and vanished for good.

U333 (Kptlt. 'Ali' Cremer) turned up eventually, but didn't do much more than survey the situation from a distance. This was perhaps just as well because Cremer was most peeved and used his Morse lamp to curse everybody around. Apparently he had been sending radio beacon signals for fifteen hours, but hadn't been heard. Even the sea in a moderate force 4 wind was too much to contemplate getting men out onto the open deck of this small Type VIIC, so it was agreed that both boats should part company and try again when conditions improved. This was the first time medium-sized, seagoing boats had gone as far as the western Atlantic and the effort had shown them to be better suited for long-distance voyages than had originally been thought. However, their small size left them pitching and rolling in an alarming manner, which put the idea of working on the exposed upper deck out of the question. The weather settled down, but not before U98 under Kptlt. Wilhelm Schulze also put in an appearance. Once the heavy seas subsided, U333 was filled up, but then came the problem of repairing some sections of the hosepipes. There were two of them, running side-by-side, one for diesel fuel and the other for lubricating oil. The entire 165 metres of pipes had to be hauled onto the comparatively small deck for a close inspection. This was not only hard and dirty physical work, but finding space for such a long length was not easy either, especially as the men had to examine it closely.

Despite being in an unfrequented part of the ocean, the refuelling did not go without interruption. Luckily this came at a moment when rough seas prevented a U-boat from being attached to the end of the oil pipe. Suddenly, shortly before 0900 hours on 22 April, when a dull night was clearing to turn into a brilliant day, two lights were spotted in the haze covering the horizon. Wilamowitz immediately took evasive action, showing them his smallest silhouette. His assumption that the lights were on board a harmless freighter with neutrality markings rather than on something with aggressive intentions proved to be correct and the lights vanished again into the morning mists. Despite the later clarity of vision, the sea remained too rough to attempt a refuelling with U98, so it was a case of waiting for two further customers – U571 (Kptlt. Helmut Möhlmann) and U582 (Kptlt. Werner Schulte) – to put in an appearance. The weather later calmed sufficiently to pass over some essential stores including forty canisters for personal respirators. U-boats were still without ventilation systems and these cumbersome devices had to be worn during prolonged dives, even when sleeping, to prevent the air turning too foul. They contained potash or sodium hydroxide to absorb carbon dioxide as it was breathed out.

A brief pause to add a personal digression: I stopped writing the above paragraphs to check Helmut Möhlmann's first name and had just started typing it when Horst Bredow from the U-boat Archive telephoned. 'Helmut Möhlmann's son has just been here,' he said, 'He lives in the United States and doesn't speak German; could you please send him some English language U-boat Museum brochures?' I was dumfounded at the coincidence.

As the weather calmed, the men of U459 worked feverishly to pump diesel fuel as well as lubrication oil to a number of boats while others were busy ferrying a multitude of stores. The time needed to transfer goods and pump liquids was considerably improved since the first disastrous attempt with U108. Refuelling U564 under Kptlt. Teddy Suhren, for example, took only two hours and twenty minutes compared to the unbearably long ten-hour struggle with U108's slipping towing hook. This timing was cut even finer for U69, which was refuelled in one hour with another hour and a half needed for the transfer of solid provisions. Wilamowitz was more than well pleased with his men, who worked exceedingly hard under the most atrocious conditions without complaining. Suhren, incidentally, had put on quite a bit of weight since he received the Knight's Cross as First Watch Officer of U48 and during this voyage had already been in the Atlantic for a swim. Finding one of his men was having difficulties repairing a hatch, he clambered down from the conning tower to help, only to be washed overboard. Luckily his men reacted very quickly, threw him a life belt and fished him out again, but not before he had discarded his boots and heavy leather clothing.

U459 was one of the first boats to be fitted with a large deep freezer room and this started adding considerable problems at this stage of the voyage. Deep freezers were a new innovation in those days, found only in a few specialised commercial undertakings. Ordinary fridges were still a novelty of the future for many, so none of the men had any experience with this type of food preservation and did not know about the ferocity of its freezing capabilities. Even fishmonger's shops would have had iceboxes rather than fridges. The ice for these was delivered on the back of a lorry, rather than being made by the fridge. The vast majority of households wouldn't have had refrigerators until long after the end of the war.

When the packaged frozen food was waiting by the quayside before being stowed inside the U-boat, it collected condensation on the outside. This was then placed slightly wet into the freezer with fresh, unpacked meat placed on top. Today even the majority of children could predict what was likely to happen, but the men of U459 didn't discover their impossibly huge lump of ice until they wanted to remove a few items. Crowbars, hammers, wrenches and cold chisels were brought in to separate portions. What was more, the constant rolling and pitching meant men were often thrown off balance at the critical moment as they tried to hit something and some blows accidentally struck the men or the machinery rather than the frozen food. Men suffered from bruising, but the freezer objected more strongly to such harsh treatment by breaking down completely. Luckily most of the food had been extracted by that time.

Working on and in U459 had indeed become most uncomfortable. With so many men on the upper deck being constantly drenched by waves washing over them, they accumulated vast mountains of soaking wet clothing and there was not enough room in the engine compartment to dry it. As a result it became necessary to start work by putting on already damp or sometimes even wet clothing. Wilamowitz cursed, saying none of his customers wanted fresh water, so one of the two extra big stills should be replaced by a specially ventilated drying cupboard. But this was a job for the dockyard and could not be done at sea by the men themselves. So they had to cultivate an indifference to the unpleasant conditions. Wilamowitz made the point in his diary that he considered this too detrimental to health in the long run.

The crowd which collected around U459 was rewarded with a calm north-easterly of force 1–2, making the transfer of goods much easier, but even this pleasant weather didn't prevent U571 from wrapping the oil pipes' hawser around one of its propellers and then fouling it under the hydroplanes. The Allies left the U-boats in a tense peace to sort out their problems without interference. For much of 1942 they did not interrupt during serious mishaps like this. However, the natural enemy, the Atlantic itself, wasn't obliging for long and the wind intensified again to whip up heavy breakers, which started washing over the upper decks. Recovering the fuel pipe became quite a serious problem. The twenty men on the upper deck spent most of their time sliding over wet planking or swimming by the side of it. They would all have vanished into the teeth of the weather had they not been firmly attached to strong lifelines.

If this was not enough, the gremlins made every effort to test the men to their limits. Suddenly, without much warning, smoke poured through the engine room. Foul smells from leaks venting noxious gasses into the interior were not uncommon and the men often reached for their personal breathing gear to deal with such troublesome situations. On this occasion, however, things were different. The flickering brightness of flames quickly told them they had a fire on their hands as well and every effort was required to prevent the situation from getting out of control. Luckily the men reacted quickly enough to put it out again. A close investigation showed condensation had resulted in wires at the back of the main motor switchboard short-circuiting. The war diary hardly goes into details, other than to mention how Maschinenmaat (Petty Officer of the Engineering Division) Wetzel did especially well to extinguish the flames.

Refuelling continued as before. Boats turned up to be supplied with fuel, lubricating oil if they needed it, and whatever provisions they were short of. Transferring the solid goods was now becoming more difficult due to an acute shortage of kitbags. Empties had to be returned, but they had seen enough service for wear and tear to have taken its toll, and some were accidentally dropped into the water to make off on their own. There weren't any shops around to buy new ones, so the men had to make do and someone came up with the suggestion of using ammunition containers. None of the customers had a need for fireworks because they were firing torpedoes without any intervention from the air. In addition to this, no one could see a reason for U459's puny artillery of two 37mm deck guns. The ammunition for these was also stored in good sized, waterproof boxes. These containers were raided, the contents carefully stowed in safe places and the boxes used for transferring water-sensitive goods.

There was certainly no shortage of customers. U352 (Kptlt. Helmuth Rathke) was being supplied when the land-based Operations Room in France sent news that U566 (Dietrich Borchert), U572 (Heinz Hirsacker) and U594 (Dietrich Hoffmann) were also on their way to meet U459. This was still being digested when U69 (Ulrich Gräf) and U558 (Kptlt. Günther Krech) announced their arrival as well. Although it was good to see new faces, the men of U459 were left feeling a little sour by the inefficiency of some new customers. U566, for example, managed to break two fuel pipes by fouling them with its hydroplanes, meaning the 165 metres of heavy rubber had to be hauled back on deck to be repaired.

At least the engineering officer came up with some good news while this was going on. After three days of concerted effort, the burnt out electric motor was back in action and would probably get the boat home, as long as it was not driven too fast. U566 (Dietrich Borchert) left again, leaving U459 in splendid isolation without any indication as to whether other customers would show up. This was so unusual that the Obersteuermann, who was responsible for navigation, had to reread the reference numbers given in the original radio signals and then double-check his own position. The weather had been relatively kind, making him fairly certain he was in the correct place and that they were zigzagging in the right naval grid square of CC37. So there was nothing for it but to sit quietly and wait.

A splendid day turned into a calm night and it was almost midnight when a lookout reported seeing a flare rise into the dark sky. It was the right colour to be an identification signal, but rather than send a reply, Wilamowitz headed cautiously towards it. After all, there was always the chance that the enemy might be playing with signal rockets or a neutral was sending a genuine distress call. Eventually contact was made with U594, U572 and U69 which seemed to have had no problems finding each other, although for some reason they did not spot the supply boat until it crept up on them during the darkness of the night. Morse lamps were used to tell them to keep their distance until first light and, rather than rush into a frantic activity, everybody settled down to get some sleep until they could see what they were doing. The duty watch and the bakery, of course, were kept busy, but the men had got used to that by now.

Ulrich Gräf was the first to close in, keeping perfect position some 25 to 30 metres behind U459, but to one side to avoid any danger of the boat accidentally running into the supply tanker. Wilamowitz made the pungent comment in his log that it was a real pleasure to watch this after the messed-up manoeuvres of the past. His joy was short lived, however. Heinz Hirsacker caught both pipelines with his hydroplanes, cutting about 50 metres off the end. There was nothing for it other than to haul the whole contraption onto the deck of U459, retrieve the section still attached to Hirsacker and then to repair the damage. The men did everything they could to prevent oil from spilling onto the surface of the sea so as not to provide the enemy with noticeable evidence of their presence. Getting seawater into the pipe system did not matter, as the bottoms of the oil tanks were open to the sea all the time so that water could replace the oil in the tank as this was being used up. Therefore any water in the system was just returned to the sea, albeit a little dirtier than when it was picked up. Wilamowitz was delighted with the performance of his men in dealing with these crises, but also somewhat disturbed by Günther Krech (U558) who succeeded in jamming the fuel pipe so tightly under his own hull that it was rather difficult to retrieve without causing more damage. Once again the repair gang had to work feverish overtime while Wilamowitz reported that this had so far been the clumsiest boat as far as manoeuvring was concerned.

The next boat, U103 under Kptlt. Werner Winter, presented even greater sorrow for U459. There were no problems with the picking up of the pipeline and U459 was moving slowly forward, trailing the pipe, so there was no need to throw a rope from one boat to the other. It was a case of slowly closing in on the buoy at the end, hooking it and hauling the pipe on board. It quickly became apparent however that U103 could maintain neither steady speed nor course. Instead the boat was swinging from side to side and slowing down or speeding up until the pipes were stretched to their limit. Then, creeping slowly forward, U103 created the danger of making loops in the pipe. Wilamowitz, who was responsible for the entire undertaking, no matter what seniority the other commander might have had, wondered whether he should attempt to compensate for this variation, but decided it would be best to maintain a steady speed and course. Changes with the supply boat would only make things worse for the inexperienced men at the other end.

This was an occasion where he could have done with a pump capable of working automatically at variable speeds rather than the few fixed stages that were available via the control panel. Getting the pressure just right was not easy and on one occasion the pipe seemed to inflate like a balloon, but the pump was shut down before the bubble burst. The controls were inside the boat and, with water often washing over pipe and deck, meant that it was not easy to spot when things were going wrong. After a while, parts of the pipe slipped over-board and vanished into the depths and U103's mishandling became even more worrying. It seemed impossible for the boat to maintain 3 knots for passing over provisions. Again the boat crept too far forward and then lagged behind. Considerable time and patience were neces-sary before Wilamowitz ordered the process to be abandoned.

Today it is difficult to understand Wilamowitz's comments about the handling of U103 and U558. This was Werner Winter's third voyage with U103 and Krech was on his seventh with U558 when these refuellings took place. On top of that, both commanders received the Knight's Cross during the next few months, indicating that they were certainly no dimwits. However, several of the old lags have made derogatory comments about poor boat-handling abilities and this performance can perhaps be explained by there not having been enough opportunities for men to have practiced precision manoeuvring in confined spaces.

Seeing U103 vanish into the distance brought considerable relief, not only because the most awkward customer had left but also because the men guessed that they were now going home. But, as often happens at sea, things were not quite so easy and it was not long before a request came in to supply U753 (Korvkpt Alfred Manhardt von Mannstein). This was more than a mere nuisance. U103 had destroyed enough of the hosepipe for the remainder to be too short to make a safe connection. Luckily U459 had a spare hawser and the men worked feverishly to patch enough pipe from the bits. This went very well, but then there was no sign of U753. In the end there was nothing for it but to request radio beacon signals. This was done by choosing a special number at random and asking the other party to find it in their secret codebook and transmit the correct letters of Morse for the radio direction finder to get a bearing on. The majority of people in the German Navy were under the impression that both Britain and America were capable of determining the location from where such signals came from, and the men were not happy about sending them. It made them feel a little like a sitting duck in the middle of a target. However, the alternative was to leave colleagues floundering in far-off waters and that would have been even worse. As the search continued, it looked very much like a case of both boats having been given different positions. It was a really big cursing job. Once they had sighted each other there was not enough time to clarify the nature of the problem. Oiling had to start at once before the enemy could put an end to the procedure. Diesel oil was pumped through what was left of the pipe, but getting a fairly small amount of thick lubricating oil over was more difficult. Using the containers from the fresh water still eventually solved the problem. The large, 30-litre water cans were filled with oil and passed over without difficulty, although handling them on deck was not the easiest.

So far, the hatches in the deck had been opened only once on an exceptionally calm day, but now and on the majority of previous occasions, water washed over the upper deck to make opening of the lower hatches suicidal. Instead, everything needed to be transferred by passing it up the conning tower and down the outside before it was loaded into inflatable dinghies to be pulled from one boat to the other. U459 had it a little easier than the recipient as it had a special derrick constructed in the conning tower for hoisting up the heavy loads. Getting heavy items down a vertical ladder was certainly not the easiest of undertakings and everybody who had been to sea before wondered what would happen if the enemy put in an appearance at such a critical moment. At least the men of U459 were rewarded with an exemplary performance from U753, giving them a good positive feeling for the homeward run. They arrived in Lorient shortly after first light on 15 May 1942, almost exactly eight weeks after leaving Kiel.

13

1942 - CLOSING THE AIR GAP OF THE MID-ATLANTIC

Attacks against convoys had been getting progressively more difficult since the autumn of 1941, when Britain introduced H/F D/F or 'Huff Duff', a 'High Frequency Direction Finder' capable of automatically determining the direction from which even very short radio messages were coming from. This was a major breakthrough and incredible aid in the convoy war. U–boat patrol lines maintained radio silence while searching for their targets and then started sending messages the moment they were about to launch their attack. H/F D/F installed in escorts and in some merchant ships not only gave a warning that an attack was about to start, but it also gave the exact direction that it was going to come from. Thus it was possible to employ escorts with radar in just the right spot to eliminate false echoes from wave tops and reflections from the ships within the convoy. Escorts could then force the U–boat under and, working together in pairs, one would locate the submerged boat with Asdic, its underwater submarine detector, while the other dropped depth charges on the unfortunate victim. The initial problem for a single destroyer working own its own was that Asdic loses contact with the target once it gets too close and therefore ships had to run in blind, giving the submerged U–boat a chance to turn, drive to a fast speed and hopefully get out of the way of the blast.

The significant influence of H/F D/F was hidden from the Germans by the seasonal bad weather of autumn 1941 and the war at sea had changed considerably once U-boats invaded the eastern seaboard of the United States. It was the summer of 1942 when U-boat Command was seriously hit by the increasing prevalence of this new invention, and even then it took a while to digest the news that the short-range surface attack at night was not going to work any longer. The narrowing of the mid-Atlantic air gap, which made it possible for Britain and America to provide convoys with almost continuous cover all the way across, made a far more obvious impression than this secret radio direction finder.

What is particularly amazing is that one Royal Navy commander sent a lengthy report about his malfunctioning H/F D/F back to base, giving the exact details of its performance and this vital signal was intercepted and decoded by the German Radio Monitoring Service. It even ended up on the desk of Kpt.z.S. Hans Meckel, who was kept so busy that he did not have the time to study everything he was given. After the war, when he learned of this most significant happening, he was the first to make this story known and it was he who drew the author's attention to it. Sadly, U-boat Command had reduced its staff to the barest minimum in order to maintain secrecy and therefore did not have the back-up staff to deal with many vitally important changes in the war at sea.

U221, under Oblt.z.S. Hans-Hartwig Trojer, a seagoing Type VIIC boat, left Kiel on 1 September 1942 for its first war cruise. Trojer had been 2nd and 1st watch officer in U34 under Wilhelm Rollmann since shortly before the beginning of the war and he had also served as watch officer in U67 under Heinrich Bleichrodt for six months. Both of them were renowned commanders, so he could not have had a better start in U-boats. He also had the advantage of having commanded a small coastal boat for a little over half a year. This meant he brought the right skills for the job and gained the Knight's Cross of the Iron Cross shortly before he was killed in action at the end of September 1943, a little over two years after first setting out with U221. There were no survivors when U221 was sunk. The entire crew died with him.

The 5th U-boat Flotilla in Kiel under Karl-Heinz Moehle supplied the necessary equipment and stores needed by boats on their way to the front, so this was the last stopping off point before making for the treacherous North Atlantic. Progress was slow, with the boat usually managing less than 150 nautical miles per day and the oncoming weather was sometimes so appalling that a six-hour stint on the surface produced no more than 35 nautical miles over the ground, meaning that the boat was approaching Newfoundland at about 7 miles per hour. (1 nautical mile is 1.15 land miles and 1.85 kilometres.) This time the lack of progress was due almost entirely to the weather, with hardly any interruptions from aircraft or surface ships. This was considerably different to Trojer's first attempt to sail west at the beginning of the war. During his first voyages as watch officer, patrolling aircraft and an abundance of small fishing boats constantly hampered progress around the north of Scotland. Now it appeared as if the seas had been swept clean and the most exciting thing that happened was the barometer dropping rapidly. This was so fast that the men could almost see it move. When the needle finally stopped, no one believed that barometers could indicate such low numbers. It was a bad omen and it didn't take long for everybody to realise that the gadget had not broken. The Atlantic was indeed capable of producing these incredibly low depressions of unimaginably appalling weather.

The monotonous passage of time was taken up with practicing everything Trojer could dream up to keep the men on their toes. As always, the necessary maintenance work also kept men busy. It was not until the eighth day at sea that the alarm sounded for real. An aircraft with a searchlight broke the peace of the night. It was still at a reasonable range of 3 kilometres, homing in on the U-boat when watch officers and the lookouts came tumbling down while U221 crashed into the depths. Nothing happened and Trojer returned to the surface, convinced that his lookouts had spotted a cloud thinning in front of a bright star and from then on they no longer responded to the vivid light in the sky. The lookouts proved their worth a little later when one of them spotted some drifting mines and then a sailing ship. Not sure what to make of it, the men of U221 gave it a wide berth and, just to complete the picture, an aircraft appeared the following day as well. Again, there were no repercussions and the voyage continued after a short period in the depths.

Eleven days after setting out, U221 encountered a mass of fishing boats sailing as a group with noticeable smoke coming out of their funnels. At about five-minute intervals this increased most dramatically into a thick black display cloud. The performance seemed weird, almost as if they were deliberately trying to lure U-boats towards them. There were too many for an attack so Trojer ignored the smoke. The following day there were the first signs of more attractive activity in the form of an aircraft circling in the far distance, suggesting that something was going on beyond the horizon. Around this time U-boat Command formed the Pfeil group with a view to intercepting Convoy ON129. Finding these east-bound ships was not easy as the sea constantly washed over the top of the conning tower, making it almost impossible to see a great deal: just holding binoculars in front of the eyes was more than difficult. It was physically exhausting, yet persistence brought a reward and shortly after 0900 on 14 September the lookouts caught their first glimpse of the objective.

They had cast off at 0700 in Kiel, so they had now been at sea for a full two weeks without achieving anything more than merely finding a target. The old days, when war cruises sometimes lasted only two or three weeks, were long over. The next trick after having sighted the convoy was to find out what it was doing and with visibility down to 3–4 miles, that wasn't terribly easy. After a little observation it became obvious that there were four columns of thirty or forty ships with at least one corvette at the front. There were also a number of aircraft, which constantly forced the U-boat into the depths. To make things even trickier and more frustrating, the convoy was making excellent use of the weather. Instead of sailing in a straight line or general zigzag, the ships appeared to be taking every opportunity of heading into the abundant showers to cover their movements. This leaping from one area of poor visibility to another made the hunt most irritating.

It was not always the enemy that threw a spanner into the works. On this occasion it was a signal from U440 under Hans Geissler. He was only about 20 or so nautical miles away, saying his boat was no longer capable of diving after receiving a severe battering from Convoy SC99. What was more, U440 was the second boat to have been driven away from SC99. U216 under Kptlt. Karl-Otto Schultz had also been forced away. Getting close to merchant ships was becoming increasingly difficult for experienced commanders and impossible for the majority of new men appearing at the front. For a while U221 abandoned the convoy to help their stricken comrades, but the diving problem seems to have been rectified because U440 later put into Brest without help from U221.

In the meantime, visibility around the convoy worsened, making it impossible to keep contact with the merchant ships and the hunt was finally called off so that boats with sufficient fuel could concentrate on finding other targets. One of the big problems was that U221 kept encountering escorts and in reasonable weather there were also air-craft, which made the tracking of merchant ships virtually impossible. When the hunt was abandoned, the storm and the waves were so rough that it would have been impossible to shoot any torpedoes, so the men of U221 were not too sad at having lost their lucrative target. Just keeping the boat on the surface for recharging the batteries was incredibly hard work. Deck plates were torn off and containers on the outside opened despite being tightly screwed shut. Even bits of the conning tower fairing vanished, torn away like a sheet of paper. The inside of U221 looked as if a riot had passed through it, with smashed crockery in every corner. There were also a number of unpleasant injuries, but none of them were seriously life threatening and there was always the consolation that the men could dive deep into the calmness of the depths to recover from their ordeal and enjoy a meal in peace. Their counterparts on the escorts were not so lucky. They had to endure the incredible motion, the persistent wetness and the unpleasant cold without respite. They certainly seemed to be worse off than the U-boat men.

It was just before first light on 24 September 1942 when the next convoy (SC100), already reported by U258 under Kptlt. Wilhelm von Mässenhausen, heaved into sight. Although the storm had subsided by that time, a bright full moon combined with brilliant visibility made it far from ideal for a surface approach and since the position of the convoy in relation to the U-boat was perfect, U221 dived for a submerged attack. Once again the torpedoes didn't produce any results (a problem encountered by many U-boats) despite having been aimed at a couple of overlapping ships. These ships were too slow and too close to miss. Yet Trojer did miss. He was preparing for the second shot when the hydroplanes jammed. Just at that moment, as the engineer officer reported the matter by calling up into the conning tower from the central control room, Trojer caught a glimpse of the escort turning towards his extended periscope. There was no choice – he had to abandon the attack and go deep. The waters of the mid-Atlantic were so clear that anyone on the surface could easily make out the hulk of a submarine at periscope depth.

Now follows the amusing bit. If one were to write this in a novel, then readers would claim that the story was too far fetched. Yet this is true. It did happen. The boat dived by making itself bow heavy with as many men as could be spared. Then they were ordered to rush back to their action stations to make it level off again. Following this intricate manoeuvre, when the boat was balanced at a depth of about 70 metres, the men set about finding the problem with the jammed hydroplanes. Imagine their surprise when they discovered that a large packet of icing sugar had collected enough moisture for a thick liquid to ooze out of the bottom and drip onto some vital moving parts before setting hard again and putting a vital part of depth-keeping gear out of action. There can't have been many incidents during the war where a submarine was prevented from attacking by a bag of sugar.

The corvette that came bearing down on U221 didn't spot the U-boat and therefore it was possible to reload torpedo tubes before having another go at the convoy. The opposition must have noticed that there were U-boats in the vicinity. Once back on the surface, U221 was constantly harassed by aircraft. All of them were large land-based bomber types, probably with a good supply of depth charges in their bomb bays. In the end all four attacking U-boats were driven off and left to curse empty seas. Getting close to ships was certainly becoming more difficult and every ounce of skill had to be applied to avoid becoming a target for the escorts. What the U-boats didn't know at the time was that the sentries had strict instructions not to leave their position around the convoy. They could push U-boats under, but there were not enough of them to hunt U-boats to death. That would have left a gap in the defences that other submarines could easily penetrate. So escort commanders had orders to put U-boats down and then return to their place around the convoy as quickly as possible.

As September was drawing to a close, U221 had been at sea for thirty days, making it increasingly necessary to refuel. Convoy SC100 did lose a number of ships but even with post-war records comparisons, it is difficult to establish exactly who shot at what. There was no way any U-boat could remain in position to observe any damage and men had to rely on the far-off sounds as they tried hard to evade the hunters. The important experience gained was that U-boats could still shoot at merchant ships if they got close enough. The big problem lay in reaching that shooting position. There were many occasions where U-boats saw merchant ships from a range just a little too far away for accurate aim. Trojer made the point that the underwater hunts were difficult because he had to rely on the commentary from his sound detector, who was nearly always also the radio operator. This was confusing and could really only be used for locating far-off ships as it did not provide accurate-enough details for a submerged attack. Therefore Trojer preferred to remain on the surface, even if this made life a bit more stressful.

It is virtually impossible to define the length of 'a good shooting distance'. Even U-boat commanders found this difficult. To give one example, 'Teddy' Suhren of U48 once asked permission to shoot at a ship. The commander, Heinrich, better known as 'Ajax' Bleichrodt, refused on the grounds that it was too far away and could not be reached. Suhren cursed and said quite openly in front of the men that they had hit smaller targets even further away. So, to prove Suhren wrong, Bleichrodt acquiesced and gave permission for a single shot. To his utter surprise the torpedo did hit after an exceptionally long run.

U221 met the supply submarine U116 under Oblt.z.S. Wilhelm Grimme for a couple of days at the beginning of October. This was no purpose-built supply submarine but a hastily converted Type XB minelayer. Being the largest U-boat type of the Second World War and having a lot of outside mineshafts, which could be filled with storage containers, made these conversions ideal and many helped to keep pace with the convoys. U116 never made it back to port and its loss has never been explained. There was no signal, no reports of any one having attacked a submarine, nothing. Shortly after this meeting U116 vanished into the depths of the Atlantic while on its way home.

After this refuelling there were so many U-boats milling around in the same area that the positions of convoys were frequently communicated, but finding them in time always proved more difficult than the training schedules had suggested. The escorts now seemed to be occupying the positions where the U-boats liked to lurk in order to follow the merchant ships. Therefore U-boats had to shadow from greater distances and once this vital spy had been pushed under, it was often too awkward to regain contact. It made it too easy for the convoy to change course without its shadow noticing. This problem of losing a convoy due to it suddenly changing course after pushing a U-boat under could also work in favour of other hunters whose position was not yet known. This happened to U221 when the 13 October was less than one hour old. Suddenly, without warning, a convoy loomed out of an intensely dense rain shower.

The watch officer on duty thought an escort ahead of the merchant ships had spotted U221 and the sound detector was manned as the boat dropped into the depths. Yet, despite the proximity, nothing happened and U221 resurfaced. Trojer had not yet climbed out of the hatch when he spotted a destroyer coming straight towards him. Luckily it was approaching from the rear, where there was a gap in the conning tower wall. Had it been anywhere else it would have taken him a few more valuable seconds to spot it. Full speed ahead and alarm was the order. Once again the boat dropped into the depths. This time the destroyer passed harmlessly over the top and again nothing happened. There were no repercussions. U221 surfaced again with the convoy some 2 kilometres ahead and a couple of irritating escorts towards the rear. Not an ideal position, but it was about 0130 in the morning of a dark night with moderate waves, making it difficult to spot the low silhouette of a submarine, even at close range.

The radio operator sent off a sighting report while Trojer concentrated on finding the best targets. Two years earlier this would have been an easy case of sailing with the convoy in relative peace, but now the commanders in such a position were far more concerned with a multitude of small fast warships around them. Instant action had to be taken as soon as these showed an interest in the intruder. The advantage of being inside a convoy was that one could dive and then have a period of relative peace while the convoy passed overhead and the escorts couldn't attack. This gave many U-boats the opportunity to dodge sideways and hopefully get away. So, for a man with Trojer's experience and confidence, this awkward situation was not at all bad. The constant juggling with position around the convoy lasted for several hours until almost 0600 when U221 fired its first torpedo. This left at exactly 0556 hours, the second shot at 0622, another at 0623, and the fourth at 0710. That was the end of this part of the action – for the time being. U221 was lucky in managing to get another shot at the same convoy during the following night, with the torpedo going off at 0004 hours and then another at 0012, 0013 and two at 0032 hours. This was an incredible performance. Five ships and one escort were sunk. Three of the other U-boats also came close enough to sink one target each. It was an incredible performance under tremendously complicated conditions. The problem was that a large number of other U-boats spent an equally long period at sea but came home empty handed.

It must be remembered that U221 was one of the most success-ful boats of its time and there were far more which never even got close enough to a convoy to launch torpedoes. To overcome this new trend, Germany developed two new types of torpedo. One was specially designed to attack convoys and the other was fitted with a sound detector that would allow it to home in on propeller noises. These were used mainly against escorts.

The new anti-convoy torpedo was introduced towards the begin-ning of 1943, when convoys started reporting a disturbing new phenomenon: torpedoes were no longer running in straight lines but curving their way through convoys instead. They were promptly given the name of 'curly', but turned out to be nowhere near as dan-gerous as historians have made out. Known officially in Germany as 'FAT' taken from *Feder-apperat-torpedo* (spring-apparatus torpedo), many people thought that the initials stood for *Flächen-absuchenden-torpedo* (Surface searching torpedo). The idea was that these were aimed in the usual way, but once past their target they would start running in loops rather than continuing in a straight line beyond the far side of the convoy. The distance to the target and whether it should run in a right-hand or left-hand loop was adjusted before firing. U221, still under Hans Trojer, used such torpedoes during the third war voyage, which left from St Nazaire on 27 February 1943. The first days at sea were peaceful without interruptions and the first target on 7 March was a single ship, making it unnecessary to use this new weapon. A spread of two normal torpedoes was shot to sink the 3,015-ton freighter *Jamaica*.

Shortly after this, U221 joined a newly formed patrol line searching for Convoy HX228. Sighting an aircraft and then a corvette, the radio operator was ordered to transmit a brief sighting report and shortly afterwards the location, course and speed of the convoy. Trojer did not want to waste any time in which escorts might locate him and decided to go in for an attack at the earliest opportunity. This was made slightly easier for him as his movements were covered by a snow squall. His plan was to fire a Falke torpedo from the rear tube and then aim the bow tubes at other worthwhile targets. This Falke torpedo was a forerunner of the later, more sophisticated T5 or Zaunkönig, which homed in on the sound made by the target. Unfortunately for Trojer the wrong information was dialled into the torpedo calculator, known as the 'fruit machine' in Britain. As a result the effort ended in a miss. The curly torpedoes from the bow tubes did their job, creating three massive explosions. One of these ships had a great deal of ammunition on board and exploded with such terrific blast that U221's periscope was damaged by heavy objects hitting it. The submarine itself was submerged at the time and therefore missed the worst of the blast. The men inside felt its severity however: some were thrown against bulkheads and for a moment many thought that the end of their days had come. The Royal Navy reacted terribly fast and an escort came bearing down on the U-boat before Trojer could orientate himself for another shot. The blast had been such a shock to the system that the periscope could not be retracted and U221 dived with it still extended. The blast from the depth charges was so severe that it forced the slightly bent periscope back into its housing and in doing also sheared off the sixteen screws securing the eyepiece section at the bottom. Later, when Trojer tested it again, he found the cross-wires had been pushed to the side as well.

There wasn't enough damage to contemplate returning home and U221 continued with operations. The ships sunk from Convoy HX228 were *Tucurinca* (5,412 GRT), *Andrea F. Luckenbach* (6,565 GRT) and *Lawton B. Evans* (7,197 GRT) was hit, but was not prevented from reaching Britain, where the damage was repaired. In addition to the new torpedoes, U221 also carried a new electronic aid in the form of a radar detector. These devices were useful in indicating the presence of warships and aircraft, but did not contribute a great deal to the finding and sinking of targets. Theoretically they should have been used to help locate convoys, but this became rather tricky because even when a single radar signal was detected, it could be emitted by one of any number of escorts and all of them could turn their attention on the U-boat. Conditions had changed considerably since U221 first put out to sea and even passages in what had been relatively safe areas were now becoming dangerous. U-boat men had been used to aircraft bearing down on them, but now U221 experienced the same aggressive behaviour from ships. Escorts were often spotted heading for the U-boat at great speed and dropping enough accurate depth charges to seriously hamper operations. In its rear tube U221 had a Falke-type torpedo, which homed in on sound and would put off an attacking escort. Once again, all that happened was that the weapon passed under the attacker, rather than hitting it.

On 18 March the helmsman made a mistake and steered U221 right under the sinking 7,191-ton freighter *Walter Q. Greshamor* or the 8,293 GRT *Canadian Star*. Both had been hit by FAT or 'curly' torpedoes in quick succession and it was difficult for the submerged submarine to determine exactly what was happening to whom on the surface. Once again the earlier and by now well-known pattern of retaliatory attacks followed and there was no way U221 could escape unscathed. Escorts quickly pounced and all the men of U221 could do was to make a long list of damage reports. They were lucky inasmuch as Trojer had enough experience, skill and determination to dodge the main blasts. Despite this, it still meant that this time it would not be case of turning the boat around quickly in port and leaving again for another bash at sea. There were going to be plenty of opportunities in port for the men to concentrate on hitting the local bars and even enjoy some home leave. One has to bear in mind that U221 was one of the more successful boats in one of the biggest convoy battles of the war. The meagre successes mentioned here were supposed to cut off the Allies' supply routes.

After the war, Kpt.z.S. Otto Köhler and Fregkpt. Karl-Heinz Nitschke, talked about U377 being hunted for dreadfully long periods of up to thirty-six hours or longer. Köhler remarked that it was an incredibly long time to go without sleep and the build-up of carbon dioxide numbed the brain to make even plain thinking difficult. On one occasion Nitschke, the engineer officer, measured the foulness of the air and announced that according to the book, life was no longer possible in the high concentration of carbon dioxide that was then inside U377. Despite this, Köhler ordered extreme silence while he dodged another set of depth charges. 'Deep down,' Köhler said, 'I kept wishing that the next set of bombs would finish us off. It was painful just to keep going.'

U221 arrived back in St Nazaire on 28 March 1943 after having been at sea since 27 February, a period of twenty-nine days. Hans Trojer was awarded the Knight's Cross of the Iron Cross. He came back from one more patrol after this before U221 vanished into the depths during an amazing duel with an aircraft. The U-boat gunners killed two of the aircrew and set one of the fuel tanks on fire so that the plane had to be ditched far out at sea. The airmen survived in their life raft for eleven days before being picked up by HMS *Mahratta*.

14

THE BIGGEST CONVOY BATTLE OF ALL TIME

In March 1943 the fast convoy HX229 ran into the slow convoy SC122 and almost 100 ships faced the teeth of a wolf pack, making the ensuing clash the biggest convoy battle of all times. Many historians have labelled this as the climax of the Battle of the Atlantic, although the performance of individual boats had dropped drastically since the first successful period of the autumn of 1940.

In February 1943, Kptlt. Klaus Hartmann was a year older since commissioning U441, his first command. A lot had happened in those twelve months to turn him from an average officer into a hardened sailor. At the age of thirty, he was a comparative latecomer to U-boats. He had been serving in the light cruiser *Nürnberg* for almost a year when the war broke out and after that spent some time in *Wilhelm Bauer*, the first purpose-built submarine escort ship, before starting his specialised training during the summer of 1941. The next stage was being thrown straight into bitter action in the North Atlantic convoy routes. It was not too unusual for promising officers to become commanders without having been through the watch officer stage of the promotions ladder. Tackling those convoys was quite disappointing in many ways. The days of wine and roses were over and although statistics show that U-boats were sinking a large number of ships, the overall success was due to there being a vast number of them. Individually they were producing meagre results. Only a few U-boats came within striking distance of the enemy, and the majority came home empty handed. The number of U-boats at sea climbed steadily throughout 1942 until September, when it reached the psychological barrier of 100 and remained at that incredible high throughout the coming months. The astonishing and disappointing thing, as far as Hartmann was concerned, was that these incredibly high numbers were at sea for over half a year before the first large-scale battle took place.

Despite one concerted effort after another, none of these vast wolf packs ever managed to strike at a convoy in force. Reported merchant ships always evaporated into thin air or struck the wolf pack at the extreme end of the patrol line, and this was happening at a time when Britain could not read the secret U-boat radio code. One of the most amazing and significant events of the war took place during the last few days of 1942, when three plucky men from HMS *Petard*, Anthony Fasson, Colin Grazier and Tommy Brown boarded U559 to salvage its four-wheel Enigma machine with the current code books and thus made it possible for Bletchley Park to crack what they called 'Shark'. Both Fasson and Grazier went down with U559 and the canteen assistant, Tommy Brown, who had lied about his age when he joined up, was killed in a house fire while on leave a short time after this momentous event. U441 joined in what was to become the biggest convoy battle of the whole war, at a time when Britain was starting to decode German radio signals faster than the radio operator of U441 could turn the jumbled letters into meaningful phrases.

U441 and U440 cast off from Brest shortly after 1600 hours on 27 February 1943 to follow a minesweeper for the next two and a half hours until an escort flotilla took over to help them through the increasingly dangerous Bay of Biscay. Once well clear of land, U440 ordered 'fast ahead' in order to pull away from the U441 and soon both of them were left on their own to face the ravages of what had already become one of the most hostile areas for U-boats. On this occasion, however, progress was good and it was just ten minutes before midnight when the new electronic receiver indicated that it was picking up radar signals from a source in their vicinity. The old wooden and by now famous Biscay Cross had already been superseded by a special water- and pressure-resistant aerial fitted to the top of the conning tower, making it easy to slip into the depths before the U-boat came within range of the enemy's radar set. The reason for this was that it was possible to pick up radar impulses over a far greater distance than that from which the radar operator could expect to receive an echo. Consequently, this new invention for picking up enemy radar impulses was indeed much more than a terrific morale booster – it had become an essential lifesaver. The assumption that the radar impulses had come from an aircraft was confirmed by the absence of propeller noises. So it was not necessary to remain submerged for long and an hour later U441 was back on the surface, continuing with its westward voyage along a route dictated by the land-based Operations Room.

As usual, U441 dived again shortly before daybreak. Sun up and sun down were both difficult periods for U-boats inasmuch as it was tricky to spot attackers against a low sun and the peculiar lighting around these times was not conducive to spotting small objects on the water or in the sky. It had always been policy to ride these few difficult minutes out in the safety of the depths, but now things had become hot enough in the Bay of Biscay for U-boats to remain submerged during daylight hours and U441 continued peacefully below the waves. A few far-off depth charge detonations were heard, but nothing came close enough to disturb the men. A deep diving test was carried out and then tests on other parts of the machinery. U441 surfaced again shortly after 2000 hours to continue westward on the surface at a slightly faster cruising speed than that at which the electric motors could propel the submerged boat. Five hours later, the radar detector again suggested that an aircraft was operating in the near vicinity and U441 crashed back into the depths for an hour or so to allow it to pass. The next few days continued in a similar vein, without anything coming close enough to worry the men. At midnight on 3 March, the positions given in the logbook changed from 'Biscay' to 'Atlantic' and a short signal was transmitted with their position to inform U-boat Command's Operations Room that U441 had safely passed the dangerous Black Pit of Biscay, as it was now being called. This time the Operations Room was in more upheaval than the boats. The U-boat chief, Karl Dönitz, had been promoted to the role of supreme commander-in-chief of the navy with the title of Grand Admiral and was therefore moving from Paris to Berlin, but this went so smoothly that hardly anyone at sea noticed the commotion.

Britain was on the verge of being able to read the German Enigma signals again. In any case, the secret Submarine Tracking Room in London had been able to understand the significance of the short passage reports, such as the one transmitted by U441, and therefore it was not long before aircraft were sent out to find the boat responsible. British direction finders could determine the approximate latitude that these signals were coming from and survivors from U-boats had unwittingly disclosed the approximate longitude from where the passage signals were made. So, it was a simple matter of directing Coastal Command to the appropriate area. This time weather conditions were in the aircraft's favour. There was a moderate wind with low cloud, making it possible to approach visually without radar while remaining out of sight of the U-boat.

Each U-boat usually carried four officers – the commander, engineer officer and two watch officers – but the day was divided into three watches, so the third watch officer was usually the Obersteuermann (navigator). (Like the commander, the engineer officer was always at hand when any type of manoeuvring was necessary, so they did not stand normal watches.) Although the Obersteuermann was a warrant officer, he was usually better qualified than the commissioned officers because he had often been in the navy for ten years or more before embarking on a difficult specialised training course in order to climb out of the lower ranks. The main difference in qualifications was that officers had to have had a grammar school education while warrant officers would have joined as ordinary seamen and were then promoted out of the lower ranks. However, this rigid pre-war rule was waived once the war started and a number of promising warrant officers went on to hold commissions. Indeed Wilhelm Spahr, the Obersteuermann of the famous U47, which sunk the battleship *Royal Oak* in the Royal Navy's anchorage at Scapa Flow, went on to become a commander.

On this occasion, the aircraft bearing down on U441 was less than a kilometre away. That was too close for diving and the third watch officer, the Obersteuermann, manned the anti-aircraft gun before following the lookouts down below. There was enough ammunition clipped in place for him and the single gunner to have a go at putting the attacker off its aim. Everything happened too fast and then, at the critical moment of opening fire; the aircraft approached behind the radar detector aerial, making it awkward to shoot. The Obersteuermann was not so much concerned with breaking the aerial, but more anxious about possible ricocheting metal flying back at him and at the gunner. Guns from the aircraft were blazing away, but luckily did not even touch the U-boat. Once the aircraft was out of gun range, the watch officer ordered the gunner below before following him and closing the hatch, allowing U441 to drop into the depths. Unfortunately for the men in U441, the depth charge aiming was a good deal better than the shooting and the Obersteuermann had hardly reached the central control room when a shuddering and almost deafening detonation threw the boat into total darkness.

Somehow the confusion caused by the delay in diving resulted in the diesel engines having been shut off, but the electric motors were not yet engaged. At this critical moment, when there was hardly any movement, surface tension was strong enough to prevent the boat from sinking. There was nothing for it other than to order everybody into the bow compartment to upset the delicate balance and allow the hulk to slide beneath the waves. Hartmann calmly told his men that things seemed to be getting a bit hectic and ordered that the boat remain in the depths until nightfall. It was a case of enjoying a peaceful meal in the depths rather than putting up with the jostling of the waves. There were further depth charges, but the aircraft had no way of locating the submerged U-boat and seemed to be throwing its weapons blind and a long way off.

The relatively peaceful pattern of the past few days repeated itself for the next twenty-four hours. Once again the weather was creating the same conditions that allowed the aircraft to approach so closely. Therefore Hartmann remained submerged for the latter part of the following day. Later, things were still plodding along in their usual slow routine when the radar detector warned of an approaching aircraft and U441 hurriedly slipped into the depths. The pile of incoming radio messages included details of a patrol line being set up in the mid-Atlantic with the rather inconspicuous name of Neuland, and orders for U441 to take up a new position in that line. Each commander had strict instructions not to use the radio unnecessarily in the vicinity of such a wolf pack. U441 was only some 220 nautical miles from its allocated position and since other boats were much further away, had plenty of time to get there. In fact, having also been given permission for 'free manoeuvre', Hartmann went via a slight diversion in the hope of getting away from the incessant air cover. He thought that there was no point hanging about unnecessarily in the same area for too long when Coastal Command was making the mid-Atlantic so uncomfortable. It was the end of the day before more definite news came from a German Kondor reconnaissance plane, which provided further details about the anticipated convoy target. The merchant ships were far enough away for U441 to continue with its most leisurely pace at the most economical cruising speed. The only change in the monotonous daily routine came when the diesel engines were run at fast speed for a short period to test that all the nuts and bolts were still in place and to blow any soot out of the exhausts. In addition to this, there were also a few occasional practice dives to keep the men on their toes. The weather remained calm and there was no interference from aircraft, making the rest of the day quite uneventful.

It was shortly after 0900 hours on 6 March 1943 when things suddenly became more dangerous, although the majority of men in U441 were completely unaware of the danger. The sea was still as calm as a duck pond, with only a few ripples on the surface, but visibility was closing in rapidly. Once surrounded by the grey mist, Hartmann found things were too risky to hang about on the surface and ordered the boat into the depths. U441 had hardly levelled off when the sound detector picked up the distinctive high-pitched whine of a turbine from what was possibly a destroyer. Waves washing against the hull, U441's own diesel engines and all manner of noises from inside the hull made it difficult for the sound receiver to work while on the surface and it appeared as if the far-off destroyer was experiencing similar problems. It kept stopping to shut its engines down, suggesting that it was looking for something specific rather than escorting a convoy. Whatever it might have been up to, U441 was far away enough to be out of range. In any case, absolute silence had been ordered, which would have made it extremely difficult to hear the submarine with passive sound detectors, even if they were much closer together. Yet despite this wide margin in U441's favour, the encounter still felt most unpleasant.

U119 (Kptlt. Alois Zech) had reported an attack from a destroyer earlier and this snooper was probably the same thorn in the flesh. Luckily it vanished slowly into the vastness of the empty ocean, and it was noon the following day when the boat took up its position in the planned Neuland patrol line. Yet there was not much to write home about even having reached the critical area. Conditions remained good and without interruptions apart from the occasional radio message. There was nothing much the officers could do other than keep plotting the possible course of the convoy and positions of other boats around them. Even alterations broadcast from the Operations Room were easy to comply with without having to break the ordered radio silence. The only discomfort came from the natural elements; the strengthening wind could be felt inside the stuffy extremities of the submarine by a gradually increasing roll and pitch. The seas became rough enough to throw the lookouts off balance and one of them was thrown against the periscope support, knocking him into semi-consciousness. He was helped below for treatment of a severely bleeding forehead, but as it turned out, the damage was much less than the volume of blood suggested at first. Another man, suffering from severe tonsillitis, was far more of a worry. This could be infectious and be passed on to everybody else, but the beasties turned out to be somewhat choosy and didn't fancy the idea of spreading among such an unwashed crew.

This period of sitting in a patrol line, constantly obeying orders from the Operations Room with regard to position changes, but being unable to contribute much to the general proceedings, was most frustrating. The line gradually grew as more boats appeared, but there were no signs of the enemy, making life most tedious. It was lunchtime on 10 March when details of the first positive sighting came through the radio. Sadly for the men, the information was too raw to act upon. It said where a convoy had been sighted, but not what it was doing. It was one of those irritating situations where someone had sighted a sign of a convoy, smoke for example, but without catching a glimpse of the ships themselves and therefore was too far away to help the rest of the pack. The vital piece of news came an hour later from Oblt.z.S. Hans Hunger in U336, giving both the position and course of the convoy, but not its estimated speed. Hartmann was free to make his own decision and therefore immediately calculated a collision course with the merchant ships. This had hardly been done when the land-based Operations Room ordered everybody to a faster speed and, at the same time, demanded an immediate weather report from Paul-Karl Loeser in U373. Such demands were always somewhat ominous. They suggested something had gone wrong somewhere and the U-boat Command wanted to know whether the boat was still alive.

Slowly more convoy sightings filtered through and it was not long before Oblt.z.S. Albert Langfeld in U444 passed on the speed of the convoy via radio. Things were starting to look good for the U-boats. By early evening on 10 March there was enough information for the wolf pack to converge. Several boats were within contact, but the peaceful calm did not last long. The merchant ships had hardly been engulfed in darkness when the ether erupted with news of attacks. Sadly the messages were of the wrong sort. They came from U-boats reporting attacks against them from escorts, indicating that the opposition was well prepared for an onslaught. Quickly it became obvious that getting anywhere near the convoy was going to be tricky.

As usual, the diverse information from different boats suggested that there could either be two convoys in roughly the same area or that everybody was making a huge number of navigation errors. Whatever, there was no running commentary and U441 was left lurching in the dark. Several detonations were heard around midnight, suggesting that a slight variation in course might be advisable, but despite the excited atmosphere all around, there were no indications of any targets. During the early hours of the morning, the situation started to become so uncomfortably critical that everybody started cursing everybody else. The big decision was whether to continue with the collision course or whether it might be better to deviate and look elsewhere. The decisive point, where the merchant ships could have slipped past undetected, had been reached and information from other boats suggested that the convoy had safely bypassed the patrol line. It could now be some distance behind U441.

The action to be taken in this game of nerves was decided by only one person – the commander. Cursing as more signals came in, Hartmann ordered U441 into a silent dive to listen with the sound detector.

A noise was quickly picked up, but not the commotion he was hoping to hear. The faint tone of a lone merchant ship with thumping reciprocating engines made another agonising decision necessary. Should U441 continue to hunt for the convoy or tackle this straggler? Hartmann chose to make for the noise, but the boat had not gone terribly far when the horizon lit up with a yellowish glow. Hartmann responded by ordering a higher speed in order to head towards the commotion. Flashes from detonations became more frequent, but U441 was still far too far away to hear any rumblings. Yet as the minutes rolled on and U441 climbed over the old horizon, all the men could see was more empty sea. The brilliant display from a short while ago vanished like a mirage. It was more than frustrating.

'Silent Dive' was the order.

Propeller noises could be heard, but once again these came from a single thumping merchant ship, not from a convoy. Then the high-pitched whine of a torpedo caused Hartmann to have a quick look through the periscope. There was nothing there, nothing at all, not even a seagull pretending to be a plane on the attack. Arriving back on the surface, the men were greeted by more detonations and flashes of various kinds, but again no targets. All around them U-boats were attacking and even broadcasting how they were planning on using the newer anti-convoy torpedoes, but the sea remained empty for U441. Even running towards the telltale signs at high speed did not produce any results. By this time it was slowly getting light, meaning a bright slither of light blue rested on the horizon above a still, black sea and even these perfect conditions didn't reveal any targets.

Soon the men of U441 found themselves on a moderate sea with reasonably clear sky, giving them a field of vision of about 8 nautical miles all around. They could see as far as a faint haze obscuring the far distant sky. Conditions remained good, but still there were no targets. Hartmann cursed once more. Tired from a lack of sleep and from the physical effort of a long spell on duty, he had to resign himself to the fact that he had run past the merchant ships without seeing them. It was infuriating, but the situation did not allow for any let-ups. The hunt had to continue. Unable to make out where the merchant ships were, the men in U441 hoped that a radio bearing signal would be transmitted from one of the boats still in contact with the convoy.

Earlier orders, prohibiting the use of radio once in the patrol line, prevented Hartmann from asking for directions.

The men in U441 were concerned with the lack of reconnaissance information. Something somewhere seemed to have gone wrong; things weren't going according to the plan they learned at commanders' school. To make matters worse, it was not long before the Operations Room sent a terse signal for reports from all boats still in contact with the convoy. Nothing happened other than a huge smoke cloud rising into the far distant sky. Without further ado, U441 turned towards it, hoping to get a look in on the action. At that critical moment, just as the engines were battling with high power and shooting very noticeable bow waves over the reasonably calm sea, an aircraft was spotted flying from right to left. At first the men thought they were in luck and had not been spotted. Things looked good until the lookouts saw it turn and disappear into the low clouds. There was no choice: U441 had to dive, to seek out the safety of the depths and to vanish from the surface before the attacker re-emerged from its cover. Once down in the depths, the radio operator called out the good news that he could hear propeller noises, but there was something unusual about the faint vibrations in his earphones. They sounded more like a diesel engine, suggesting that another U-boat was nearby rather than a surface ship. Whatever, there wasn't much the men in U441 could do about it other than to remain absolutely silent and hope that the impending depth charges would not hit too close to home. Luckily they didn't. The aircraft must have found an empty sea once it emerged from its cloud cover.

U441 remained down below for so long that anyone in the air would have lost interest in flying over an empty sea, but on surfacing an hour or so later found another large, land-based aircraft circling above it. The men on the top of the conning tower watched as it dropped a number of bombs and then flew out of sight. This time the lookouts were also rewarded with the sight of a number of mastheads in the far distance, but this news had hardly been digested when another large aircraft screamed down on them. U441 crashed into the depths once more, and were surprised to find life quiet and calm. There were no depth charges. They guessed that it had been the same plane from earlier which must now have expended all its weapons against other boats. Hartmann remarked that in situations like these, it was good to have colleagues who had taken the sting out of the bee. It was around midday before the air was considered safe enough for resurfacing, but by then the starboard clutch was giving them trouble. Men were still working feverishly to fix it, meaning that it would be better to remain in the depths until the problem had been rectified.

As it happened, a number of progress reports came flooding in from boats that had succeeded in attacking. These at least gave some more useful details of the convoy's progress. The situation was not as straightforward as it might sound, however. For a start, the people who attacked were usually also pushed under, meaning that they could not get a clear view of the proceedings and no one seemed to know the whereabouts of the convoy core. It seemed very much a case of U-boats knocking off stragglers. In any case, there were still two problems: first, the damaged clutch prevented Hartmann from running even at a fast cruising speed, and second, he needed more definite positions than the contradicting figures sent by the other boats. The best course of action was to stay put until some more definite news came in. Limited visibility due to fog and intermittent snow showers did not help to clarify matters and the rest of the day passed without any definite decisions being taken. Most of the men fell into an uneasy sleep.

It was shortly after 1800 hours on 11 March when what looked like a fairly empty merchant ship appeared out of a snow shower on the horizon. Once again the weather was with the opposition. Just then, when Hartmann could have done with some poor visibility to get closer to the target, he found himself in crystal-clear surroundings. Despite this, formulating an attack plan took only a few seconds and by the time U441 had dropped out of sight, Hartmann realised that he had acted so quickly that he hadn't estimated the ship's direction or speed – essential information for a successful underwater hunt. The sound detector helped to confirm that U441 was heading towards the target. The only problem was that despite a fairly high speed, it didn't seem to be getting any nearer. When surfacing again an hour or so later, only the tops of the masts were still visible on the horizon. The ship, obviously heading away from the U-boat, was now in such a position that it could no longer see the tiny hunter.

This meant that U441 could run on ahead without being spotted unless the opposition started zigzagging. As it disappeared into a snow shower again, the men had to hope that it wouldn't change course while they stepped on the gas – now it was a case of nerves and sheer calculation. At the appropriate time U441 dropped into the cellar again to use the sound detector to make sure that they were still on target. As luck would have it, twilight was setting in, but Hartmann was still hoping to catch a glimpse of his target before it got too dark. The ship vanished, appeared again and then the situation was perfect. U441 was making for its first shot of this momentous voyage. Imagine the feeling on board as the tenseness was suddenly interrupted by an almighty detonation; Hartmann watched pieces of his target fly into the air without firing a single shot!

'Surface.'

At that moment, as lookouts poured out of the hatch, another powerful detonation followed. It seemed unbelievable, but someone else was chasing the same ship and got there first. This really was one of those moments where the men felt like sinking one of their own U-boats, if they could only have found it. It was more than infuriating. It was downright exasperating.

Hartmann was still cursing himself and everybody else when U377 under Kptlt. Otto Köhler reported the presence of a convoy in roughly the area where it should have been; this positive sighting was good enough for the men of U441 to forget their misfortune and head towards it at high speed. The routine of sighting the shadow or silhouette of a ship, not being able to identify it properly and at the same time not being able to get close enough, continued until the early morning when a number of confusing radio signals suggested that there was no convoy at sea but a vast concentration of independent stragglers instead. All of them were that little bit too far away to reach easily.

Then, when the men in U441 thought they were getting close, they were pushed into the depths by the radar detector. This indicated the presence of what could be at least one aircraft. The black sky of night had changed into a dull grey, but the majority of people would still remain in the comfort of their own beds when lookouts spotted an aircraft with four engines. It did not take long before the damn bee changed course and headed straight towards U441. Luckily the men reacted very quickly and the subsequent detonations were far enough away not to worry them. What made matters worse was that there was no let-up in the radio signals coming in, all reporting attacks on merchant ships, but all U441 could manage was to miss the action by inches. Surfacing a short time later, it became clear that there was not one land-based aircraft, but a whole squadron of them. What was more, the weather conditions were ideal for aircraft. At a range of 3 kilometres, a twin-engined aircraft dropped out of low cloud and came bearing down straight towards U441, suggesting that it had spotted the U-boat ages ago and had manoeuvred into a favourable position before making its final run in to attack. Strangely enough there followed no detonations, making Hartmann wonder whether the opposition had run out of depth charges.

Another frustrating day passed with nothing much happening except the land-based Operations Room sending a signal encouraging the men not to give up. Slowing down to an economical cruising speed, the men of U441 continued the search in an orderly fashion, hoping some action was going to come their way. It did, but not the way they had hoped. First, the chain working one of the diving tank vents snapped, meaning a repair was necessary, and then heavy seas bent the radar detector aerial on the top of the conning tower. This didn't seem to stop it working, but made it impossible to bring the contraption back into the housing when diving. Fast underwater speeds, as well as the force from nearby detonations, could render the gadget useless. This did not feel comfortable at all since the device had been very useful during recent days and nights in warning of impending air attacks: on each occasion U441 had succeeded in dropping into the depths before the attacker could bring his weapons to bear. The weather also put an end to any thoughts of chasing merchant ships. With a gale force 7 on the surface, it was not the friendliest place to be. Keeping up the speed demanded by the Operations Room was impossible, although U441 made every effort to battle against the raging seas. The only consolation was that U441 picked up messages from other U-boats in contact with the convoy saying that they were also unable to maintain their shadowing positions.

There was no shortage of news trickling in as radio signals with sighting reports were flooding in all the time and, if this was not enough evidence of other U-boats in the area, the lookouts reported sighting one struggling with the mountainous seas. A recognition signal was quickly answered and then a brief exchange identified the boat as U406 under Kptlt. Horst Dieterichs. Another tense moment arose shortly after U406 had drifted out of sight and as another typical German U-boat silhouette was spotted in the distance. Being shortly past midday now, it was necessary to first establish the new recognition signal with which to challenge the grey wolf. This was not answered at first and then there followed some unrecognisable Morse, putting Hartmann into a somewhat tricky predicament. He turned immediately to present what was possibly a British submarine with the smallest target before repeating the new recognition signal several times, hoping that the other boat was German and would realise it was not responding according to regulations. The weather was too wild to do much else other than curse and make detailed notes of any possible identification features. The boat looked typically German, but Hartmann knew the British had captured U570 some eighteen months earlier and this particular U-boat might not have a German crew. The possibility may have been slight, but it was always better to be safe than to be sunk as a result of one's own negligence.

This boat too vanished back into the grey vastness of the mountainous Atlantic while the nerve-wracking monotony of the chase continued. The proceedings were interrupted only by a steady influx of German radio signals and by large, land-based Coastal Command aircraft. Aircraft spotting was definitely growing in popularity, although there was never enough time to hang around long enough to enjoy them from close quarters. When they did come within grasping range, things tended to get rather unpleasant. Eventually, when merchant ships came into sight and U441 had the opportunity to fire torpedoes, things happened rather quickly. The action was almost over before it started, with the majority of men in U441 not even having realised that they were participating in one of the most significant events of the war; an event that historians would dissect for years to come and which would fill the history books for future generations.

The night the chase started was just one of those nights. U-boat Command had instructed remaining boats to move at high speed in order to form two new packs with a view of intercepting another convoy.

However, although the weather was reasonably kind, the surface of the water was somehow whipped into an incredible swell, making it exceedingly difficult to maintain the required speed. As the boat slid down into a trough, it hit the next waves with a shuddering blow while the spray just carried on, sweeping over the top of the conning tower and stinging the eyes of the men on watch. Then, as the whole boat tilted in the other direction, men slid aft as the bows rose up to climb on to the next crest. With both hands often holding on to binoculars, safety belts were more than essential not only to prevent men from being washed overboard, but also to support their weight against the raging water and to prevent them from falling over.

The second watch of 19 March 1943 was getting ready to go on duty at 0400 hours when another U-boat was sighted. The signalman instinctively grabbed the Morse lamp to send a recognition signal when someone muttered, 'No light, there's something else there.' Straining their eyes, the men made out a few small darker blotches and, focusing on them, they quickly realised they were looking at the black shadows of several merchant ships. Two minutes later everybody in U441 was on full alert, while the diesels hammered heavily to drive the boat into a favourable attacking position. Things had to move fast now, and time was of the essence. It would soon be light enough to make a surface approach impossible without being seen. Two escorts were also identified and the other U-boat was seen to take a diverging course as well. Hartmann didn't dare use his signal lamp and was therefore hoping desperately that the other boat had also spotted him; otherwise there was the possibility that things would become unpleasant for both of them. Being slightly ahead, he didn't ease off and considered himself in an ideal position to strike the first blow. At 0433 hours a short signal announcing his intentions to attack was sent according to standing orders.

At about the same time, one of the escorts started throwing depth charges, making Hartmann wonder whether it had found the other U-boat, but he didn't allow himself to be put off his plan. As was often the case, at this most critical moment of the attack the convoy turned slightly, making it considerably more difficult to get a good shot, but Hartmann was still not going to be put off his objective. To make matters even more frustrating, the sky cleared to produce a magnificent moon, shining brightly over a by-now moderate sea and U441 was lying directly between this brilliant light source and the merchant ships, making itself a sitting duck for a large number of observers. As was usually the case, minutes quickly started dragging into what felt like hours. Time appeared to stand still. Sometimes things happen too quickly, but now it seemed as if everything was glued into a solid block without movement. It seemed ages before U441 was able to manoeuvre into a good position to broadcast what Britain called a 'curly warning'. The special anti-convoy torpedoes were designed to run in a straight line for a preset distance and then, if they missed their target, they would turn in loops rather than continuing in a straight line. The reason for these twists was to make the torpedo more likely to collide with a ship in convoy, rather than getting lost in the empty space beyond it. Bearing in mind that a torpedo could cover a distance of over 10 kilometres and they were shot from about 1 kilometre, it is easy to see that the looping mechanism increased the chances of hitting something, including the U-boat that fired it. Of course, these loops could also be a great threat to any other U-boats in the vicinity and therefore commanders had to broadcast these very important warnings.

It was 0550 hours when the first curly torpedo left Tube I bound for a 5,000-ton freighter. Strangely enough, the men inside the boat heard a detonation a few minutes later, although no one on the top of the conning tower noticed any effects and Hartmann did not give permission for the prepared success radio signal to be transmitted. The next shot followed a few minutes later from Tube III. This time the target was an 8,000-ton freighter with passenger accommodation. The results were a little more distinct, in the form of intense spray erupting aft of the stern mast. It was accompanied by a brilliant flash of light and then by a dense cloud of smoke squelching forth from the superstructure. The third target received two torpedoes from Tubes II and IV. Neither produced the expected result, and Hartmann ordered the boat to be turned in order to fire the rear tube. This was aimed at a 7,000-ton freighter. Again it was not possible to observe a hit. Although these shots were recorded in Jürgen Rohwer's Axis Submarine Successes, the targets have not yet been identified and it looks as if none of the ships were sunk.

Conditions were calm enough for Hartmann to order the reloading of all tubes straight away, without waiting for the boat to drop into the calmness of the depths. Although it seemed unlikely that he would manage another shot at the convoy before daylight, he was hoping to get in front and perhaps try a submerged attack. Escorts seem to have been alerted, but this time U441 was in luck and was able to hide in a patch of exceptionally poor visibility under a shower cloud. The escort was not put off however, and eventually Hartmann took the boat down to seek the safety of the depths.

The first target was seen to be sinking, but there was not enough time for a detailed study of the results. Confusion was ruling the roost, making the men certain that one of the sinking ships had not been aimed at and therefore must have been caught by an anti-convoy torpedo while it was looping through the columns of merchant ships. This time it seemed unlikely that this torpedo had come from another U-boat because the curly warning was still in force and should have prevented other boats from closing in on the convoy. Luckily these thoughts were not interrupted by aggressive action from the escort, which was just over 2 kilometres away shortly before U441 left the surface. It seemed highly likely that U441 had not been spotted. The still peaceful surroundings did indeed suggest the men had got away without being seen. They were counting their luck when the first detonations echoed through the boat, shaking the interior seriously, as if the deafening noise was not enough to warn them they had been caught. Recovering from the shock, the men realised the detonation was far enough away not to be too troublesome. The next set of depth charges were considerably closer, however, and the men started wondering how long it would be before they received some fatal punishment for their audacious action on the surface. Obviously the mob on the surface was short of neither depth charges nor time. A few minutes later another eight charges detonated, then another set and another. Any ideas of a submerged attack had to be abandoned and everybody settled down in silence to receive their punishment, rather like naughty children queuing by the headmaster's study awaiting a mass caning; only this was far worse. Eighteen more attacks followed. A total of forty-nine depth charges were counted between 0654 and 1130 hours.

The majority of these were far enough away not to be anywhere near life threatening, but the loud propeller noises made it inadvisable to surface. In fact, the opposition was close enough to prevent U441 from reloading torpedoes: the sound detectors on the surface would almost certainly have heard the torpedo mechanic swear. So this had to be put on hold until more peaceful times could be guaranteed. At around midday the men thought they should be clear of the pests on the surface and were slowly adjusting their minds to going back up top for some fresh air when more depth charges told them they were not alone. It was obviously best to remain quietly in the cellar. It was getting on to 1400 hours by the time the torpedoes were reloaded and U441 stirred with enough confidence for a look through the periscope at what was going on. Poor acoustic conditions had been in evidence for some time and although these could have made it difficult for the escort to hear U441, it also worked the other way round and made it very awkward for the radio operator at the sound receiver to work out what was happening around the U-boat.

Despite the long, enforced respite deep down in the cellar, not all was lost. Convoy sighting reports came flooding in almost faster than the radio operators could decode them. The idea of shooting on ahead of the positions given and waiting for a submerged attack in daylight during the morning of 20 March looked feasible. In addition to this there were good prospects of tracking some of the many stragglers reported by the other boats. If their messages were correct, there should be a vast number of independents chugging along on their own without escort protection, making more than ideal targets as long as those dreaded aircraft were kept at bay. The moon was still shining brightly in the late-night sky, suggesting the weather was not likely to help in any way and the Royal Air Force would have a brilliantly clear sky. What was more, the airmen were not restricting their activities to nice sunny days. To drive home the fact that they were a force to be reckoned with, a four-engined plane forced U441 down into the cellar at 0335 hours on 20 March.

Later, another aircraft put paid to the idea of manoeuvring in front of the convoy, but it did not prevent the search for stragglers. Shortly after midday on the 20th a Sunderland crashed out of low cloud about 2 kilometres away, aiming itself at the U-boat. Once again the third watch officer, the Obersteuermann, was on duty to warn off the aircraft and to order the gun crew into action. The log states that the 37mm anti-aircraft gun was manned and opened fire when the aircraft was at a range of 1,000 metres. Bootsmaat Pakura watched as only the first two or three shots and the last two missed their target. The other fifteen of so punched forcefully into the huge fuselage. The aircraft appeared to respond to this impact by turning away sharply and flying past U441 at a distance of about 500 metres. Although theoretically a sitting duck, it was far too fast for the gunner to aim at. After all, U441 was not a steady gun platform and had a slippery deck, rolling and pitching enough to put anyone off such steady eye work. In addition to this, several men were needed to operate the weapon and coordinating this was not always easy, especially as there had been only a few opportunities for practising.

The Obersteuermann didn't hesitate. He instantly realised this was a golden opportunity to vanish from the scene and ordered the alarm button to be pressed. Thirty-five seconds later, the duty watch collected itself from the floor of the central control room, while the depth gauges indicated that there was already a good deal of water above the top of the conning tower. All this efficiency didn't prevent the opposition from tossing a well-placed depth charge in their wake. This blew out the main circuits of the hydroplanes, putting them out of action; the downward plunge had to be corrected by ordering the men to the stern. Unfortunately this also upset the trim, or balance, of the boat and instead of going down, it started rising again. It broke through the surface for a short period before dropping once more. This yo-yo movement was still in full swing when various semi-serious damage reports flooded into the central control room. Luckily none of them impaired the U-boat's immediate diving qualities and were quickly ironed out so that the search for independents could continue a few hours later. As a consolation, more radio reports of U-boats damaged by aircraft flooded in once U441 was back on the surface, providing the men with ample evidence that their suffering was considerably lighter than what their colleagues around them had to put up with. Obviously the Royal Air Force was intent on doing a bit more than merely annoying the occasional U-boat. This time the planes had mounted an all-out attack in the mid-Atlantic to protect their vital convoys. It was not good news for U-boats.

Shortly after U441's devastating experiences, on 31 March 1943, sixty-one merchant ships of Convoy HX231, with escort group B7 under Sir Peter Gretton, left Newfoundland. Despite numerous attacks from U-boats, this group managed to fend off almost every one. This was the first convoy of the war that managed to drive off almost all attacking U-boats, and marked a significant turning point. Never again were U-boats in a position to seriously interfere with a group of merchant ships crossing the infamous Atlantic. One month later came the Black May of 1943 when the number of U-boats sunk rose dramatically to over forty and the U-boat Commander-in-Chief diverted his forces to less volatile areas. Having digested these awful losses, he ordered flotilla commanders to instigate a secret ballot that was secret from non-seagoing personnel and secret inasmuch that no pressure would be put on the men to influence the way they were going to vote. The result was overwhelming support to continue with the U-boat war, despite the heavy losses. Although the U-boat Arm lost about two-thirds of its men, the misery they endured was only a small fraction when compared to the appalling torture suffered by millions of people across the world. Considerably more people were to die in the most horrendous circumstances during the last twelve months of the war than throughout the preceding fifty months.

THE HITTING POWER OF THE U-BOATS IN THIS BOOK

Key

⇧: On surface
⇩: Submerged
sm: sea miles

The following rounded-up data gives some basic details about the hitting power of the U-boats mentioned in this book. It is hardly necessary to know their exact specifications when studying the war at sea, but further technical details can be found in a number of the books listed in the 'Further Reading' section.

Type II

Small, coastal submersible

Size

IIC:	250 / 291 tons
IID:	250 / 314 tons
Length:	44 metres
Beam:	4.1–4.9 metres
Depth:	3.8 metres

Armament
3 bow torpedo tubes: 5 torpedoes
1 x 20mm anti-aircraft gun

Speed

⇧:   12 knots

⇩:   7 knots

Range

IIC: ⇧ 12kt / 1900sm

                       ⇧ 8kt / 6550sm

                       ⇩ 4kt / 35sm

IID: ⇧ 12kt / 3450sm

                       ⇧ 8kt / 5650sm

                       ⇩ 4kt / 56sm

Crew

3 officers / 22 men

Type VII

Seagoing submersible

Size

VIIA: 626 / 915 tons

VIIB: 753 / 1,040 tons

VIIC: 769 / 1,070 tons

Length: 64–76 metres

Beam: 6 metres

Depth: 4.5 metres

Armament

4 bow/1 stern torpedo tubes: 12 or 14 torpedoes

1 x 20mm anti-aircraft gun

Later 2 x 20mm twin anti-aircraft guns and

1 x 20mm quadruple or 1 x 37mm anti-aircraft gun

Speed

⇧:   17 knots

⇩:   7 knots

Range

VIIA: ⇧ 16kt / 3,000sm; 10kt / 6,200–6,800sm

VIIB: ⇧ 17kt / 3,850sm; 10kt / 9,700sm

VIIC: ⇧ 17kt / 3,250sm; 10kt / 9,700sm

                       ⇩ 4kt / 80sm

Crew

4 officers / 40–52 men

Torpedoes carried
Bow tubes: 4
Bows under floor: 4
Bows over floor: 2
Stern tube: 1
Between motors: 1
In outside storage containers: 2 (1 in bows and 1 in stern)

Type IX

Ocean-going submersible

Size

IXA:	1,032 / 1,408 tons
IXB:	1,051 / 1,430 tons
IXC:	1,120 / 1,540 tons
Length:	76.5–76.8 metres
Beam:	6.5–6.8 metres
Depth:	4.7 metres

Armament

4 bow/2 stern torpedo tubes: 22 torpedoes including 4 in outside containers
1 x 20mm anti-aircraft gun
Later 2 x 20mm twin anti-aircraft guns and
1 x 20mm quadruple or 1 x 37mm anti-aircraft gun

Speed

⇧:	18 knots
⇩:	7+ knots

Range

IXA:	⇧ 18kt / 3,800sm; 10kt / 10,500–11,350sm
IXB:	⇧ 18kt / 3,800sm; 10kt / 12,000–12,400sm
IXC:	⇧ 18kt / 5,000sm; 10kt / 13,450–16,300sm
	⇩ 4kt / 63sm

Crew

4–5 officers / 40–52 men

FURTHER READING

Bailey, C.H., *The Royal Naval Museum Book of Battle of the Atlantic: The corvettes and their crews: An Oral History* (Stroud: Alan Sutton and Naval Institute Press, 1994).

Banks, A., *Wings of the Dawning – The Battle of the Indian Ocean* (Malvern: Images, 1996). Includes information about U852.

Beesly, P., *Very Special Intelligence* (London: Hamish Hamilton, 1977 and New York: Doubleday, 1978). An interesting book dealing with Admiralty intelligence written by an officer who served there as the deputy head of the Submarine Tracking Room.

Brennecke, J., *Jäger – Gejagte* (Jugendheim: Koehlers Verlag, 1956). One of the great early classics about life in U-boats, written by an ex-war correspondent.

Busch, H., *So war der Ubootskrieg (U-boats at War)* (Bielefeld: Deutsche Heimat Verlag, 1954). Also one of great early classics about the U-boat war.

Busch, R. and Roll, H-J., *Der U-Boot-Krieg 1939 bis 1945.* Vol. 1, *Die deutschen U-Boot-Kommandanten* (Hamburg, Berlin, Bonn: Koehler/Mittler, 1996). (Published in English by Greenhill as *U-boat Commanders*.) Brief biographies produced from the records of the German U-boot-Archiv. Sadly, the English edition has been published without the numerous corrections recorded by the archive.

——, *Der U-Boot-Krieg 1939–1945* (Hamburg, Berlin and Bonn: E.S. Mittler & Sohn, 1999). German U-boat losses from September 1939 to May 1945 from the records of the U-Boot-Archiv.

Compton-Hall, R., *The Underwater War 1939–45* (Poole: Blanford, 1982). The author was the director of the Royal Navy's Submarine Museum and this is by far the best book describing life in submarines.

Connel, G.G., *Fighting Destroyer – The Story of HMS Petard* (London: William Kimber, 1976).

Dönitz, K., *Ten Years and 20 Days* (London: Weidenfeld & Nicolson, 1959).

Frank, W., *Die Wölfe under der Admiral* (Oldenburg: Gerhard Stalling Verlag, 1953). Translated as *Sea Wolves – The Story of the German U-boat War* (London: Weidenfeld, 1955). An excellent book, one of the early classics.

Gasaway, E.B., *Grey Wolf, Grey Sea* (London: Arthur Barker, 1972). About U124.

Gretton, Sir P., *Convoy Escort Commander* (London: Cassell, 1964).

Hadley, M., *U-boats against Canada* (Kingston and Montreal: McGill-Queen's University Press, 1985).

Harbon, J.D., *The Longest Battle* (Ontario: Vanwell, 1993). The Royal Canadian Navy in the Atlantic 1939–1945.

Herzog, B., *60 Jahre deutsche Uboote 1906–1966* (Munich: J.F. Lehmanns, 1968). A useful reference book with much tabulated information. Contains a lot of technical details.

——, *U-boats in Action* (Shepperton: Ian Allan and Dorheim, Podzun). A pictorial book with captions in English.

Hirschfeld, W., *Feindfahrten* (Vienna: Neff, 1982). The secret diary of a U-boat radio operator compiled in the radio rooms of operational submarines. A most invaluable insight into the war and probably one of the most significant accounts of the war at sea.

——, *Das Letzte Boot – Atlantik Farewell* (Munich: Universitas, 1989). The last journey of U234, surrender in the United States and life in prisoner-of-war camps.

——, and Brooks, G., *Hirschfeld – The Story of a U-boat NCO 1940–46* (London: Leo Cooper, 1996). A fascinating English language edition of Hirschfeld's life in U-boats.

Högel, G., *Embleme Wappen Malings deutscher Uboote 1939–1945* (Hamburg, Berlin, Bonn: Koehlers, 1997). Published in English as *U-boat Emblems of World War II 1939–1945* (Atglen: Schiffer Military History, 1999). An excellent work dealing with U-boat emblems, especially those that were painted on conning towers. Very well illustrated with drawings by the author who served in U30 and U110.

Kemp, P., *U-boats Destroyed* (London: Arms and Armour, 1997).

Konstam, A. and Showell, J.P. Mallmann, *7th U-boat Flotilla – Dönitz's Atlantic Wolves* (Hersham: Spearhead, Ian Allan, 2003).

Milner, M., *North Atlantic Run* (Annapolis: Naval Institute Press, 1985).

Moore, Capt. A.R., *A careless word ... a needless sinking* (Maine: American Merchant Marine Museun, 1983). A detailed and well-illustrated account of ships lost during the war.

Mulligan, T.P., *Neither Sharks Nor Wolves* (Annapolis: United States Naval Institute Press, 1999 and London: Chatham Publishing, 1999). An excellent book about the men who manned the U-boats.

Niestle, A., *German U-boat Losses during World War II* (London: Greenhill, 1998).

Paterson, L., *U-boat Combat Missions* (New York: Barnes and Noble, 2007). Contains some good photographs and many first-hand accounts of U-boat life.

Preston, A., *U-boats* (London: Arms and Armour Press, 1978). Excellent photographs.

Price, A., *Aircraft versus Submarine* (London: William Kimber, 1973).

Robertson, T., *The Golden Horseshoe* (London: Pan Books, 1966).

Rössler, E., *The U-boat* (London: Arms and Armour Press, 1981). Translated from: *Geschichte des deutschen U-Bootbaus* (Two volumes) (Bonn: Bernhard and Graefe Verlag, 1996). An excellent technical book about the development of U-boats from 1850 to the modern German Navy.

Rohwer, J., *Axis Submarine Successes of World War II 1939–45*, (London: Greenhill, 1998).

——, and Hümmelchen, G., *Chronology of the War at Sea 1939–1945*; Greenhill, London, 1992. A good, solid and informative work. Well indexed and most useful for anyone studying the war at sea.

——, *The Critical Convoy Battles of March 1943* (Weybridge: Ian Allan, 1977).

Roskill, Capt. S.W., *The War at Sea* (London: HMSO, 1954, reprinted 1976). Four volumes: The official history of the war at sea, 1939–45.

——, *The Secret Capture*, (London: Collins, 1959).

Savas, T.P., *Hunt and Kill – U505 and the U-boat War in the Atlantic* (New York: Savas Beatie, 2004). This book is of special interest because at least eight distinguished authors contributed specialist information to provide an in-depth history of this well known capture.

Sharpe, P., *U-boat Fact File*, (Leicester: Midland Publishing, 1998). A useful book that should really be brought up to date. Contains a great deal of operational, personnel and technical data.

Showell, J.P. Mallmann, *The German Navy in World War Two* (London: Arms and Armour Press, 1979 and Annapolis: Naval Institute Press, 1979 and translated as *Das Buch der deutschen Kriegsmarine*, Stuttgart: Motorbuch Verlag, 1982). Covers history, organisation, the ships, code writers, naval charts and a section on ranks, uniforms, awards and insignias by Gordon Williamson. Named by the United States Naval Institute as 'One of the Outstanding Naval Books of the Year'.

——, *Hitler's Navy* (Barnsley: Seaforth Publishing, 2009). A revised version of *The German Navy in World War Two* with additional text and new photos.

——, *U-boats under the Swastika* (Shepperton: Ian Allan, 1973 and New York: Arco 1973 and translated as *Uboote gegen England* (Stuttgart: Motorbuch, 1974). A well-illustrated introduction to the German U-boat Arm, which is now one of the longest-selling naval books in Germany.

——, *U-boats under the Swastika* (Shepperton: Ian Allan, 1987 and Annapolis: Naval Institute Press, 1987). (A second edition with different photos and new text of the above title.)

——, *U-boat Command and the Battle of the Atlantic* (London: Conway Maritime Press, 1989 and New York: Vanwell, 1989). A detailed history based on the U-boat Command's war diary.

——, *Germania International*; Journal of the German Navy Study Group. Now out of print.

——, *U-boat Commanders and their Crews*; The Crowood Press, Marlborough, 1998.

——, *German Navy Handbook 1939–1945* (Stroud: Sutton Publishing, 1999).

——, *U-boats in Camera 1939–1945* (Stroud: Sutton Publishing, 1999).

——, *U-boats at War – Landings on Hostile Shores* (Hersham: Ian Allan and Annapolis: Naval Institute Press, 2000. Translated as *Deutsche U-Boote an feindlichen Küsten 1939–1945* (Stuttgart: Motorbuch Verlag, 2002).

——, *German naval Code Breakers* (Hersham: Ian Allan, 2003).

——, *The U-boat Century – German Submarine Warfare 1906–2006* (London: Chatham, 2006). Translated as *Geschichte der deutschen U-Boot-Waffe seit 1906*; Stuttgart: Motorbuch Verlag, 2008).

——, *The U-boat Archive Series* (Milton Keynes: Military Press, 2001–2007) www.militarypress.co.uk – a set of seven reprints of secret wartime material essential for studying the war at sea.

Smith, M. and Erskine, R., *Action this Day* (London, New York: Bantam Press, 2001). One of the best books written about code breaking at Bletchley Park.

Taylor, J.A., *Bletchley Park's Secret Sisters* (Dunstable: The Book Castle, 2005). Psychological warfare in the Second World War.

U-Boot-Archiv, *Das Archiv* (German language), *The U-boat Archive* (English language). A journal now published once a year for members of FTU, Deutsches U-Boot-Museum, D-27478 Cuxhaven-Altenbruch. Please enclose two International Postal Reply Coupons if asking for details. www.militarypress.co.uk.

Verband Deutscher Ubootsfahrer, *Schaltung Küste* (Journal of the German Submariners' Association).

Watts, A., *The U-boat Hunters* (London: MacDonald and Jane's, 1976).

Williamson, G. and Pavlovik, D., *U-boat Crews 1914–45* (London: Osprey, 1995). A most interesting book with excellent colour drawings and black and white photographs.

Wise, J.E., *U505 – The Final Journey* (Annapolis: Naval Institute Press, 2005). A well-illustrated and detailed history.

Witthöft, H.J., *Lexikon zur deutschen Marinegeschichte* (Herford: Koehler, 1977). An excellent two-volume encyclopaedia.

Wynn, K., *U-boat Operations of the Second World War* (London: Chatham, 1997).

INDEX